THE
LIVEABOARD
GUIDE

ADLARD COLES
Bloomsbury Publishing Plc
50 Bedford Square, London, WC1B 3DP
Bloomsbury Publishing Ireland Limited
29 Earlsfort Terrace, Dublin 2, D02 AY28, Ireland

BLOOMSBURY, ADLARD COLES and the Adlard Coles logo
are trademarks of Bloomsbury Publishing Plc

First published in Great Britain 2012
Second edition published 2019
This edition published 2026

A catalogue record for this book is available from the British Library

Library of Congress Cataloguing-in-Publication data has been applied for

ISBN: PB: 978-1-3994-1733-4; ePub: 978-1-3994-1734-1; ePDF: 978-1-3994-1735-8

2 4 6 8 10 9 7 5 3 1

Lovingly designed and typeset by Tony's wife, Vickie
Printed and bound in China by RR Donnelley Asia Printing Solutions Limited

To find out more about our authors and books visit www.bloomsbury.com and sign up
for our newsletters
For product safety related questions contact productsafety@bloomsbury.com

THE LIVEABOARD GUIDE

3RD EDITION

Living Afloat on the Inland Waterways

TONY JONES

ADLARD
COLES

LONDON • OXFORD • NEW YORK • NEW DELHI • SYDNEY

Dedicated to Puck, the best boat dog.
2009–2024

Tony at Bagnall Lock Bridge 49,
on the Trent & Mersey Canal.

CONTENTS

INTRODUCTION

Welcome aboard! If you've just bought this book then I welcome you as a dear friend. If you're new to boat life this enthusiastic welcome may seem excessively generous, but if you spend enough time around boat folk you will come to cherish these friendly welcomes from people you might previously have considered strangers. That's just the way we are.

In the years since the first edition of this book was published in 2012, the liveaboard lifestyle has become incredibly popular – primarily because of the cost of housing, and the quality of life to be experienced at the cheaper end of the market. At least 15,000 people live aboard according to a recent Canal and River Trust survey, with the concentration of those located in the South of England. The number of boats in London more than doubled in the eight years up to 2018, with an estimated 10,000 people now living aboard in the capital alone, according to the 2013 'Moor or Less' report from the Environment Committee. The rise in the number of liveaboards has been both staggering and obvious to anyone spending time on the waterways.

Making the decision to live aboard is the beginning of a steep and never-ending learning curve. Don't let that worry you too much, though: boating and stress don't sit together well at all. You will find that there's plenty of help available for new boaters and reading this book is a great place to start. You will quickly realise that there are many different ways to achieve a pleasurable liveaboard

life, and the choices you make now will greatly influence your lifestyle. The aim of this book is to help you create a liveaboard lifestyle that will suit you.

The first questions to ask yourself are 'Why do I want to live on a boat?' and 'Will boat life suit me?' Most people who choose to live aboard will cite increased freedom, reduced living costs and a less complicated lifestyle among their reasons for choosing a boat for a home. Boat life can certainly deliver these rewards, but they come at a price. Living aboard can be rather hard work, complicated and frustrating and has the potential to seriously affect your bank balance, whether because of expensive repairs or by restricting your earning potential. It's not all rolling countryside and the easy life. It's important to conduct some research beforehand and to be prepared for the ups and downs of life aboard a boat. It's all too easy to end up being bound to a complicated and expensive boating headache if you aren't adequately prepared. The decision to live aboard is not one that should be made lightly or quickly and there's much to learn and consider if you intend to avoid the many potential pitfalls. But for those who have the right outlook on life and are willing to do their homework, a rewarding and peaceful lifestyle awaits.

This book focuses on the practical aspects of living aboard a boat and presents the pros and cons in all their glory. Alongside each chapter you will find stories, opinions, anecdotes and advice from a range of liveaboard boaters. Many of the boaters quoted here have lived aboard for a number of years. Their methods are tried and tested and their advice is grounded by experience and expertise. Their advice may or may not work for you, but it will help you to determine whether you're suited to boat life and, more importantly, what kind of boat life is right for you.

BOAT FOLK

In every community there's a broad spectrum of characters and circumstances and boat life is no different. However, boating does seem to attract people of a certain type and there are some commonly encountered profiles. For example, it's common for boaters to live alone, mainly because of the space constraints of life aboard, but there's also a rambling 'free spirit' inherent in the lifestyle. Another reason for the prevalence of single boaters is that living aboard is sometimes a consequence of a divorce, leaving one partner (statistically usually the husband) with a share of equity large enough to buy a boat. That said, it's common enough for couples to live aboard too, especially as boat folk are often easy-going types who can rub along in the confines of a boat quite happily.

Although not particularly common, you may find whole families living aboard. Usually these are small families comprising only three or four people, sometimes one parent, sometimes two, and usually only one or two kids.

Young people may also become liveaboard boaters as they look for cheap places to live, while at the other end of the scale boat life is often the refuge of retired people who are seeking to downsize, sell their home and see out their days on the equity. Many of these retirees become constant cruisers, making good use of their new-found free time. However, growing old and infirm aboard a boat can be difficult and ultimately dangerous, and it's important to have a contingency plan in place for when boat life may no longer be a viable option.

Boat folk are a varied and eclectic bunch with many differing circumstances and lifestyles, but by reading this book you will see that there are a few common threads that unite us all.

MEET THE BOATERS

Every boater is different, so it would be impossible to provide bespoke information to suit each individual's needs and circumstances. Instead, scattered through this book you'll find real-life experiences and recommendations from a wide selection of different boaters with different profiles and expertise.

They're all lovely folk, and they'll almost certainly be as helpful and friendly if you meet them in person out on the cut.

Tony, Vickie and Puck – Nb The Watchman.

Martin, Jules and Reggie – Nb Strait and Narrow.

Richard and Lucia – Nb Kelly.

Hannah, Ant and Mabel – Nb The Corridor.

Kev and Saffi –
Nb The Grey Lady.

Adrian, Kim and Pepper – Nb Hugo.

Justine and Woody –
Nb Frog With A Heart.

Robbie Cumming – Nb Naughty Lass.

Mike – Nb Aldebaran.

Steve and Eileen – Nb Sophie.

Charlie, Wendy and Bella – Nb Philip George.

Sarah – Nb The Book Barge.

Canal Cruising Company.

John – Nb Sound of Silence.

Jo and Troy – Snaygill Boats.

BEEN THERE, DONE THAT
HOW DID YOU COME TO LIVE ABOARD A BOAT?

ROBBIE CUMMING
Nb *Naughty Lass*

I was looking for a job in London while dating a girl who lived there. A mutual friend was trying to sell her narrowboat and asked me would I like to live on the boat rent free in exchange for keeping it warm, secure and also moving (as it was registered on a continuous cruiser licence). My initial thought was boats were for hippies or holidays, so it probably wasn't for me, and I didn't really have a burning desire to live on one. But as soon as I got on board, the smell of coal fires and diesel engines, the closeness to nature and the general feeling of freedom was almost overwhelming. I was surprised at how friendly and helpful the boating community is, especially in London. Within three months the boat was sold, my relationship ended, and I'd failed to get a London job. But I at least knew one thing: I wanted to live on a narrowboat!

DARREN AND DEBBIE
Nb *Dunster*

After years of looking around and seeing the rat race consume us, we looked into an alternative way to live. A life on the canal appealed above all others because of the tranquillity brought about by the water itself.

RICHARD AND LUCIA
Nb *Kelly*

We bought our boat while we still lived in a house. However, after one of our first big trips we realised that living on the canal network was what we wanted to do. We'd spent three months travelling from Leeds to London, Bristol and back via the western canals, and after that experience there was no turning back. There was so much more to see and do that we just couldn't wait to be back on board and under way. So we put our stuff in storage, rented out the house and moved aboard Kelly. Eight years later we are still enjoying every minute.

STEVE AND EILEEN
Nb *Rahab*

We bought the boat as a retreat, a refuge from the hustle and bustle of modern life. Although we're not near retirement age just yet, our intention was to eventually get a bigger boat to live on when we retired. Before long we found ourselves spending more and more time on board until eventually we thought, 'Why wait?' So that was that! At first we worried that if we lived aboard full-time the magic might wear off, but in fact quite the opposite has happened. Living aboard has its own joys and adventures that aren't apparent when you only use the boat occasionally.

BEEN THERE, DONE THAT
HOW DID YOU COME TO LIVE ABOARD A BOAT?

KEV AND SAFFI
Nb *The Grey Lady*

After my wife died I was a bit lost, rattling around in a big old house that was so full of memories. As a former Royal Navy diver, I've always been around boats and the idea of living aboard was comforting. I felt at home as soon as I stepped aboard.

HANNAH, ANT AND MABEL
Nb *The Corridor*

We'd been renting for years and had loads of hassle, mainly with landlords selling houses from under us. We were saving for a mortgage deposit, but it wasn't easy while renting and moving house so often. We chose to live on a narrowboat because it offered a more stable path toward eventually owning a house, with the boat potentially becoming a future deposit.

The utilities are largely pay-as-you-go, giving us more control over what we spend. And beyond the practicalities, we were drawn to the idea of travelling and living on the water. It also suited our desire for a simpler lifestyle. It turns out we prefer it and decided to make it permanent.

Tony's *towpath tales*

One of the things that makes boat life so special is the sharing and considerate small-village-community culture that has almost disappeared from land-based living. Indeed, the canals are often referred to as one long, linear village community, and having spent time meeting people across the length and breadth of the system I can tell you that this is a good description.

The boating community has come to my aid on many occasions, but one example sticks in my mind as being particularly exemplary. It occurred a few days after I bought my boat as I was travelling south on the Grand Union Canal.

I had filled up my water tank before I left the marina, but somehow my cold-water tap in the galley was dry. Confused, I pulled alongside a water tap where a seemingly knowledgeable-looking chap was tinkering on his boat and asked for some advice. 'I'll bet you have two water tanks!' said the fellow, whose name turned out to be Danny. He went on to explain that some boaters don't like the look of the rust and cobwebs inside their old steel water tank so installed a more hygienic plastic one beneath their front deck.

After inserting the hose and turning on the tap, Danny and I settled into the easy conversation that can commonly be found with folk on the waterways. Almost half an hour and two cups of tea later I stepped into my boat and heard an alarming splosh! Instinctively I swore loudly, bringing Danny rushing over. Popping his head through the door he saw what was causing my alarm, and then he said the most beautiful words a man has ever said to me: 'Don't worry son, your boat isn't sinking.'

After a little investigation we found that the plastic tank was no longer watertight, so the water had been simply filling up the hull of my boat. Danny then spent a whole weekend helping me bail out the water, remove the ruptured tank and repair my plumbing. By way of thanks I offered to take Danny and his girlfriend out for dinner, but Danny would hear none of it. Even our two evenings spent at the pub were not a chance to reciprocate as Danny pointed out that this was his town and, while I was there, he would be buying the beers. 'You can buy the beers when I visit you,' said Danny. 'And I drink a lot!' he warned.

Cont.

As the beer flowed, I spoke to Danny about what it was like to live aboard, hoping to make the best of his expertise and experience. 'Let me tell you something about boat life,' he said. 'There's an old boating tradition that says you should never eat the last slice of bread. You should always throw it off the back of your boat for the ducks to eat. That way, when you're broke and you have no food and are on your arse with nothing to eat, there will always be a big fat duck hanging around near the back of your boat. All I'm doing here by helping you is throwing bread off the back of my boat. If you're going to make a success of living aboard I suggest that you do the same.'

His advice hit home and it has held me in good stead ever since.

Mrs Duck says 'Pay it forward'.

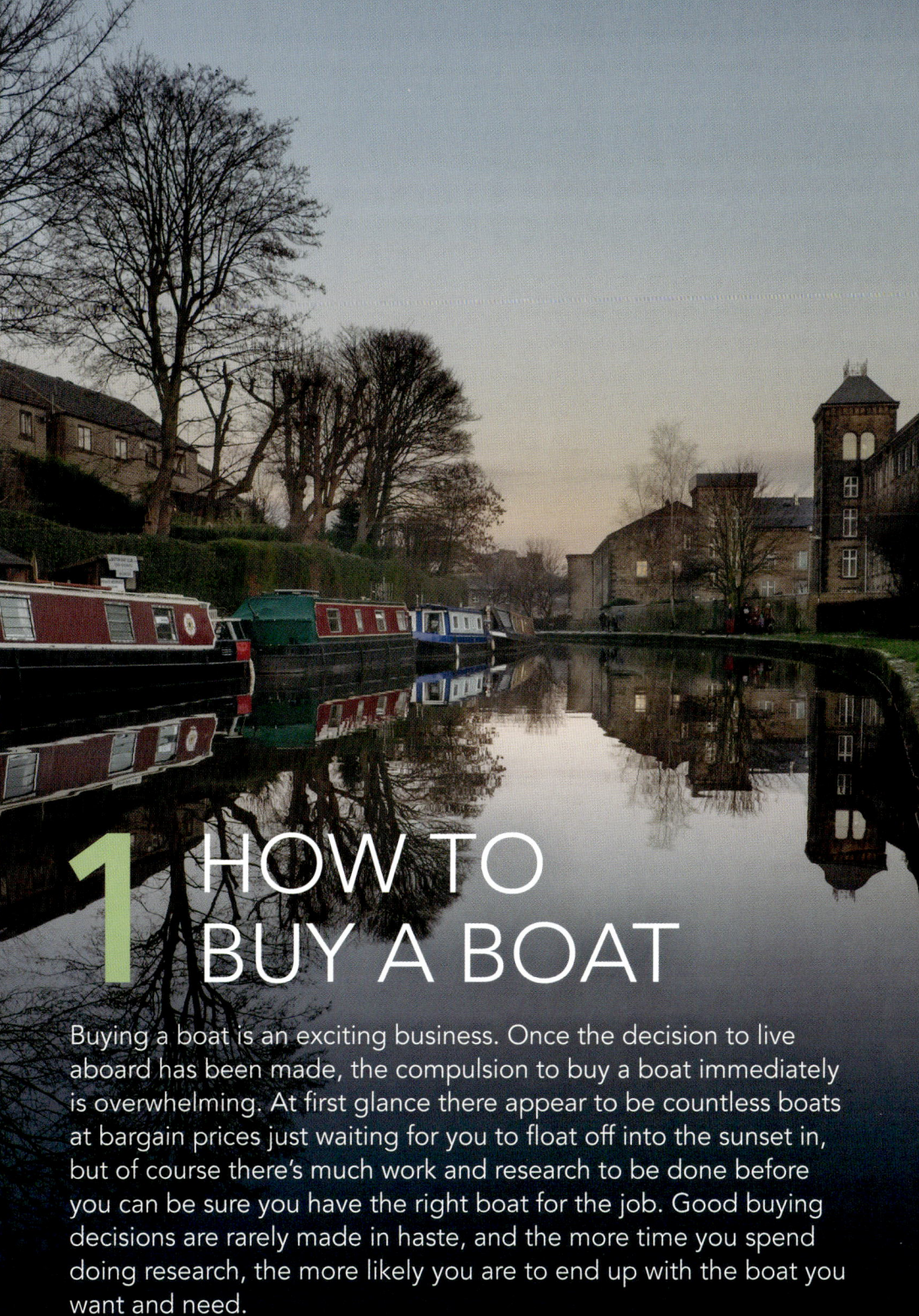

1 HOW TO BUY A BOAT

Buying a boat is an exciting business. Once the decision to live aboard has been made, the compulsion to buy a boat immediately is overwhelming. At first glance there appear to be countless boats at bargain prices just waiting for you to float off into the sunset in, but of course there's much work and research to be done before you can be sure you have the right boat for the job. Good buying decisions are rarely made in haste, and the more time you spend doing research, the more likely you are to end up with the boat you want and need.

TYPES OF BOAT

Although there are many different styles of boat to be found on the inland waterways, some are seen more frequently, and for good reason. While all of them could be used as a liveaboard vessel it's easy to see how some are more suited to that purpose than others. Bigger isn't always better!

NARROWBOATS

Narrowboats are the most popular choice for liveaboard boaters for reasons that will become obvious as you continue to read through this book.

There are four main styles of narrowboat:

Traditional stern

Traditional stern narrowboats, or 'trads' as they're commonly called, have only a small aft deck just big enough for one person at the tiller. The engine room in this type of boat will be either in front of the back deck or in a dedicated engine room in the middle of the boat, but in both cases it's inside the cabin.

PROS
- Considered by purists to look more authentic than other styles of boat.
- Lots of internal, secure and lockable space.
- Engine hole is covered and protected from rainwater.

CONS
- Access to the cabin from the engine room can be tricky in some trad boats.
- Access into the engine bay for repairs can also be tricky in trad boats.
- Little space for crew to socialise with the helmsman while underway.
- Some kind of signalling system is required to communicate with crew inside the boat – for example, when approaching locks or bridges, or when in need of tea!

Traditional stern – just room for the tillerman.

Cruiser stern – enough room to socialise.

Semi trad – the best (or worst) of both worlds.

Cruiser stern

Cruiser stern boats feature a large back deck big enough for crew and passengers to socialise near the tiller when underway. The engine in a cruiser-style narrowboat will invariably be under this large back deck.

PROS
- Usually easy access into the cabin from the tiller.
- Plenty of space for company to stand or sit with the helmsman near the tiller.
- Lots of room for canine companions.
- Pram-hood covers create a useful space to remove wet coats and muddy boots.

CONS
- Rainwater will usually find a way into the engine hole and require occasional pumping out.
- Reduced secure interior space.

Semi-trad

Semi-trads enjoy the best of both worlds, with the open space of a cruiser stern and the style of the trad. The back deck is enclosed at the sides but has an open top.

PROS
- Looks like a trad at first glance.
- Plus all the benefits of a cruiser stern.

CONS
- All the same negatives as a cruiser but, unlike on a cruiser, the deck is not practical for deckchairs.

💡 Vikings?
Some people call narrowboats 'barges', but canal folk are quick to correct this. A barge is wider with a beam over 6ft 10in. Others erroneously call them 'longboats', but thankfully Vikings are a rare sight on the cut.

Semi-cruiser

A relatively recent variation on the semi-trad style is the semi-cruiser. It's a bit of a variation on the crossover theme, with a large back deck for socialising and sides that are built up to some degree – often incorporating storage and seating.

PROS

- The practical back deck is great for socialising and storage – seemingly the best of all worlds.

CONS

- Interior lockable space is reduced and outdoor storage is less secure.

Semi-cruiser stern – a practical back deck.

Tug style – with a long bow deck.

Tug

Tug-style boats have large, flat foredecks and are reminiscent of old working cargo boats. Sometimes these are covered with traditional canvas covers secured with ropes.

PROS

- They look fantastic.

CONS

- The tug deck is useless for liveaboard purposes.

Tony's *towpath tales*

It was 2006, and my wallet was throbbing as I flicked through the pages of boats for sale on the internet. As far as I could tell there were dozens of boats around the right size and many were well within my budget. In fact, I could probably buy a boat and still have a fair amount of cash left over. Thankfully I had a friend with some considerable experience on hand to offer advice and to deter me from making bad decisions. Mike had been boating since 1977 and had lived aboard for several years. He was also aware that my compulsion to spend in haste might well cause me to repent, and would certainly compromise my leisure.

First, I was advised against any boat that was less than 50ft long. While living on a smaller boat is possible, a large one is always more comfortable and convenient. Secondly, I was advised against buying any boat bigger than 59ft. Large boats have large running costs, and while the difference between a 59 footer and a 60 footer is negligible, Mike knew that once you break the 60ft threshold it's difficult to hold back. A long discussion was had about trads versus cruisers before we decided that internal lockable space was more useful than somewhere to sip Martinis with guests. Even after I'd filtered the field to include only those that

qualified, there still appeared to be many boats well within my £30,000 budget. After much debate I was persuaded to spend £25,000 on a boat that Mike recommended instead of purchasing the £18,000 boat I coveted. 'Trust me,' Mike said. 'You'll thank me one day!'

And certainly I do. Back then I was not at all discerning about boat styling or fit-out quality and couldn't see £7,000 of difference between the two boats. Nowadays I look at my boat, the lines of its hull and the interesting character of the fit-out and I can see why Mike was so insistent. But I have to admit, I wasn't entirely convinced until he said, 'If you don't buy that boat, then I will!'

Tony's first day aboard.

OTHER BOATS

Although narrowboats are by far the most popular choice, plenty of other types of boats are suited to living aboard, some more so than others.

Wide beam

The style of wide beams is based upon that of the narrowboat and they're usually built by the same boatbuilders with the same features and equipment. Instead of having the standard width of 6ft 10in, the wide beam boat will usually be over 10ft wide and sometimes as wide as 15ft. Wide beams for leisure purposes are a relatively new concept so predictably have modern-style interior fit-outs, but there are a handful of historically interesting wide beams still in existence, such as the Leeds & Liverpool Short Boats. With all the space of a small apartment, wide beams are popular with those whose primary focus is a comfortable home rather than extensive cruising as these boats can't navigate the narrow canals on the network. Indeed, wide beams over 6ft 10in can't travel between the northern and southern sections of England's network, as there are several narrow pinch-points around the Midlands area that restrict wider boats. To make the journey, such boats would need to be moved by road or be seaworthy enough to navigate coastal waters, and while taking them to sea is possible, flat-bottomed boats aren't built for 'lumpy' water.

PROS
- Lots more space with a more comfortable and conventional 'apartment' feel inside.

CONS
- Limited cruising range due to their width.
- Higher costs for mooring, licence and insurance.
- Fewer boats with old-style character available.
- Considered to be less classic and traditional by purists (unless you opt for a historically interesting vessel).

Wide beam

Leeds & Liverpool short boat.

Dutch barge

These are a stylish alternative for those who want more space but still aspire to a classic style. The most original Dutch barges are refurbished industrial or fishing vessels from the Netherlands, but home-grown newly-built Dutch barge-style boats are now available too.

Dutch barge.

PROS

- Beautifully classic boats with lots of character.
- Wider with more interior space.
- Ideal for cruising coastal seas and European rivers.

CONS

- Limited inland cruising range caused by width, draught and wheelhouse height.
- Increased mooring, licence and insurance costs.
- More expensive than suitable liveaboard narrowboats.

GRP cruisers and yachts

Although GRP (glass reinforced plastic) boats are seen frequently on the inland waterways they're mainly used for summertime leisure cruising and are rarely a choice for liveaboard boaters.

The boats seen on canals aren't usually large enough to accommodate a liveaboard lifestyle, nor are they easy to keep warm. That said, a handful of desperately hard-core GRP owners do live aboard their craft on canals, but most GRP liveaboards live at sea or, more rarely, on rivers.

GRP cruiser.

An unusual liveaboard boat.

The unconventional

You do occasionally see unusual and interesting boats used as liveaboards on the inland waterways. Small military, industrial and fishing vessels have enough space to be converted and often have interesting features and fit-outs. Such boats are usually owned by people with the necessary skills to maintain them, as unlike more traditional boats neither spare parts nor support are readily available.

💡 Go everywhere

To have access to the whole of the inland waterways network, your boat should be no longer than 57ft and no wider than 6ft 10in in order to fit into the smallest locks on the inland waterways. However, boats up to 62ft can navigate the vast majority of the network, so you're not going to be missing out on much if you opt for a 62 footer. Beware, though. Boats of 62ft will need to consider the shape of their stern and the state of the lock walls at certain times of the year if they're to navigate these short locks safely.

NEW OR PRE-LOVED?

The choice between new and used boats is not simply dictated by budget. While new boats usually have a higher price tag, there are many other factors to consider too. Most new boats, like most new houses, are built to a template with little variation from an established theme. The shape of the hull, internal fit-out and the choice of facilities, utilities and equipment are usually set to the boatbuilder's stock style. As with new houses, most new boats are built to a tried-and-tested design, but the most prestigious builders do produce outstanding and beautiful boats – at a price.

Buying a new boat will usually mean waiting your turn in the builder's schedule. This could mean anything up to a couple of years, particularly for boats by popular build companies. But if you aspire to your dream boat from a specific builder it's worth the wait.

Another option is a 'sailaway' – a new-build boat for sale at a stage of pre-completion. This can be anything from an empty steel shell to almost any stage of fit-out; insulation, windows, lining, electrics and paint jobs are all options that could be either included or left for you to do yourself, depending on your budget and ability. If you have the skills to fit out a boat yourself, this can be a great way to get your ideal boat at a bargain price. Be aware that fitting out a boat requires more than an average level of DIY competency; working on a boat is different from working on a house in terms of method, skill set and regulations.

A boat build in progress, Kingsground Narrowboats.

💡 Str-e-e-e-tch

It's possible to 'stretch' a boat by adding a new section into the middle. There's little finesse to the process, which is done by simply cutting the boat in half before welding a new section of steel in the centre. The interior is then fitted out to make good inside. Although few boatyards take on this kind of work and few owners consider it, preferring instead to buy a more suitable boat, that's exactly what Tony and Vickie did. (See Chapter 4 to find out more.)

The Watchman's *stretch in progress.*

Financially speaking, buying a new boat can be rather complicated. Most experts recommend the enormously practical British Marine Federation staged-payment contract to efficiently manage the transaction and exchange of money.

In addition, it's essential that both you and the builder have a complete understanding of exactly what features and additions you have ordered and how much they'll cost.

Visiting the builder at intervals to check progress is vital to ensure all is going to plan, as mistakes and omissions can be difficult to correct retrospectively, and some mistakes are impossible to spot or amend once the next stage of the build has begun. Bear in mind that it's not unusual for the scheduled completion date to move, which can be the fault of the boatbuilder or the client making changes. And at least one or two boatbuilders go bust each year, often leaving prospective owners out of pocket and with a heap of headaches.

Second-hand boats, like second-hand houses, have an inherent character installed by the string of previous owners. This character can make the boat either desirable or unattractive, depending on both your and the previous owner's tastes and requirements, but all older boats have a character that new boats off the conveyor belt will often lack.

HOW TO FIND YOUR IDEAL BOAT

Used boats vary enormously. It's surprising how much variation can be installed into such a small space and how critical those variations can be for an aspiring liveaboard boater. The only way to appreciate the variety is to view and compare lots of boats, and the best way to do this is to visit one of the large brokerages. There are several large brokerages located around the country where it's possible to step aboard and view lots of boats in a single day.

Second-hand boats with a liveaboard heritage will often have useful features already built in and included in the price, such as powerful inverters, lots of storage space and fewer caravan-style convertible bunks. It's worth viewing boats both above and below your budget to get a good idea of what you can get for your money, but be prepared to be amazed at how prices can vary as if there's seemingly no science to the pricing process at all.

There are several options to explore when looking to buy a liveaboard boat. Most boats for sale will have a sign in the window stating as much, so a walk along the canal will often be the first step to whet your appetite. While there, you should speak with boaters and other waterways regulars too, as the towpath telegraph is often the quickest and most reliable source of boating information and news. Boat owners, marina staff, boat hire companies and chandlers will usually have their finger on the pulse of what is happening locally.

ONLINE

The largest selection of boats for sale can, of course, be found online. There are several large web-based brokerages, and boats are often offered for sale on eBay. Checking online has many advantages: not only can it be done from the comfort of your armchair at no expense, but it's also a great way to swot up on the features and equipment you're likely to find when you view a boat in person. It's also a good way to get to grips with the technical jargon that is commonly used during the boat-buying process.

Online listings sometimes include a diagram showing how the boat is laid out, details of facilities and features and a selection of photographs. A word of warning, though – be careful when buying boats online, and particularly on eBay, where scams seem to be particularly prevalent. The usual checks and balances for online shopping may suffice, but in a boat purchase transaction extra caution is recommended because of the large sums of money involved.

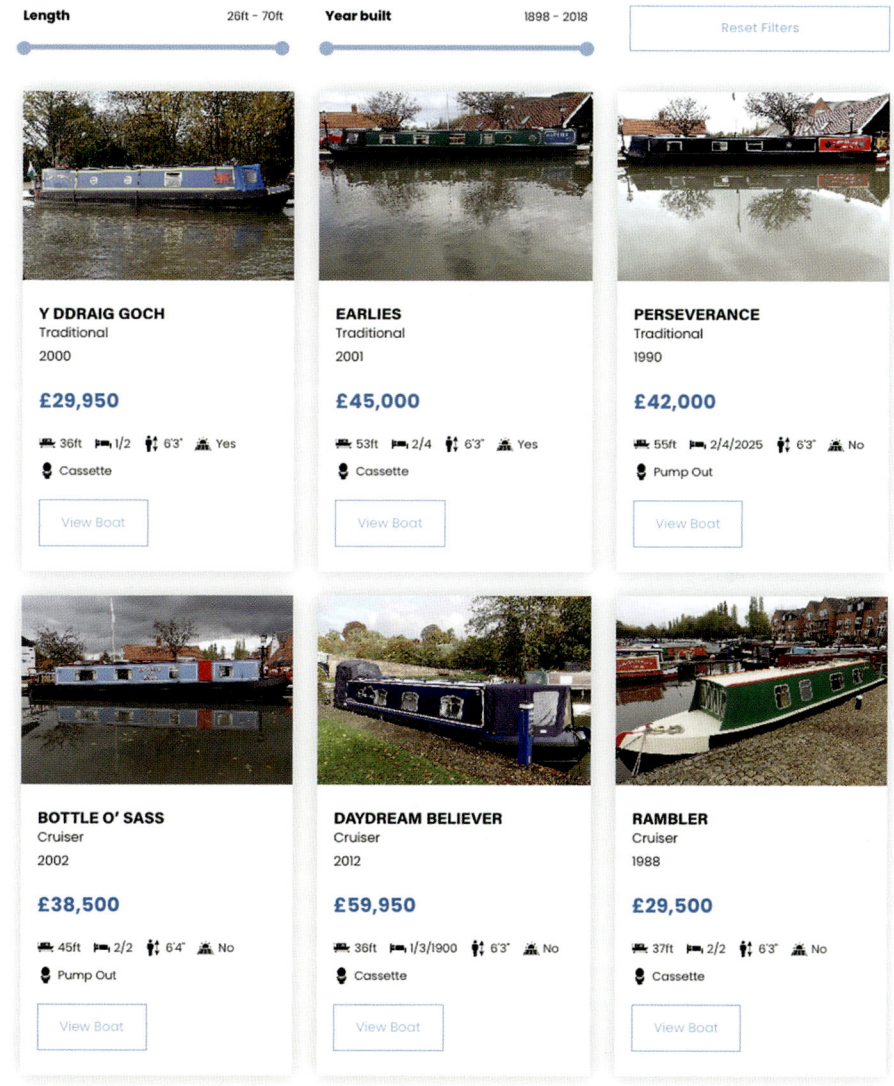

Braunston Marina's online boat brokerage.

Braunston Marina's boat brokerage.

'REAL LIFE' BOAT BROKERAGES

There are so many boats listed for sale on the web that you will likely buy your boat via one of these online brokerages. However, there's no substitute for stepping aboard and viewing boats in person. The vessels you look at online are likely to be found at locations scattered around the country, which makes viewing them logistically difficult, so a visit to a large 'real life' brokerage is always a good idea.

There are several sites around the country where you can view a large selection of boats all in one place. It's an enjoyable way to spend the day and there's always the possibility that you will find your ideal boat there, but be sure to compare many boats across a range of prices and styles before falling in love with one and making the decision to buy.

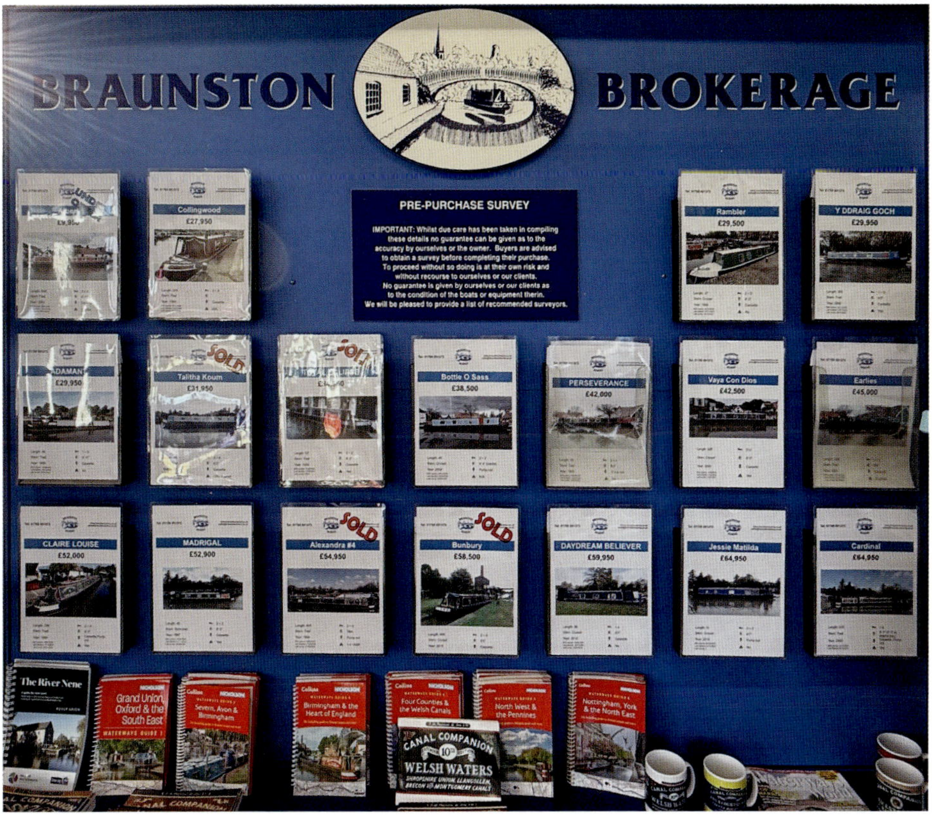

BOATING PRESS

Boats are also offered for sale in the popular boating magazines and newspapers. While there's less room for photographs and lengthy descriptions, these listings are still a good place to look to add to your list of 'possibles'.

BEEN THERE, DONE THAT
ADVICE FOR FOLK LOOKING TO BUY THEIR FIRST BOAT

JOHN
Nb *Sound of Silence*

If you're intending to renovate an old boat you need to make sure you have a plentiful supply of three things: time, money and skill. Unless you're dedicated and proficient in many areas of DIY, you should be wary of cheap boats that need lots of 'doing up'. These boats are a bargain for a reason and lots of people take on such projects only to sell them at a loss, still unfinished. If you're going to live aboard you would be advised to buy a boat you can step onto and start living on immediately, one that has all of the facilities you need. You can upgrade and make good in stages, but it's no fun living on a building site. Boat renovations always cost more and take longer than you expected.

ADRIAN, KIM AND PEPPER
Nb *Hugo*

Accept the fact that you're moving into a small space and be ruthless when deciding what items to bring on board. Spending your life tripping over and/or searching for things and generally not being able to move about freely will make life challenging. Living aboard a boat is a totally different lifestyle and the items you bring aboard need to be in sync with it.

JO
Snaygill Boats

Hire a boat like the one you want and spend a couple of weeks living aboard. While this isn't quite the same as a long-term liveaboard life, it will give you a good idea of what it's like to live with the facilities you have. Can you get along with a cassette toilet or would you prefer a pump-out? Do you need a boiler or is a calorifier suitable? Knowing the answers in theory isn't the same as having experienced them up close and personal.

JUSTINE AND WOODY
Nb *Frog With A Heart*

If you have the skills and the time it's worth buying a sailaway. By doing the fit-out work ourselves we saved lots of money and came out at the end with a brand-new boat exactly to our perfect specifications. No compromises and all within a modest budget. The price you pay is the hard work that is necessary to do a good DIY fit-out.

MIKE
Nb *Aldebaran*

Your dream boat will probably be the second boat you own, having noted the faults and imperfections of your first.

ROBBIE CUMMING
Nb *Naughty Lass*

My advice is to be patient. It took me two years to find *Naughty Lass*, but I didn't just spend that time waiting for an ad to pop up. I did everything I could to get hands-on experience and become part of the community. I joined a group online and posted that I was looking to help boaters with maintenance jobs in return for knowledge about boat maintenance. This gave me an opportunity to spend time on boats to get a better idea of what I liked or didn't like.

Robbie Cumming and his boat, Naughty Lass.

LEGWORK

Only once you have seen a good range of boats will you be in a better position to discern a viable liveaboard from a selection of unsuitable ones. This is when the serious work begins as you can now arrange to view boats that could potentially become your liveaboard home.

Murphy's Law states that boats which closely fit your ideal specifications will be moored many miles away, so it's worth being ruthless when deciding which to view. However, many boat owners have found their ideal boat in the most unlikely of places, and most fell in love after being flexible with their list of unconditional 'must have' features.

PAYING FOR YOUR BOAT

Suitable liveaboard boats start at around £15,000 to £20,000 for a serious 'doer-upper' and most cost significantly more. Many liveaboard owners bought their boats using equity from the sale of a house, particularly those who sold and moved aboard in the early noughties as property values were rising fast. Often those who sell their house to buy a boat are 'downsizing' for either economic or lifestyle considerations. It's fair to say that those who are actively seeking to enjoy a boating lifestyle are usually better suited to boat life than those who are forced aboard for purely financial reasons.

For boats at the cheaper end of the market, a personal loan is an option, but be aware that these boats might require some investment before it will be a comfortable and low-stress home. Marine mortgages are available for those who want to spend a little more than can be raised from a personal loan, and many boat brokerages can arrange these for you if you buy a boat from them.

Be aware that marine mortgages can have comparatively high interest rates and are a secured loan, meaning that, as with a house mortgage, you can lose your home if you default on payments. Some even require home equity as an assurance and all will require a substantial deposit. It's also worth remembering that some liveaboard lifestyles can affect your bank balance, particularly if you move around a lot or have an expensive mooring near your place of work. All loans will need to be repaid so it's important to factor in these specific boating issues.

 Ex-hire boats

Ex-hire boats are often available on the second-hand boat market. These boats will invariably have been kept looking tidy and most (but not all) will have enjoyed a strict and regular maintenance schedule. However, all ex-hire boats will have suffered a hard life at the hands of inexperienced and often careless boaters. They'll also be fitted out to be suitable for boat hire rather than for long-term liveaboard owners.

BOAT-BUYING CHECKLIST
Is the boat big enough?

Most liveaboard boaters agree that 45 to 50ft is a minimum comfortable-sized narrowboat for one person. Remember that bigger boats have bigger running costs for expenses such as moorings, licensing and maintenance.

Admin

When do the licence and Boat Safety Scheme certificate expire? If the expiry date is imminent, it may be possible to negotiate on the price of the boat.

Proof of ownership

Can the seller prove that the boat is theirs to sell? Ask to see their original receipt and some administrative history such as insurance and licence documents. Be sure to get a receipt/bill of sale when you hand over the money to buy the boat.

Survey

Do the sellers have a recent survey for you to look at? While it's likely that you will still need to commission a survey of your own prior to purchase, you can use the information from an old survey to help you decide if you're still interested enough to keep the boat on your list of possibles. When making an offer 'subject to survey' the seller may be more likely to contribute to any repairs the survey has highlighted if your offer was close to the original asking price. If a boat survey shows a thin or pitted hull steel thickness this does not necessarily mean you should write it off. It's possible to overplate a boat, and while this is an expensive process, it may be a viable option for a suitably priced boat if the rest of the vessel is an attractive proposition. Beware that overplating is a specialist skill and that the extra steel will likely affect how the boat sits in the water. There have been instances where overplated boats have sunk when cruising rivers because they have a deeper draught and less distance between the waterline and any holes in the hull. Some surveyors advise against overplating, preferring instead to recommend removing and replacing any suspect steel.

Engine and gearbox

Make sure you take the boat out for a short cruise to check the engine and gearbox for problems. If you aren't mechanically minded, be sure to take someone with you who knows what they're looking and listening for. Gearbox problems are common with narrowboats as the drive plates deteriorate through constant forward and reverse gear changing.

Blacking

When was the boat last blacked? If it's due another coat of blacking soon this could be another price negotiation point. Get local quotes for blacking, including dry dock or haul-out costs, and negotiate accordingly.

Paintwork

A new external paint job is expensive. While few second-hand boats have pristine paintwork, be sure to take its condition into account when negotiating the price and working out a maintenance budget.

Resale value

Some boats depreciate in value more quickly than others, but it's difficult for new boaters to discern between a classically attractive boat and a mass-produced one. Outrageous paint jobs, quirky customisations and specialised adaptations will affect the value of a boat. Someone with lots of boating experience who does not have a vested interest in the sale is the best source of advice.

Refurbishment

If you're looking to move aboard immediately, it's important that the boat you buy has everything you need in full working order. Heat, power, water and sanitation are essential from the moment you step aboard, so make sure these utilities don't need a major overhaul. While it's reasonable to expect to do a little refurbishment, if you can't step aboard and start living immediately, your liveaboard dream could become a delayed and expensive headache.

Underway.

WHAT WILL I GET FOR MY MONEY?
Less than £15,000

Cheap narrowboats aren't good and good narrowboats aren't cheap. You can occasionally find unloved used boats on sale for less than £15,000, but these will invariably be small boats with a good few years on the clock and in a poor state of repair. In most cases, the best thing to do would be to rip out the interior and refit from scratch, and even then you'll usually end up spending much more than the finished boat will be worth. Alternatively, it might be possible to make gradual improvements, but in any case, bringing one of these narrowboats back to life is a labour of love. If you have the time, skills and money to invest it can be a rewarding endeavour, but if you're looking for a cheap way to get afloat then boats at this end of the price range are rarely a good choice.

£15,000 to £35,000

We're still in the shorter, older boat market at these kinds of prices, so it's unlikely you'll find anything less than 15 years old. That said, you might get lucky and find an unloved gem that needs a bit of TLC. The styling, features and fit out will likely be commensurate with the boat's age, so expect Alde boilers, hip baths, and tongue and groove interiors. Don't expect reverse layouts, bow thrusters or diesel heaters unless they have been retro-fitted and you're at the upper end of the price range. Upgrading fittings can be costly, but sometimes this will be necessary as the original equipment ages to the point where parts are no longer available.

If you take on one of these boats you'll need to be ready to either do some work or pay to get it done, and this process can sometimes tarnish the excitement of new boat ownership. If you can tolerate this disappointment, apply your time and skills or pay for someone to do it, then it's possible to make it work. Getting a full survey is strongly recommended at this point on the market as only then can you be confident about the state of the hull and the working order of the engine and fittings. On the plus side, the fit outs from this era of boat building are usually of a good quality, with attractive solid wood rather than MDF. And if you're looking for country-cottage styling, you're certainly in the right place.

£35,000 to £50,000

If you want to get started straight away without taking on major renovation work, then you'll likely be looking at used boats nearer the £35,000 to £50,000 mark. These boats will still probably be at the older end of the boat market, and likely mid-length, but a bit of diligent searching and luck will find you a boat that's ready to go. You'll almost certainly have to spend money on upgrading and refurbishing parts of the boat, so you'll need to consider that when comparing the market. The best boats at these prices will need a paint job, but maybe we should consider that a good thing. Such a boat will often be well cared for and have decent specifications inside. They'll usually be keenly priced because a good paint job isn't cheap. It's unlikely that you'll find a used wide beam at this price, but if you do it'll need a lot of TLC.

£50,000 to £70,000

In this price bracket you'll usually find slightly larger used boats that are 40 feet long or more, with the longer boats being, predictably, more expensive.

However, there are plenty of choices to be had here, and by weighing up the length, price and age you can find some attractively neat boats in this price range. And occasionally, if you're in the right place at the right time, you'll find a real gem.

They'll usually be in a reasonably good state of repair commensurate with their age but you should expect some maintenance and refurbishment costs. Some repairs to worn-out running gear and utilities are likely and might not be immediately obvious at the point of purchase, but you should expect them nonetheless. You'll find 'value' wide beams available at this point in the market, usually at the upper ranges of the price scale.

£70,000 to £100,000

Now you'll be looking at some rather smart used boats that will have been well cared for and be in good shape. You'll find nearly-new smaller boats or tidy-enough larger boats with a few more years on the clock. Most will be less than 10 years old, so of an age where modern features become commonplace.

This is also the price range where you'll find plenty of boats that were built with liveaboards in mind, rather than those built when the leisure-cruising market was more prolific some years previously.

There's no guarantee that boats at this price won't need repairs, but the likelihood of serious defects diminishes as you climb up to the top end. Decent used wide beams can be found at these prices too.

BEEN THERE, DONE THAT
BOAT BUYING TIPS

CHARLIE AND WENDY
Nb *Philip George*

So many people end up buying boats that turn out to be either unsuitable for their needs or riddled with troubles which cost a fortune to put right. If you're new to boating I'd strongly recommend recruiting some help with your purchase. An experienced boater will be able to offer advice on the best type of boat with the right fixtures and facilities for your needs. More importantly, they can also help to identify problems with the boats you go to see.

They'll invariably know where to look for the common problems which, if you haven't seen them coming, could plague you and your bank balance. Electrical headaches, leaking windows, faulty plumbing, blocked toilets, worn-out engines, knackered heating systems and, most worrying, dodgy solid-fuel stoves. Most of these will just cost you money – and a faulty stove could cost you your life.

£100,000 to £150,000

At this point you get to choose from the best used narrowboats and wide beams, and there are also a few new boats with a reasonable spec (including length) too. Used boats will be in excellent condition and are likely to include many of the features you covet. A new boat at this price might not have every feature your heart desires, but if you're not too picky you could find just what you're looking for. If you're lucky, at this price you might find one of those special, cared-for vintage or prestige boats that those in the know might be seeking, and boats with electric or hybrid engines begin to make an appearance in this price bracket too.

£150,000+

At this price, the world is your oyster. A boat built to your specific requirements with exactly the features and fittings you would like is easily attainable if you're willing to pay the price. The most important consideration at this end of the market is to know exactly what you're looking for. Getting the boat of your dreams requires you to nurture a good relationship with an experienced boat-builder.

2 WHEREVER I LAY MY HAT

It's often said that finding a suitable mooring is one of the most important tasks facing boat owners, and with living aboard becoming an increasingly popular lifestyle choice, suitable moorings are in high demand.

A common piece of advice for new boaters is to secure a mooring even before you buy a boat, but this in itself can be a challenge. Most marinas sell mooring space by the foot, so it makes economic sense to put the longest boat possible into the space that they have available. The first question you will be asked when enquiring about moorings is 'How big is your boat?', and if you haven't bought your boat yet, you may be asked to enquire again when you know the answer.

One way to get around the problem is to reserve and pay for a mooring space large enough for your prospective boat and be prepared to swallow the extra cost if you eventually buy a smaller one. However, buying a boat can take time and, as stated before, should not be rushed, so parting with cash month after month for a mooring spot you aren't using flies in the face of frugal boating.

> ### 💡 Big boat problems
> Small boats fit into big mooring spots, but big boats don't fit into small spaces. That's why it's more difficult to find moorings for bigger boats.

If you do buy the boat before finding a suitable mooring you will need to move quickly and will probably have to make greater compromises in order to do so. You might fall lucky and be able to secure a good mooring straight away, but there's always the risk that no convenient spots are available, leaving you mooring on the towpath until space becomes free, and this can take months or even years in popular locations. Lingering on visitor moorings and 'bridge hopping' (see page 54, *Free moorings*) will soon attract the attention of Canal & River Trust (CRT) agents, so the prospect of this being your only option should not be taken lightly.

THE BIG ISSUE

Official residential liveaboard moorings can be quite costly, but thankfully they're becoming more commonly available. Marinas wishing to offer residential moorings need to apply for and be awarded proper planning permission, but in many areas this type of planning status for 'dwellings' is prohibited.

Those boaters who do secure a residential spot potentially have all of the amenities of a land-based home, including a postcode and postal service, telephone landline and sometimes the opportunity to pay council tax. However, liability for council tax is ambiguous where liveaboard boaters are concerned, and the Residential Boat Owners Association has defended several cases where liveaboards were faced with a bill. The general rule is, if the terms of your mooring stipulate that your boat is likely to be moved to a different mooring spot, you aren't liable for council tax.

Those marinas offering official residential moorings will often supplement the fee with an amount chargeable for council tax, but it is relatively small compared with the amount paid by householders. You could say it's a small price to pay for hassle-free residential mooring.

Case Study: MERCIA MARINA

'We have full planning permission for 360 residential berths,' says Tony Preston, Sales and Marketing Manager at Mercia Marina. 'Achieving residential status is often considered the "holy grail" for many boaters, as it unlocks access to essential services and benefits such as registering with doctors and banks, obtaining car insurance, getting post and deliveries, receiving the benefits you're entitled to, using local authority recycling centres, etc.

'Residents are required to move their boats to another berth in the marina twice a year, but by doing so no council tax is payable. Perhaps the greatest benefit of living at Mercia Marina is becoming part of a vibrant, friendly, and active community. The camaraderie here mirrors the spirit of the canal.'

BEEN THERE, DONE THAT
FINDING A MOORING

ADRIAN, KIM AND PEPPER
Nb *Hugo*
We purchased our boat from Braunston Marina and, as a brokerage customer, they guaranteed us a mooring as part of their sales offering.

KEV AND SAFFI
Nb *The Grey Lady*
I've been lucky enough to get a mooring in a couple of different marinas by simply enquiring. It goes without saying that being friendly and polite certainly helps smooth the way.

JUSTINE AND WOODY
Nb *Frog With A Heart*
We had plenty of time to find a marina while our boat shell was being built, which is just as well as we had to find a mooring where we would be allowed to work on the boat. Some marinas have strict rules so it was important to get permission for us to be banging and sawing. Eventually, for one reason or another we ended up continuous cruising, and quite happily too.

STEVE AND EILEEN
Nb *Rahab*
Our first mooring came with the boat when we bought it. While it was expensive and not particularly convenient for us, we did at least have a mooring, so we could look for something more suitable at our leisure. We found the boat club where we currently moor as we were walking up the towpath. There was a sign with a phone number, which we called, and three months later we were moored there and living aboard. One of the things we like about our new mooring is that our boat is not too far from the car park. At the last place it was quite a walk and carrying shopping between the two was a nightmare. To make matters worse, the path was paved with gravel, which meant that pulling a trolley was almost impossible. We didn't live aboard at that stage, so it wasn't too much of a problem, but I'd hate to have to go through that ordeal regularly as a liveaboard.

💡 Face to face
It's unwise to enquire about liveaboard moorings by phone or email. It may be necessary to set up an appointment by phone, but don't enquire about costs or space, and certainly don't declare your liveaboard status. Face-to-face meetings are preferable, as some mooring providers will have a policy of vetting new arrivals.

On paper, many mooring providers don't offer residential moorings, and while some will strictly enforce a no-liveaboard policy, others will 'unknowingly' accommodate discreet liveaboards. Even some moorings owned by CRT are classed as residential, which entitles boaters to stay on their boat all year. The definition of 'residential' is so ambiguous that it's easy for marina owners to find a loophole, especially when, as is usually the case, most boats leave the marina for some weeks or months during the course of any given year so their owners can't be accurately described as permanent residents.

It's wise to do some research and look for signs that people live aboard before meeting with the owner or manager of the site. Ask other boaters about the local liveaboard options, but avoid asking boaters from the site you're coveting until you know how the land lies. When a meeting has been arranged be careful about asking 'Can I live aboard here?' as the answer is often an official no, but there's usually a way to achieve an unspoken understanding. Some will ask outright if you live aboard and explain that living on site is not allowed and that you must vacate your boat for a set number of days per year, while others have a higher tariff for 'high-use' boats.

Answering questions honestly and complying with the rules laid down by the site is always the best policy to avoid issues further down the line. It may be that you can comply with the regulations by taking your boat out to cruise the local waterways for a few weeks or months each year.

Bosworth Marina on the Ashby Canal.

💡 Fat boat, fat wallets

Most mooring providers will charge extra to moor a wide beam. It can sometimes double the price of a narrowboat.

This is a most agreeable means of toeing the line, and as long as you don't hog popular visitor moorings you're unlikely to attract the attention of CRT agents. (Boaters with a permanent mooring seem to attract less attention than those registered as continuous cruisers for some reason.) Perhaps your partner is based locally and you spend occasional nights there? Add in a few weeks of holiday away from your boat and you will almost certainly have negated any enforceable definition that you live at your marina.

Mooring providers aren't obliged to give you a mooring so you should make your application as attractive as possible. Some places, clubs and private marinas especially will discriminate against untidy looking boats with the view that these will 'lower the tone' of the establishment. A boat roof lined with piles of firewood, pushbikes, loud unruly dogs, a TV aerial and bags of rubbish can hint that you're likely not only a liveaboard, but a messy one at that. Presenting a good image and reading between the lines when discussing moorings, can be the difference between their site being full or them being able to squeeze your boat in somewhere.

When looking for a mooring there are so many factors to consider that it's inevitable that you will need to compromise somewhere, but by being flexible and objective a solution can usually be found. In an ideal world you would find a friendly, perfectly located and well-managed mooring with great security in a beautiful location with great facilities and lots of accessible local resources. And it would be inexpensive too. In reality you will probably need to compromise and your personal circumstances will dictate which of these areas you can be most flexible in. It will come as no surprise that you will usually get what you pay for.

💡 Step aboard

When buying a boat, ask if the mooring can be transferred to you as the new owner. Some mooring providers are eager to do this as it means they'll not be losing money while they look for another boat to fill the empty spot.

This is often the easiest way to start, and even if the location is less than ideal it buys some breathing space while you look for a more convenient spot.

But beware of contracts that tie you down for a long period of time.

A typical liveaboard boat.

💡 Boatyard facilities

Boatyard moorings will often have invaluable dry dock or crane-out facilities on site. Wide beam owners should be aware that dry dock facilities for wide boats are less frequently available and crane costs can be more expensive too.

💡 Jo, Snaygill Boats

We don't have planning permission to offer residential moorings so can't accommodate liveaboards, but every now and again it becomes evident that someone is living aboard on site. Of course, we understand that boaters will occasionally overnight here, but we are always clear when we welcome new boaters that we can't accommodate liveaboards. It's awful when you realise that a new customer has been less than honest when claiming they don't live on their boat.

PAY TO STAY

PAY-TO-STAY MARINAS

Large, commercially run purpose-built marinas are popping up everywhere. Most will offer the basic utilities a liveaboard boater will need, such as electricity hook-up, water point and usually a pump-out station. Some feature a separate shower and toilet block, and many marinas now boast laundry facilities, convenient parking, chandlery supplies and even wireless internet access, dog washing facilities and berth-holder events. These features, coupled with the location, will dictate the price you pay. Most marinas of this type have floating-pontoon access and boats are moored close together, but rarely on-line or abreast.

Gallows Bridge Boatyard, Leeds & Liverpool Canal.

PAY-TO-STAY BOATYARDS

A short distance from any large marina you will find a boatyard and these are usually a cheaper mooring option where space is available. Being a working boatyard the premises will invariably have a more 'industrial' ambiance, and it's worth remembering that working with steel boats is often a noisy business. Moorings at facilities like this are often supplementary to the main boatyard income and boats will be packed into every available space. Often they'll be moored two and sometimes three or more abreast. Facilities are often limited. Electricity supply may come via a cable run from the nearest power point, and filling with water might mean shuffling boats to the nearest tap. Don't be surprised if you need to visit the nearby large marina to get a pump-out.

That said, moorings at boatyards have the benefit of knowledgeable and handy boat maintenance experts on site, and while you should not expect a discounted rate for working on your boat, you will often receive preferential treatment.

PAY-TO-STAY BOAT CLUBS

Another less frequently available option is a boat club mooring and these can be surprisingly good value for money. Boat clubs are usually run as a not-for-profit organisation and manage to keep fees low because boaters are expected to contribute to the upkeep of the club, negating the need to pay management and staffing costs or turn a profit.

Most clubs have a long and proud history and many have evolved from humble beginnings on the towpath to a point where they have the best facilities available. Some, such as Craven Cruising Club, which has two mooring locations on the Leeds & Liverpool Canal, offer no facilities at all beyond a few mooring rings and a security gate. Others have facilities rivalling even the best-equipped marina, from dry docks and covered boat-painting areas, to clubhouses with bars where social events are held throughout the year. A pint at one club I know of costs just £2.50, largely thanks to the boat-club members who volunteer their bartending services to keep the cost of a pint so low.

As I've alluded to previously, one of the main attractions of mooring at a boat club is the price. It's not unusual for moorings at boat clubs to cost half of an equivalent spot in a marina or boatyard. It's something that Jerry Holland from South Pennine Boat Club in Mirfield near Huddersfield has thought about a lot. 'The cost of moorings can be a deal breaker for people who want to get into boating – especially relatively younger people.

💡 Liveaboards

Many boat clubs won't allow boaters to live aboard on site. This is often due to a condition of their lease, but some are also eager to preserve the traditional character of their club. While some will turn a blind eye or have one or two residential boats for security purposes, many will not allow liveaboards at all.

Case Study: STRAWBERRY ISLAND BOAT CLUB

Doncaster, South Yorkshire. Sheffield & South Yorkshire Navigation

One of the best-known boat clubs is Strawberry Island Boat Club, which recently celebrated its 50th anniversary having begun its life from rather humble beginnings. The first clubhouse on the site was an old Yorkshire keel barge, which was duly licensed to serve alcohol as one of the first items on the club's agenda. The barge served its purpose admirably during the club's early years as members cut back the jungle that had taken over the adjacent land, cleared the sunken and abandoned boats, dug out moorings and built a rudimentary slipway using reinforced concrete beams.

Since then the club has installed a boat crane that members can use at a rate far more attractive than the prices charged by marinas and boatyards. The barge-based clubhouse has also been superseded by a purpose-built premises, which satisfies the social requirements of the club, including attractive bar prices.

Andrew Denny, the *Waterways World* news editor, wrote about the ceaseless work that's been done over the last 50 years to upgrade the club, saying, 'The bridge over the old lock chamber, workshop, sanitary and waste disposal station, series of clubhouses, car park, lighting, power and freshwater services, hard-standing, tree and shrub planting, grassed areas and new pontoon moorings – these were all done entirely by members participating in the regular weekly work parties. Keeping the work in-house doesn't just save money, it also creates a sense of camaraderie. These days the work parties are usually just one morning a week, followed by a lunch prepared for the group by volunteers in the clubhouse. The motto of the Strawberry Island Boat Club was "If a contractor enters through our gate, we have failed".'

And there's no getting away from the fact that most boaters are older folk, so I feel it's important for us to make boating as attractive as we can for youngsters. Maybe boat clubs with cheaper moorings are one way we can do this.'

Boat clubs usually have a strong social ethos with all of the pros and cons inherent in any close-knit community. This means that club members tend to stay members for many years and moorings aren't frequently available as a result. Most clubs run an extensive waiting list.

Case Study: AIREDALE BOAT CLUB

Bingley, West Yorkshire. Leeds & Liverpool Canal

I was four years into my boating life before I'd heard of the existence of boat clubs. I was introduced to a friend of a friend who was a member at Airedale Boat Club in Bingley, Yorkshire, on the Leeds & Liverpool Canal. I was continuously cruising at the time, but hearing about the club's wonderfully cheap moorings in this beautiful corner of the world, I decided that a mooring at ABC was exactly what I needed.

As one of the few 'younger' members I was recruited to perform many of the heavy-lifting tasks during working weekends, which I enjoyed immensely. I was assured a steady supply of tea and cake throughout the day and as a relatively new boater at the time I was keen to listen in on the conversations of those who had been out cruising during the summer season, soaking up their wisdom and advice as best I could.

The club's social calendar was extensive and always well attended. Little excuse was needed for a party or function. You could guarantee that Christmas, Halloween, anniversaries and birthdays would elicit an invite, and there'd often be quizzes or games, too.

The only downside of mooring at a boat club is the normal clunky and inefficient mechanisms you'll experience at any committee-run organisation, but this was a small frustration in what was an otherwise fabulous boating experience.

The AWCC

The Association of Waterways Cruising Clubs represents the interests of 6,000 inland waterways boat owners, through the membership of more than 100 cruising clubs. The association acts as a forum for boaters to address the many issues, both local and national, which can affect their club and their enjoyment of cruising inland waterways. Boat clubs must become affiliate with the AWCC in order for their members to access a number of benefits.

💡 Join the club

You can find information and contact details for almost all of the UK's boat clubs on the AWCC website, and many clubs have their own website.

www.awcc.org.uk

On-line moorings.

PAY-TO-STAY FARM MOORINGS

Waterside private landowners, often farm owners, sometimes offer moorings as a small enterprise, usually for only a handful of boats. Predictably, the facilities provided vary widely from site to site and are unlikely to feature boating-specific services. Interestingly, one such site fell under the care of the local council who, upon realising the site was home to liveaboard boaters, set about legitimising the residential status of the moorings. By charging the lowest rate of council tax the moorings became bona fide residential, thus eliminating the earlier ambiguity and subterfuge.

PAY-TO-STAY CRT ON-LINE MOORINGS

On-line mooring, i.e. being moored on the canalside, is one of the cheapest mooring options as these moorings usually have no facilities at all. While this might sound like the worst possible option, on-line moorings have several distinct advantages. First, they're usually pretty cheap, so if that is a primary focus for you then on-line mooring might be your best option. Secondly, as a bona fide mooring you will not have to worry about being moved on in the same way that continuous cruisers often will. Thirdly, this type of mooring is widely available and often in the most surprisingly picturesque of locations. And lastly, you will usually have boating neighbours on the same stretch of canal, amounting to a ready-made community.

Pontoon-style moorings.

Of course, without an electrical hook-up it's important that you have an engine and an electrical system that you can rely on, but this should be true of all boaters. Similarly, the need to travel for pump-out and water should not be too much of an inconvenience for boaters who are well organised and prepared, and most will relish the opportunity to start their engines and undertake some actual boating, no matter how short or irregular.

On-line moorings are frequently available directly through CRT and are acquired via tender through a sealed auction bid. It's possible to get a bargain if you aspire to a mooring location that is for some reason less popular, and it's often advisable to check demand and prices with others at the site.

💡 Security

On-line moorings are often situated on the towpath, where the general public have access. While security is not often an issue where moored boats are a familiar sight, it's worth checking whether there's a regular local problem.

No mooring is totally secure and problems can potentially occur anywhere. A good boating community is usually enough to discourage all but the most hooligan of elements.

PAY-TO-STAY END OF GARDEN MOORINGS

Many boaters aspire to own their own mooring, either at the end of a garden or by owning a piece of land next to the water. Indeed, these types of moorings are only an option if you own both the house and the boat you want to moor there. CRT will charge a fee to moor on their water, usually 50 per cent of the fee levied for similar moorings in that vicinity.

> 💡 **Short-term moorings**
>
> Many marinas and boat clubs will offer short-term moorings for set periods during the year. These are available because a regular moorer is away cruising for a given period and filling the space is a good way to earn extra revenue. Some places offer moorings during winter as people hunker down after the cruising season, and it's worth securing these as early as possible.

FREE MOORINGS

Yes, it's possible to incur no mooring costs whatsoever, but there's a different price to pay. Free visitor moorings are available at thousands of places on the waterways network and these will normally have mooring rings, bollards, cleats or metal piling that can accommodate mooring hooks. It's also possible to moor at the water's edge wherever this is practicable and the land is not privately owned. However, these moorings aren't permanent and the amount of time you're allowed to stay there ranges from a maximum of 14 days to as little as a few hours. These visitors' moorings are intended as just that.

Boats without a permanent mooring are termed 'continuous cruisers' and there are rules governing the mooring such activities. A continuous cruise is a slightly ambiguous activity, but the craft used is defined by Canal & River Trust as a 'boat [that] travels widely around the waterway network without staying in any one place for more than 14 days (or less where local CRT signs indicate a shorter period)'. The specifics aren't set in stone, and while CRT has done its best to define the rules for continuous cruisers, there are many boaters who endeavour to inhabit a grey area within the regulations.

The rules state that the boat must move to a new location at least every 14 days, with a 'new location' being defined as a new district rather than a different mooring spot in the same area. The guidance states: 'The necessary movement from one neighbourhood to another can be done in one step or by short gradual steps. What the law requires is that if 14 days ago the boat was in neighbourhood X, by day 15 it must be in neighbourhood Y. Thereafter, the next movement must normally be to neighbourhood Z, and not back to neighbourhood X (with obvious exceptions such as reaching the end of a terminal waterway or reversing the direction of travel in the course of a genuine progressive journey).'

Free moorings on the Leeds & Liverpool Canal.

Some continuous cruisers who need to be in a particular area will often resort to what is known as 'bridge hopping', moving short distances in a given area before returning to the original location. This is rarely a successful strategy and will soon attract attention from CRT enforcement staff, the resultant stress being a veritable coffin nail in the carefree boating lifestyle most of us aspire to. The only way to avoid the hassle is to abide by the rules and move to a new neighbourhood every 14 days. The definition of a 'neighbourhood' varies with geography and not by mileage. In urban areas a new neighbourhood might be the next town a short distance away, whereas in rural areas the distance could be far greater, and this is where some boaters feel there's a grey area. 'A sensible and pragmatic judgement' is required according to the CRT's guidelines.

The mooring rules are overseen by enforcement staff from CRT, whose interpretation of the regulations seems to vary enormously according to reports from boaters from across the country. Specifically allocated visitors' moorings are more strictly enforced, as are the stopping places on all of the busy parts of the network. Patrols are less frequent on quieter and less desirable stretches of water, but consistently stubborn overstayers will soon attract attention and, sometimes, a charge for overstaying.

💡 **CRT mooring regulations**

Learn more about continuous-cruising mooring regulations at:

www.canalrivertrust.org.uk/boating/license-your-boat/continuous-cruising

💡 **Quote – Troy, Snaygill Boats**

In the last few years the number of people enquiring about liveaboard moorings has increased sharply and we know that other marinas and boatyards are experiencing the same thing. Living aboard is gaining popularity fast!

💡 **Factors to consider**

- Location
- Electricity
- Water
- Pump-out
- Gas, coal and other supplies
- Local cruising options
- Train/bus services
- Shopping

- Chandlery
- Crane or dry dock
- Boat maintenance
- Laundry
- Shower or toilet block
- Internet access
- Clubhouse
- Post collection service

Tony's *towpath tales*

My boat was lying in Daventry, Northamptonshire, when I bought it. I didn't move aboard immediately and stayed for a few weeks in the place I was renting in Surrey while I searched for a mooring nearer my work in Epsom. Having commissioned the marina in Daventry to do some work on my boat's electrical system I had a few weeks of grace to find a more convenient mooring.

Eventually, I found a space in a large commercial marina located on the beautiful River Wey near Woking. This solved my immediate mooring issue, but in turn raised several other problems to be faced at a later date. The most immediate of these was that the River Wey is managed by the National Trust and living aboard is simply not allowed. I was informed in no uncertain terms that living aboard would not be tolerated, and told stories of people who had tried to get away with it only to be confronted by the National Trust.

Luckily, my circumstances at the time allowed me to get around the problem in a variety of ways. I still had use of my rented land home for a few more weeks and my girlfriend lived close enough to the marina to be convenient. Add to that three weeks of holiday spent abroad and a period where the boat was having yet more work done, and I managed to make my stopovers on the boat sporadic enough to not attract any attention for the several months I was moored there.

The second problem was financial. The cost of mooring at the marina was eye-wateringly expensive (for 2005 at least), with the annual mooring fee for my boat being in excess of £4,000. For that price I could have a residential mooring elsewhere on the network, let alone a strictly enforced non-liveaboard spot. The price was certainly reflected in the quality of the mooring and the beauty of the venue, though, which brings me onto another problem I was now faced with. By the time I had spent a few nights aboard my boat in the beautiful setting that surrounded my mooring I knew I needed a more convenient liveaboard spot as soon as possible.

The River Wey is one of the most stunning waterways in the UK, and after a short time I was sold on boat life hook, line and sinker. I had a choice: I could stick around in Surrey and keep my job, but not be able to live on my boat, or I could quit my job and set off north to some place where mooring and living aboard would be easier. So I headed north with the intention of finding a mooring (and hopefully some work) somewhere en route.

The idea of living in London has never floated my boat so I had no intention of stopping there, but I still wanted to live in the south. Having reached the Grand Union Canal I stopped in Hemel Hempstead, Hertfordshire, to enquire about moorings. Immediately I was asked if I lived aboard, to which I replied that I worked away regularly and stayed with my girlfriend often, but would be staying on my boat for periods of time in between. This seemed to satisfy the mooring manager, and I was given a spot costing approximately half of what I was paying on the River Wey; and there I stayed for over a year, venturing out occasionally to cruise the waterways around the area.

Again, my frequency aboard didn't seem to concern anyone who might care that I was living there, and I was never troubled about it.

RENTING BOATS

Renting a boat instead of buying one, or renting out a boat you own, could appear attractive. However, there's a lot to know before you undertake either of these activities. Getting it wrong could be either costly, dangerous or deadly.

Owning a boat is expensive, so no wonder the idea of renting it out could be tempting for some. Private owners feeling the pinch from the rising cost of living might relish the prospect of earning a seemingly passive income from their boat. Interest in boat rentals has seen an uptick in recent years with rising house prices encouraging more people to consider alternative housing options. AirBnB-style short lets are increasingly popular too, not to mention the post-Covid trend for staycationing creating a market.

So how viable is boat rental? What are the costs? And, more importantly, what risks are involved? My first port of call to find out more was Gareth Stephens, Head of Business Boating & Waterside Moorings at CRT.

GARETH STEPHENS, CRT.

It's possible to rent out your boat on a commercial basis and CRT has robust guidance and regulations to govern the process thoroughly. There are two main models of business that these regulations aim to cover:

1 Boats hired for navigation purposes, whether overnight or day hire.
2 Boats hired for static letting with no navigation.

Boat owners wishing to operate any of these commercial activities will require a 'self-drive holiday hire licence', or a 'static let' licence. These licences are approximately double the price of a standard private use licence.

To obtain either of these licences, boat owners will need to present:

- an insurance certificate that shows they're insured for their business activity. Any boat engaged in a commercial activity must be covered by suitable a commercial insurance policy. They'll need to obtain third party and public liability insurance cover provided by a company that is authorised and regulated by the Financial Conduct Authority and which covers liabilities of at least £2 million for each claim. A standard non-commercial policy will not be sufficient.

- a copy of their British Marine Federation Handover Audit certificate or a copy of their full handover procedure document. This is the same handover process a person would receive when hiring a boat for navigation. This is a necessary requirement even if the boat is being hired for a static letting and no navigation is planned.

- proof that their mooring provider is happy for them to operate from the site. A boat rental business must operate from a designated and approved site. If the boat is based in a marina, assuming approval is forthcoming, the marina may apply a surcharge to the mooring fee.

If the boat is located on a secure mooring site where access to the site is via a code or key system, the boater must also provide evidence that the other moorers on the site are happy for them to offer the boat for static letting. And they must show you have the right to access facilities such as fresh water, sewage disposal, rubbish disposal and fuel. It's not possible to operate such a business from the towpath or with a continuous cruiser licence.

- a Boat Safety Scheme certificate to non-private/hire boat standards. The certificate requires an enhanced inspection, which is identical to those performed on boats used in a hire fleet.

- a copy of the landlord's gas safety certificate.

BOATS HIRED FOR NAVIGATION

Boats hired for navigation purposes will also need to conform to the requirements of The Hire Boat Code. This is a code of practice for the operation of hire vessels on inland waterways that sets out the basic principles of safe operation. It also makes clear the responsibilities of each of the parties involved. The focus is on ensuring that the operator has a suitable safety management system in place to ensure the continued safe operation of the vessels under their responsibility. Any boat owner aiming to enter the boat rental or hire market should ensure they fully familiarise themselves with the code.

RESIDENTIAL MOORINGS

Long-term residential use of a mooring for accommodation usually needs planning permission. Boat owners wanting to rent out their boat for residential purposes should contact their local planning authority (LPA) at an early stage and they'll tell you if planning permission is needed. While CRT does not police planning regulations, your business could be at risk if you're found to be operating in breach of the LPA's rules.

A PASSIVE INCOME?

Renting out a boat incurs a reasonable amount of heavy lifting. In addition to the additional administrative and financial requirements, owners will also need to consider the time required to properly hand over the boat, and also be prepared for the potential of 24-hour emergency call-outs. This is why most established hire-boat companies employ the economy of scale by operating several boats, thereby spreading the cost of running the service among the whole fleet.

💡 Hiring checklist

If you're thinking about hiring a boat for static let or navigation you should check the boat has:

- The correct licence – a self-drive hire or static let licence. A private licence is not sufficient
- A commercial insurance policy
- An enhanced Boat Safety Scheme certificate
- A landlord's Gas Safety certificate
- A boat handover document

The boat may not be properly licensed or insured if the handover happens on the towpath and not at a designated mooring or if the owner can't produce the documentation listed above.

While these requirements might seem onerous to the individual boat owner aiming to monetise their circumstances, it's important to appreciate that these regulations are in place to protect the customer while they're aboard the boat. 'The minute you accept payment from a customer you have additional responsibilities,' explains Gareth. 'Anyone operating under the radar will invariably be failing in their duty and responsibility to make sure the customer is safe. Opportunist and rogue operators do exist and the CRT endeavours to shut them down as quickly as possible.

If you're concerned a boat is not licensed correctly you should contact CRT.'

The Trust recently introduced static let licences to service the recent trend and demand for such lettings but only a small number of static let licences have been issued in the five years since they were launched.

Case Study: A RENTER'S NIGHTMARE

Name withheld by request.

I'd been on a couple of short narrowboat holidays before, but my first real experience of narrowboat life was renting one through a company that acted as a letting agency for narrowboat owners. My experience was pretty bad.

I'd split up with my partner and needed to find somewhere to live as soon as possible. The narrowboat letting agency came up when I Googled and it seemed like a good way to get a roof above my head and get started with narrowboats. The person I spoke with on the phone sold me an idyllic lifestyle and I arranged a viewing a few days later. The boat looked nice enough at first glance. It needed a good clean and was a little tired in places, but it was certainly somewhere I could see myself living. The man from the agency told me that they would be responsible for all of the administration and legalities, and they'd also take care of any maintenance or repairs that needed to be done. All I had to worry about was water, diesel, toilets and fuel, and of course, pay the £1,300 monthly rent. I also had to pay £1,500 upfront as a deposit.

Things weren't good right from the start. I picked the boat up on the towpath near Hillmorton and found that there were lots of the owner's possessions still aboard, taking up valuable storage space. The stern gland also urgently needed repacking and it soon became apparent that the back boiler on the solid-fuel stove wasn't working. It took weeks for this to be fixed, meaning most of the boat was freezing because the radiators didn't heat up. Thankfully, hot water could be supplied by running the engine, but this was less than ideal too because I was in a marina and running the engine constantly was frowned upon.

The owner of the boat I was renting lived in America, while the agency owner lived in Dorset and was extremely difficult to get hold of. And when I did manage to contact him he became aggressive and accused me of breaking the back boiler. Eventually, a young lad came to fix it, but it took several attempts spanning a few weeks before it was fixed.

The handover when I moved onto the boat was sorely lacking too. I got about half an hour of tuition – essentially a whistle-stop tour of the boat, and then I was sent off into the wild blue yonder. The agency encouraged me to continuously cruise and discouraged moving into a marina. I know now that this was probably because the paperwork and insurance I had were not suitable. I never saw a Boat Safety Scheme certificate and the insurance cover looked like a standard private owner policy without mention of any commercial liability. And when the licence expired I was told that 'it had been taken care of' although I didn't see a licence I could display for weeks.

I realise now that I should have investigated the situation more thoroughly but, like many new boaters, I was naive and didn't know what I didn't know. The longer I spent living on the boat the clearer it became that it was a bad situation and likely not compliant with CRT's licensing conditions. I stuck it out for nearly six months before resigning myself to the fact I needed to find somewhere else to live. Nowadays I live on my own boat in a marina and it's quite obvious how badly run the company was and how potentially dangerous my situation was while I was renting from them. Similarly, I'm sure the agency owner would not have been liable should anything untoward have happened, and that liability would almost certainly have fallen upon the owner. My advice to anyone looking to rent a boat to live in would be to do lots of research, and then to do even more. The cost of legally renting a boat means it would probably be cheaper to rent a land-based property. I'd certainly never rent a boat to live on again.

STATIC RENTAL INSURANCE

Quinton Hall, Haven Knox Johnston. Many people bought boats during the Covid pandemic with a view to using them for staycation holidays, and then quickly realised that boats are expensive to maintain – especially with the recent increases in the cost of living having an impact on many people's budgets. As a result, many boaters are now looking for ways to monetise their boat, which is why we launched our static-hire policy.

The policy is strictly for non-commercial owners and is only used for 80 per cent occupancy volume. That means the boat can be rented out for 80 per cent of the year and must be for private use by the owner for the remaining 20 per cent. It covers only the boat – not the people using or renting the boat. Their personal risks and liabilities would be covered by the platform on which the static-let boat is advertised (eg AirBnB) and through the renters' travel insurance. The policy is only suitable for static hire purposes, which means the boat cannot be taken from its mooring by the hirer. Indeed, a clause in the policy states that the boat must be locked and secured to the mooring and therefore unable to be taken away. The owner must also have permission from the operator of their mooring or marina.

It's important to note that the policy is strictly for non-commercial rentals. We recently refused cover to a boater who wished to employ a cleaner to service their boat between tenants as employing staff would contravene the 'non-commercial' stipulations of the policy. It's also up to the renter to perform due diligence and comply with the licensing requirements of the navigation authority where they're moored.

Case Study: BEWARE OF SCAM ARTISTS

The October 2012 edition of *Waterways World* reported the story of confidence trickster John Driver who defrauded both the owner and renter of a boat. Under the business name Narrowboat Homes, Driver invited boat owners to rent out their boats to tenants for a share of the rental income.

The owner of a boat called *Canality J'aime* took up the offer but received only a handful of bank deposits before payments ceased. Attempts to contact Driver proved fruitless, so the owner located their boat and took possession.

Meanwhile, it transpired that Driver had sold the boat to an unwitting buyer who was completely unaware that Driver was not the owner of the boat and had no legal right to sell it. The first the new 'owner' knew of the situation was when they returned to find the boat gone and informed the police. Driver was eventually convicted, but both 'owners' lost around £8,000 in resolving the issue.

3 THE COST OF BOATING

'A boat is a hole in the water into which you throw money.'

Tony watches on as The Watchman's engine is lifted out for rebuild.

Aspiring boaters often ask about the financial aspects of boating. Despite the stock response being 'an arm and a leg and your firstborn child!' it's a difficult question to answer given the variety of boats, boaters and waterways. To get some idea of the costs involved, a handful of boaters were asked to keep track of their boating-related spending for a whole year. The costs listed are true of 2025 and will of course vary over time. Here is a summary.

Canal & River Trust
Making life better by water

THE WATCHMAN

72148

08/26

Standard Canal and River Licence. 1037667

THE BIG THREE

LICENCE

In order to be sure you get the most suitable and cost-effective licence you'll need to consider a few different factors.

1 WHERE DO YOU WANT TO CRUISE?
Most of the waterways in England and Wales are managed by CRT and can be navigated by boats with a Canal and River Licence from CRT. The Environment Agency manages most of the remaining navigable rivers and you'll need a different licence to navigate each individual river.

In addition, several smaller agencies manage a handful of navigable waterways, each requiring a different licence. A list of these can be found in the table opposite.

2 HOW BIG IS YOUR BOAT?
CRT calculates licence fees on the length and beam of a boat. A beam over 2.16m will incur a surcharge of 13 per cent on the licence fee, and if your boat is over 3.24m you'll be looking at an extra 26 per cent.

> 💡 **Going for gold**
> A 'Gold Licence' will let you cruise all the waterways managed by both CRT and the Environment Agency.

The Environment Agency also considers boat length and beam in its licence calculations.

3 HOW FAST DO YOU WANT TO PAY?
CRT offers a 'prompt payment' discount for boaters who pay their licence fee on time or sooner.

> 💡 **CRT rivers only**
> A rivers only licence is a cheaper option for those boaters wishing to cruise only the rivers managed by CRT. Beware that this will severely limit your boat's cruising range and is unsuitable for continuous cruisers.

Canal & River Trust
www.canalrivertrust.org.uk/boating/license-your-boat   Tel: 0303 040 4040

Environment Agency
www.gov.uk/browse/environment-countryside/boats-waterways   Tel: 03708 506 506

Basingstoke Canal BASINGSTOKE CANAL AUTHORITY
www.hants.gov.uk/thingstodo/basingstokecanal/onthewater   Tel: 01252 370073

River Wey THE NATIONAL TRUST
www.nationaltrust.org.uk   Tel: 01483 561389

River Avon AVON NAVIGATION TRUST
www.avonnavigationtrust.org   Tel: 01386 552517

Norfolk and Suffolk Broads BROADS AUTHORITY
www.broads-authority.gov.uk/boating/owning-a-boat/tolls   Tel: 01603 610734

Bridgewater Canal (Manchester) BRIDGEWATER CANAL COMPANY LTD
www.bridgewatercanal.co.uk/boating   Tel: 0161 629 8432

Manchester Ship Canal MARINE OPERATIONS DEPARTMENT
www.peelports.com/marine/our-ports/manchester-ship-canal   Tel: 0151 949 6140

Middle Levels MIDDLE LEVEL COMMISSIONERS
www.middlelevel.gov.uk   Tel: 01354 653232

Worseley, Bridgewater Canal.

Case Study: LICENCE PRICES

The Watchman is 50ft long and has a standard 12-month Canal and River Continuous Cruiser Licence with home mooring from CRT. This would cost £1,360.44 but was discounted for prompt payment online to £1,326.43.

Pitchfork is 35ft long and has a 12-month rivers only licence with home mooring from CRT. This cost £606.02, which includes the prompt payment and online discounts.

Aldebaran is 60ft long and has a 12-month Gold Licence costing £1,767.97 when paid in full in advance. If paying by direct debit, this cost would increase to £1,994.02.

Visitors' licence fees (50ft narrowboat)

1 day on the Thames – £55.00 (note: length and beam are considered)

Up to 9 days on the Basingstoke Canal – £56.00 (any boat, any size)

Up to 21 days on the River Wey – £109 (liveaboards strictly not allowed)

Cruise the length of the Manchester Ship Canal – £267 (conditions apply, call for details)

Boat Safety Scheme certificate

Boats are tested for safety by qualified inspectors every four years and compliant craft are issued a Boat Safety Scheme certificate. The test points are identical for all boats irrespective of size or type, so these variables will not affect the cost to any great degree.

The safety examination is a black-and-white affair and therefore quite easy to budget for. Although the cost of the test is not fixed, most inspectors will charge around £200 to £250, which will cover the examination and the issue of the certificate. Most fail points can be remedied with minimal financial cost and a couple of man-hours, although non-compliant gas cookers are sometimes more easily replaced than repaired. Some examiners may also make an additional charge if a second visit is required following a fail, particularly if they have any distance to travel.

INSURANCE

The topic of insuring your boat can raise many questions. Paul Knox-Johnston of Haven Knox-Johnston shared some hints and tips to consider when it comes to protecting your boat.

'Firstly, cover levels can vary quite considerably between different policies, so it's always worth checking you're comparing like with like when you get boat insurance quotes and decide which cover areas and associated values you need to protect your life afloat. Always read the small print to understand any cover limitations. It's important to remember that insurance is not a maintenance contract and will not provide cover for deterioration, wear and tear or bad maintenance.

The Premium

Key elements which come into consideration when setting a policy premium are (but not limited to):

- Value of the boat – it's worth making sure you have a realistic value for your boat which you update annually at renewal time. Insuring a ten-year-old boat at its purchase value is probably excessive and likely to raise your premium.

- Type of boat – whether it's a narrowboat, wide beam, Dutch barge or river cruiser will have an impact on the premium.

- Location – where is your boat's primary mooring? Is it canal side in a city centre or a gated marina in the countryside? A marina can offer additional security and as such can result in a discount on your premium from some insurers.

- Cruising grounds – where do you intend to cruise? Are you staying on the canal network or planning a trip on the tidal Thames. If you're heading out into tidal waters this may come at an extra cost, and it's worth checking that your policy provides cover before embarking on a river cruise.

- Usage – being a continuous cruiser may mean you have a huge amount of helming and lock traversing expertise, but it probably means you have many possessions on board and are travelling many miles amongst the less experienced. Be clear on your requirements when speaking to your insurers/brokers. Single-handed boating can be seen as a more adventurous form of life on the cut and may not be to the tastes of all insurers. Importantly, if you're intending to use your boat for any commercial purposes such as for towpath trading, or even AirBnB-type letting, you must advise your insurer as this will certainly affect the price of your insurance.

- Claim history – a history of making claims, or inversely a good no-claims bonus will impact upon the premium price. We offer an industry-leading 25 per cent no-claims bonus after five years of claim-free boating.

Contents Cover

Haven Knox-Johnston's "All Weather" fully comprehensive policy can be combined with our 'Floating Homes Contents' policy extension to cover items of a personal nature and is popular amongst liveaboard boaters. Items of a personal nature are generally considered to be those that would not normally be sold with your boat.

We offer flexible cover values from £5,000 to £25,000 and are here to help if you need to insure higher amounts. We cover contents both on and off the boat, including stuff you have in storage, anywhere within Europe and for up to 60 days per policy period elsewhere in the world. Individual items valued in excess of £1,000 (electronic items £500, bicycles £250) need to be agreed by us.

Surveys

We ask for a survey when a boat is 30 years old (40 years for narrowboats) and if cover is held continuously then no repeat surveys are required. Barges are slightly different and need to be surveyed every seven years.

Without a recent survey, some insurers may still be willing to offer third-party only insurance for older boats. This is usually adequate to obtain a waterways licence, but it would not provide cover against loss or damage to your boat or contents, so it should be regarded as a last resort.

Summary

An insurance policy is sold based on the disclosure of information at the time of purchase, so it's vital to always keep your insurer up to date if details of your

Case Study: INSURANCE PRICES

Boat	Value	Built	Approx quote
60ft x 10ft wide beam	£65,000	£65,000	£65,000
60ft cruiser stern narrowboat	£30,000	£30,000	£30,000
44ft trad stern narrowboat	£24,000	£24,000	£24,000
57ft cruiser stern narrowboat	£85,000	£85,000	£85,000
26ft GRP river cruiser	£20,000	£20,000	£20,000

All quotes assume no previous claims, marina based, zero no-claims bonus and £200 to £300 excess. Information kindly provided by Haven Knox-Johnston.

Pilling's Lock Marina, Quorn.

boat or plans change. This includes any new customisations or modifications, changes to market value or boat condition, change of mooring, location or vessel use, additional purchases and convictions. If in doubt, it's worth having a conversation with your insurer, who will be happy to help.'

MOORINGS

Moorings costs are dependent on geography, facilities and the size of your boat.

Moorings with facilities such as mains electricity, local pump-out/Elsan or laundry will cost more than a basic on-line mooring, as will moorings in picturesque or convenient locations. Most marinas will also charge different fees if moored alone or abreast another boat, and some also differentiate between frequent and infrequent usage.

Case Study: MOORINGS

Airedale Boat Club (ABC)

ABC sits on the Leeds & Liverpool Canal near Bingley, a stone's throw from the famous Five Rise Locks staircase. Most boats here are moored abreast another at a cost of £24.50 per foot per annum, and there's also a £50 per year membership fee. That means a 50ft boat would cost £1,275 each year. If you manage to secure a mooring on your own, without another moored abreast, the cost per foot increases but this is rarely an option.

ABC has electricity supply and water is available from a CRT tap on the towpath opposite. Pump-out and Elsan disposal are a short walk away, but probably further than you'd want to carry a full cassette.

The club is run as a not-for-profit organisation, which is how the club keeps mooring fees low. Boat owners are required to attend six mandatory 'mooring days' held on weekends throughout the year to carry out maintenance chores around the site and you'll be charged a fee if you miss any of these maintenance days. Repeat offenders can be evicted.

On-line moorings

These are prolific and relatively cheap, though facilities are usually limited. An on-line, offside mooring to accommodate a 57ft boat at Bilsborrow Wharf on the Lancaster Canal currently costs around £2,750 per annum – although it may cost more as this mooring is secured through an auction bid (see below). There's gated access and mooring rings, and immediately adjacent are CRT shared facilities, including a water point, Elsan and refuse disposal.

An offside mooring to suit a 48ft boat at Spode House on the Trent & Mersey Canal is currently costing around £1,643 per annum. Vehicular access is via a private road, but there are no parking facilities on site. There are mooring rings and a shared water point close by. The nearest facilities, including rubbish disposal, showers, toilets, Elsan and pump out, are six and a half miles east of the site at Fradley Junction.

Canal Cruising Company

A friendly and busy working boatyard on the Trent & Mersey Canal in Stone, near Stoke on Trent. On-site facilities include diesel, gas, metered electricity supply and pump-out. Cassette toilet owners will need to walk to the nearest CRT disposal facility each time they need to empty, some 15 minutes away. Moorings per week cost 87p per foot, plus VAT, making a 50ft boat mooring around £2,715 per year.

Case Study: MOORINGS

Apsley Marina.

Apsley Marina

Operated by Aquavista, and located on the Grand Union Canal near Hemel Hempstead. Facilities include metered electricity, water points, showers, pump-out and Elsan, a laundry facility and a convenience store. Nestled among a modern apartment block complex, a residential mooring here for a 50ft boat will cost £9,984 if paid in advance.

This residential mooring would become your legally recognised residence, so you would also receive a host of other benefits including:

- A registered UK postal address and post box.
- You can use the marina address to register for doctors and schools etc.
- Free council tax when choosing a composite council tax option.
- A secure parcel collection point for your parcels.
- One free wash and dry per week.
- One free pump out per month.

Case Study: MOORINGS

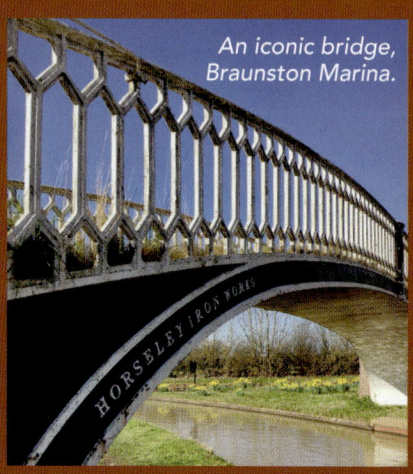

An iconic bridge, Braunston Marina.

Braunston Marina

This is one of the most iconic locations on the inland waterways and is located near Daventry near the Northamptonshire/Warwickshire border. It's steeped in history, near the centre of the network, and has all of the facilities you'd expect and more – from dry dock, boat painting and workshop services to gas, water electricity, showers, pump out, laundry. There's even a rope and fender shop that, as you enter, feels like stepping back in time.

Mooring fees cost £202 per metre, plus VAT if you pay monthly, which would make a 50-foot boat £3,670 per year, or discounted to £3,340 if you pay annually. There's also a £19 per week surcharge for 'high usage' boaters that would likely apply to anyone reading this book.

London

Residential moorings are particularly sought after and priced accordingly.

Talavera Moorings in Hackney, run by CRT, are set at a guide price of £14,000 per annum, with a recent mooring auction having a final bid of £16,000. These are linear pontoon moorings with residential status featuring a wide array of facilities, such as pump-out, Elsan, electricity, water, waste bins and even telephone and internet connections.

Many desirable locations in London, such as Little Venice, have similar 'guide price' values. However, this cost can increase significantly when these moorings become available for auction. Most mooring auctions are for three-year contracts, for the duration of which the price you bid is the price you will pay for each of those three years. After that time, the mooring price will drop back to the specified guide price on a rolling yearly basis.

For reference, the lowest guide price for a residential CRT mooring in this area is £9,500 per year, at Atlip Road in Enfield. It's also worth being aware that not all CRT moorings have residential status and they'll ask for proof of your permanent address if applying for one of their 'leisure' moorings.

UTILITIES

Utilities costs will vary with usage and a liveaboard boater will obviously spend more than a weekender or holiday cruiser.

Most marinas and boatyards will provide mains electrical hook-up points for liveaboards, usually through some type of metered facility to ascertain how much power you're using. Some apply a standard monthly charge, but this is rare. Prices vary significantly and it's not easy to compare the costs with other facilities, but I've never met a boater with an electricity bill anywhere near what you'd pay in a house.

This services bollard has water and electric.

Water provision is included in the licence fee so there's no extra expense here, although some boaters use filtration systems or water purification tablets at a small additional cost. You'll find taps located at the waterside all over the network, and these are free to use. Some boatyards and marinas will also let you fill up for free, although many do now charge a nominal fee unless you're buying bigger ticket items such as diesel.

Gas bottles come in several sizes, with the larger ones offering better value, but most boat gas lockers seem to accommodate the 13kg canisters. In addition to the gas used for cooking, some boats have gas-powered instantaneous water heaters. These increase consumption considerably, though most boaters who have them consider this a small price to pay for instant hot water.

WINTER WARMTH

The majority of older boats use a solid-fuel stove for heat, and even those that have other heating systems aboard will still have a stove in addition. The debate rages continually over which coal is best, and boaters are usually partisan and eager to compare costs and performance. Many will endeavour to find a timber yard or similar source for free or cheap kindling. While fallen deadwood can be found on and around the towpath, one should consider the impact this has on local wildlife. Many types of insect use rotting deadwood as either food or habitat, so plundering this natural resource for your fire is frowned upon by naturalists as intensive harvesting can quickly lay waste to an area.

Some boats make the most of the heat produced by their stove to provide hot water and to heat radiators by utilising a back burner system. This is an efficient way to get 'free' hot water during wintertime, but lighting the stove is not practical during summer.

Diesel-fuelled heaters are an increasingly popular option. There are several types to choose from, but many are fed from the same diesel tank as the boat's engine, making running costs difficult to obtain. Once installed, most diesel stoves have low maintenance costs, but all will require regular servicing.

ONLY FOR BOATERS
Fuel usage

Diesel fuel expenditure is difficult to estimate as usage and prices vary so widely.

Although many keep a log of the fuel they buy, few keep records of engine running hours. Recent legislation taxes fuel for boats differently depending on how it's used.

Fuel for propulsion is taxed at a higher rate than that used to charge batteries for domestic use or for diesel-powered heating. For those with a single fuel tank it's impossible to accurately measure the proportions of fuel used for each, so a sensible approximation is usually implemented. 'After much discussion within the industry it has become almost standard practice to implement a 60/40 split when selling red diesel for boats,' says Troy of Snaygill Boats. 'Customers sign a declaration of usage which we keep on file for HMRC to view if requested.'

The industry has seemingly resigned itself to the inevitability of tax relief being removed for boaters. Until that becomes the case it's the responsibility of the boat owner to accurately declare their usage proportions for tax purposes, and it's entirely legal to buy diesel at domestic tax rates if the boat will use the fuel while moored, during the winter, for example. It's

also worth noting that HMRC does not require fuel suppliers to record fuel sold in volumes of less than 100 litres, although many keep records of all sales, regardless.

PUMP-OUTS

The main factors governing pump-out costs are frequency (of boat use) and volume (of your black water tank). Many boaters negate this cost by utilising cassette-type toilets as these are free to empty at Elsan sanitary disposal points.

Both pump-out and cassette owners will utilise odour-neutralising solutions, but this cost is negligible, totalling approximately £20 to £30 per annum.

Pump-out station at Bosworth Marina on the Ashby Canal.

BOAT MAINTENANCE

How long is a piece of string? Maintaining one's boat is a major expenditure and the cost incurred here can vary enormously. Not only is the age and condition of your boat a factor but the prices charged by companies providing services can differ hugely too.

Some maintenance issues creep up slowly, while breakdowns can come out of nowhere and require immediate attention. While it's difficult to know what's round the corner, there are some constants to bear in mind when budgeting, such as replacement batteries, water pumps and stern gland packing. These are consumable items with high workloads, and they'll invariably go wrong at the most inconvenient moment. Budgeting for them makes a lot of sense. Leisure batteries can cost anything from £100 each for a cheap and cheerful model, with higher specification models costing multitudes more. A new water pump will set you back at least £100. Overhauling a stern gland will cost around £30, but it's a greasy, time-consuming job.

Case Study: LIVEABOARD COSTS

ADRIAN, KIM AND PEPPER
Nb *Hugo*

We're liveaboards and almost exclusively marina based, occasionally venturing out to cruise the local area during the summer. While I do work in the marina where we are based, we're not aboard all day every day like other boaters listed in this section, so I guess our expenditure will be less in some areas.

- Gas: £240pa
- Coal: £960pa (needed around eight months of the year)
- Diesel for heating: £240pa (needed for six months of the year)
- Insurance: £300pa

Maintenance (last year)

We're low mileage boaters so maintenance expenditure isn't too bad for us. We service our engine and our diesel heater annually, and if we add in the cost of blacking and other occasional maintenance expenditure it comes out at around £1,800 to £2,000pa.

Case Study: LIVEABOARD COSTS

ROBBIE CUMMING
Nb *Naughty Lass*

I cruise the network extensively, using marinas only occasionally. It's difficult to work out my average expenses because there are so many variables, including how often I'm away from the boat, the weather, emergency repairs or even what part of the country I'm in. So this is a bit of guesswork it should be pretty close.

- Wood, coal, firelighters, stove maintenance: £750pa
- Diesel: £300pa
- Boat licence: £1,100pa
- Boat insurance: £245pa
- Phone and Wi-Fi (2 x sim only contracts): £840pa
- Launderette: £120pa
- Toilet emptying and chemicals: £200pa
- Additional mooring costs and additional river licences: £500pa

Maintenance (last year)
- 340W Polycrystaline solar panel: £100
- 2 x 6V deep cycle batteries: £500
- 11 x custom thermal break double glazed windows: £10,000
- Boiler flue: £130
- Blacking: £1,200

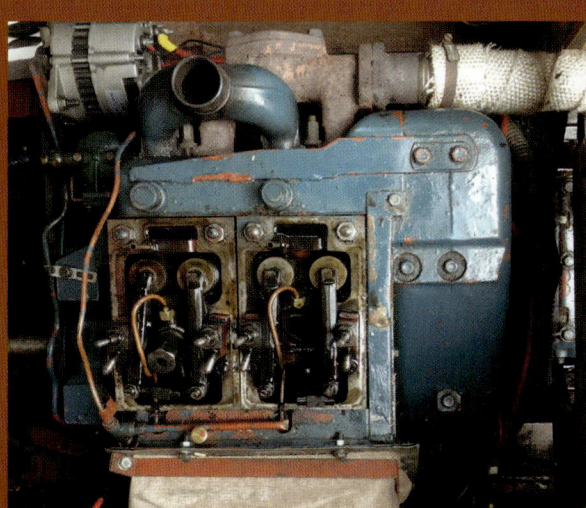

Robbie's Lister ST2 engine receiving some TLC.

Case Study: LIVEABOARD COSTS

KEV AND SAFFI
Nb *The Grey Lady*

I'm retired and live aboard full time in a large marina, though I do get out onto the cut for occasional cruises.

- Coal: £290pa (I use it only for six months of the year, and I'll let the fire go out at night).
- Gas: £82pa (I only use gas for cooking. So a bottle lasts me six months).
- Diesel: £420pa (during the winter months I use 25 litres of diesel per week for hot water and radiator heating. During the summer I cruise a bit more, but it's balanced against not using diesel for heating. I have a 300-litre tank which I fill at the beginning of the season, and the tank isn't empty by the time I fill up for the winter.
- Mooring: £3,950pa at Barton Turns Marina for my 60ft boat.
- Insurance: £540 (fully comprehensive which also covers my contents).

Maintenance (last year)

Sadly, I didn't record the money I spent on maintenance, but it hasn't been significant as my boat is relatively new. Though I did have it signwritten, at a cost of £600.

Case Study: LIVEABOARD COSTS

TONY AND VICKIE
Nb *The Watchman*

While we would normally cruise the network for at least half of the year, we've found ourselves being more marina based over the last 12 months – largely due to our heavy workload. We both work from the boat, so we're aboard almost 24/7, apart from meetings, work trips and holidays, so our expenditure will be higher than most folks'. We also keep extensive records for our tax return, so we can give lots of accurate detail about where the money gets spent.

- Mooring: £3,605pa (we spent most of the year in one marina or another).
- Licence: £1,350pa (our boat is 61ft).
- Insurance: £617pa (including contents insurance).
- Gas: £623.58pa (we use gas to heat water and for cooking).
- Electricity: £366pa (solar panels only supply our needs for the nicest parts of the year).
- Diesel: £123pa (just for navigation, and uncharacteristically low for us).
- Coal etc: £970pa (fire gets lit in late September and it doesn't go out until April. We don't do cold).

Maintenance

£2,116pa (over £1,600 of this figure is a new mattress and a new washing machine, leaving only £500 or so spent on 'proper' maintenance this year, which is pretty low in comparison to previous years when we had to do repairs and upgrades. That £500 comprised a load of items around £20 each – just routine maintenance bits and bobs such as electrical components, replacement seals, gaskets, hose connectors etc. Oh, and a set of porthole bungs for just over £100).

MAINTENANCE COSTS

Mandy Donnan is the Service Manager at Braunston Marina in Northamptonshire, so she's well placed to offer an insight into the cost of routine boat maintenance. 'Engine servicing is usually carried out yearly with a view to avoiding breakdown expenses later. A basic service – changing oil, filters, coolant and belts – will cost from around £450, and a more thorough going-over can cost more.

It may be worth learning to service your engine yourself, not only to save on labour costs but also to nurture your relationship with your boat: the cost of replacing the consumable filters and fluids comes in at around £100.

If you have an older engine you may want to keep a small pot of extra cash to make available for small repairs that inevitably become necessary.'

Hull blacking is a less frequent maintenance cost that most boaters execute every two or three years. Prices will vary of course, but Braunston's prices will give you a guide. 'We charge by the metre, with prices starting around £60 per metre for a full service job,' says Mandy. 'This includes getting the boat out of the water in the dry dock for preparation and re-blacking. So, for a 50ft boat that would cost £915.'

Those with more time and patience may plump for a DIY blacking process. You will still need to get the boat out of the water and back at a cost of approximately £300, and materials will cost around £150. You may also want to hire equipment such as a pressure washer. Another option, which is a longer lasting application, is

to treat the hull with epoxy. This costs significantly more, but requires redoing only every four to seven years or so.

There are other peripheral costs to consider while the boat is out of the water too. 'It's advisable to check sacrificial anodes and replace them if necessary,' recommends Mandy. 'Purchase and fitting for four anodes will cost around £380, depending on the type of anodes you need. And some people insist on fitting more than four! A hull survey to check the integrity of your hull's steel thicknesses is also an option at this time, particularly if your boat is approaching the age when insurance companies will require one. This will cost around £400, but different surveyors will charge different prices.'

BOAT PAINTING

Painting your boat is one of the most costly projects for a liveaboard, so it's easy to understand why many boaters

Fresh blacking and anodes checked.

choose to paint their boat themselves. As with most jobs, preparation is important and can take up a significant amount of time if it's to be done properly, and the ability to do a truly impressive paint job is not something that can be learned overnight. Most painters agree that it takes a few attempts to acquire enough skill to do a good job, which is probably why the quality of most DIY paint jobs is disappointing. So, for the purposes of this chapter, I've concentrated on information from professional boat painters as DIY jobs vary widely in their costs and finish quality.

When you're choosing a boat painter it's important to ask around for recommendations – and be prepared to join a waiting list, as the most reputable painters will be booked up for at least a year or two. Prices for professional paint jobs vary widely depending on which painter you use and how much preparation they do before the painting starts. While some painters will happily spruce up an old or fading paint job, these are never as smart as those done from scratch where the boat is taken back to the bare metal.

Andy Russell at andyrussellpainter.com is based near Nantwich and has been painting boats for over 30 years. He offers this advice:

'Boats will usually need a new paint job every eight to ten years and the price you pay will, obviously, vary with your requirements. As a rough guide my prices come in at approximately £200 per foot plus docking costs, which vary depending on where you are.

That's a full "back to metal" job, with the windows and brass work removed. From there we treat any rust, apply two-pack epoxy base coats followed by either Epifanes two-pack paint or International Perfection Pro. I also include all the traditional decoration on hatches and the bow and also lettering in my price. And when it's all done, I guarantee you'll have a fine-looking boat which will make us both proud.'

💡 Paint job price guide

An average 58-feet boat is roughly £12,000 plus docking costs.

💡 Paint job considerations

Marinas with overheads will often cost more than a one-man-band painter, and, like most things, paint jobs tend to cost more in the south of the country.

Eye-catching signwriting by Andy Russell.

💡 Resale value

The difference a good-quality paint job can make to an old or tired-looking tub is remarkable and it can have an enormous influence on the value of a boat, something worth thinking about if you intend to sell your boat at any point.

OPTIONAL EXTRAS

BREAKDOWN COVER

This is usually a sensible precaution, particularly for those new to boating, so it's a cost I always quote to the uninitiated when the question of expenditure arises. Thankfully, there are breakdown cover services available for boats, similar to those offered by the AA and the RAC for road vehicles. River Canal Rescue are the runaway leaders in the narrowboat world and they offer a range of different breakdown options depending on the level of cover required.

These start at £75 per year for a 'retainer' service, which is a 'pay on use' option. You'll pay a flat rate of £75 per callout and recovery is charged per hour, with the cost of replacement parts added too.

RCR's premium cover costs around £335 per year and it appears to have been designed to solve most breakdown related issues, including unlimited call-outs, recovery, transporting crew home, replacement parts, and an annual engine inspection.

Of course, there are several options to consider so be sure to check the details on their website, but for new boaters who are just learning the ropes, the peace of mind offered by breakdown cover is worth its weight in gold. As an alternative, many boaters simply call the nearest boatyard listed in their waterways map guidebook. While few boatyards provide a call-out service, you might save some money in return for the inevitable inconvenience this option entails.

💡 **Other random costs**

- CRT facilities key: £5 to £10
- Anti-vandal/handcuff key: £5 to £10
- Windlass: £15 to £50
- Key float: £3 to £10
- Sea magnet: £15 to £35
- Tiller pin: £15 to £50
- Stove-top fan: £15–100

BEEN THERE, DONE THAT
INTERNET COSTS

TONY AND VICKIE
Nb *The Watchman*
My internet needs were meagre when I lived alone on my boat. It was used mainly for mailing and surfing the web, and occasionally for sending a few large photo files to editors. Plus I'd watch one or two movies online each month, so my 10GB contract was plenty.

The problem arose when my graphic-designer girlfriend (now wife!) moved aboard. Her enormous design files soon ate up the allowance, so we needed a solution.

Thankfully, we happened upon prepaid unlimited data sim cards, which work out at less than £10 per month for an 18-month or two-year service. No contract needed.

CONCLUSION

How long was that piece of string again? Clearly there's no single answer to the question 'how much does it cost?' – there's such an abundance of variables to navigate that boating expenditure can vary wildly. This chapter couldn't possibly be a conclusive list of costs; I'm sure some readers will be paying more and hopefully some will have found fantastic bargains and be paying far less for the products and services I've listed. Boaters are a particularly prudent, resourceful and frugal bunch, but it's worth remembering that 'price' is not always the most important factor when making a purchase of any kind, and that 'value' should always be a consideration too.

The Watchman *and her rebuilt engine are reunited.*

4 SPACE – THE FINAL FRONTIER

There's no getting around the fact that your boat will be smaller than your house, but like most aspects of boating this can be an enormous benefit when viewed from the right perspective. 'Downsizing' one's lifestyle is a process that many people find both daunting and rewarding, and the transition from house to boat is one of the make-or-break tests for new liveaboard boaters.

The secret is to move aboard with only the bare minimum of possessions and to only bring more aboard when it becomes absolutely necessary. A good trick is to pack as if for a camping holiday. A suitcase full of clothes and toiletries will suffice for a few weeks until you work out exactly what else you need. A few items of cutlery and crockery, a handful of books, a couple of towels and two changes of bedding will usually suffice, and indeed many liveaboards never feel the need to expand much beyond this list. Moving possessions aboard in stages is the only practical way to do it, and any attempt to move aboard in one go is likely to end up in a stressful and untidy disaster.

STORAGE ABOARD

The design of most boats seems to provide plenty of ingenious nooks and crannies for storage, but many of these hidey-holes aren't easily accessible. Deckchairs can be stored under the bow deck during the winter, but crawling under there for a tool kit in an emergency is not fun. It's worth making a note of the items you use regularly and allocating them an easy-access prime storage position.

If the bed on your boat does not have storage space underneath it will not be long before you're planning a new bunk. Designing the bed to accommodate baskets or drawers below will give you instant access to everyday items like clothes, bedding and towels. The rest of the space under the bunk is less easily accessed without lifting the mattress, so this space is best reserved for items you use less often such as DIY equipment,

camping or outdoor gear and spare bedding for guests. One way to make it more accessible is to use gas-lift struts which make listing the bed far easier.

Wardrobe space is another valuable commodity and a ruthless clothing cull is invariably necessary. A 'one in, one out' policy for new clothes will mean less clearing out less often, but it's a tough rule to stick to for some people. Some boats waste valuable wardrobe space by housing a calorifier water-heating tank there. While these are a great option for leisure boaters or continuous cruisers, most liveaboards will want to have hot water available without the need to run their engine. Removing the calorifier and replacing it with an instantaneous gas water heater or diesel heater will not only free up some space, but also provide a more convenient and cost-effective supply of hot water.

ENTERTAINMENT

It's notable that many liveaboard boats don't feature a television. Whether this is because boaters are busy with other pursuits or because they have unsubscribed from the banalities of modern life is not clear, but the fact remains true. Flat screen TVs have obvious space-saving advantages, but it's worth considering models with a flip-down screen if your boat design will accommodate it.

Most boats also do without large music sound systems in favour of a car stereo unit, not only to save space but to combat the problem of vibration when you're underway. However, even car stereos are becoming obsolete in favour of laptops and phones with Spotify and Bluetooth speaker systems, thus negating the need to store an expansive collection of CDs.

OUTSIDE STORAGE

Rooftop boxes can be custom built to fit your boat and some boaters even adapt the models intended for use with cars. Both are a good storage option for items such as gardening tools, cleaning products and other low-value boating accoutrements. Similarly the dead space on the back deck of cruiser stern and semi-trad boats can accommodate lockable crates or bench boxes.

💡 Good for the soul and good for the bank balance

Getting rid of the unnecessary junk and clutter you have accumulated is both liberating and rewarding. Just think of all the money you can make by selling your excess gear at car boot sales or on eBay.

Depending on how much junk you have, you could earn a decent chunk of money towards the cost of your boat if you start the de-junking process early.

Rooftop storage can be doubly useful with the addition of solar panels.

💡 Liveaboard storage tips

- Steps make good storage areas with easy access – a tool kit can be stored here, but be sure to have a mini tool kit handy for the inevitable small jobs.

- Consider blackout blinds on press studs in corridors with high footfall. Curtains and blinds will invariably and frustratingly snag as you walk past them.

- Foldaway chairs for guests can be stored under the gunwales.

- Multi-hangers make good use of small wardrobe spaces.

- A flip-up table is a great quick-and-easy table at mealtimes.

- A 'one in, one out' policy can help to limit the size of your wardrobes and bookshelves, but it's a ruthless and difficult rule to abide by.

- Canvas covers offer extra, waterproof internal space for cruisers and semi-trads, and the cratches of all narrowboats.

- Storage containers will save time, space and your sanity.

- Vacuum packs for shrinking and storing clothes that are out of season will free up space.

- A bench seat or crate with a cushion makes a dual-purpose seat and storage area.

- If you haven't used it or worn it in the last 12 months, get rid of it.

💡 Office filing rules

Office paperwork is one of the most tempting items to hoard. Here's a rundown of how long you need to keep official documents.

- Wage slips – three months (six years if you're self-employed).
- Tax paperwork – five years.
- Phone bills – one year.
- Banking paperwork – six months.
- Receipts – until guarantee expires.
- Self-employment paperwork – six years.

Remember that most paperwork can be avoided by conducting business online. Storage then becomes a file on your laptop – but don't forget to back up!

Stern hoods are becoming a standard feature on many semi-trad and cruiser stern narrowboats. Although some waterways purists might not appreciate them, the additional covered space is enormously valuable and can be used for many different purposes. Keeping your coal, wood and dog-food sacks here will minimise clutter and mess inside the boat, and having somewhere to keep muddy boots and wet coats is similarly civilised. Chris Salisbury, from Canvasman, designs, manufactures and fits bespoke covers for all types of boats. 'People are surprised at how much practical extra space a canvas hood gives you. Your cratch becomes a useful storage area and we have even seen people use the space under their wide-beam stern hood as a dining room.'

Lockable storage
on a cruiser stern boat.

Canvas hoods for cruiser stern and
semi-trad boats can be like
adding an extra room.

NEED MORE SPACE?

I moved aboard my narrowboat in 2005 with two boxes of stuff and my laptop, and while I've slowly but surely filled the boat with 'stuff' I'd managed to keep it under control enough to not worry about the lack of space. That changed in 2018 when my then partner Vickie and I decided we'd like to live together. We both work from home, I as a writer and she as a graphic designer, so we needed space not only to live aboard but also to work aboard comfortably. We started making plans and quickly realised there was a lot to consider.

Of course, everyone's situation is different and our eventual solution might not work for you, but our journey might help you to explore your own solution. Indeed, I'm immensely thankful we didn't dive straight in with some of the ideas we'd considered early in the planning process.

WE'RE GONNA NEED A BIGGER BOAT!

I haven't written a whole section about the option of commissioning a newly-built boat because if you have the funds to do so then it would be the perfect solution. But it wasn't an option for us. We'd also written off the idea of a wide beam, not least because of the significant cruising range restrictions inherent in owning a wide-beam craft.

Initially we thought a butty would be a good solution. An unpowered companion craft that could be towed alongside or behind our 50ft narrowboat could be used as a floating office, leaving our narrowboat to be our home. A 20ft butty would enable us to have access to the entire network if we towed our butty through the locks alongside or behind.

However, it soon became clear that 20ft steel boats are rare, and none of those we found was suitably fitted out inside. We even looked into having a butty custom built from scratch – before realising what a headache towing a butty would be. Towing another boat behind is excruciatingly slow going and requires some skill to navigate through bridge holes. Not only that, but the workload involved in locking through shorter locks is such that we realised a butty was not going to work for us. We'd need to tow the butty behind until we reached a lock, then pull it alongside to go through the lock – only to be faced with the same job one mile further on when we reached the next lock. It all sounded like too much effort, and we'd miss the joy of cruising together. So that idea was binned.

The next most obvious solution would have been to buy a bigger boat, because surely an extra seven or eleven feet would solve the problem? So we started looking at bigger narrowboats online, knowing that finding one that had the right layout would be difficult. We'd resigned ourselves to doing some renovations, but we were unprepared for the slim pickings available. Most of the boats we found were so unsuited they would require an almost completely new fit-out, relegating 99 per cent of them to the 'no' pile.

Over the course of several months' extensive searching we did find a few boats that were possible contenders. Unfortunately, every one we arranged to see in person proved unsuitable for one reason or another – and here's the rub. It seemed that every time we found a boat we wanted to view it would be lying a few hundred miles away from our current location. We would give up a day to drive three hours to see a boat, only to be disappointed – and each time it ate a little piece of our soul. Not only that, but it was expensive and impractical too, given our workloads running our own businesses.

The final nail in the coffin of the 'buy a bigger boat' plan was the fact that we would need to sell my boat to fund the bigger-boat project. It would be impossible to know how much it would sell for and how long it would take to sell, thereby creating great uncertainty and a significant unquantifiable delay. Not only that, but I am rather fond of *The Watchman* and we had been more than disappointed in the boats we'd looked at in terms of quality and character. I was loath to swap my boat for another.

Stretching *The Watchman*

We knew we had to find another way to make our plan work. But by this time, we realised we were running out of options so we made some investigations. We worked out that with the budget we had we could stretch our boat, get a bigger galley, a new office, some storage space and a bigger bathroom. Plus we'd get to keep the wonderful boat we knew and loved, and had great confidence in. And, most importantly, we could get a definitive budget and timeframe for the work, so we had a set date for when we could begin our liveaboard lifestyle together.

I was quite cautious of considering a stretch for my 50 footer as I was completely in the dark about boat-stretching. I hadn't seen a boat stretch done, read about a similar project or met anyone who'd had their boat stretched. It was totally new territory.

We also decided to look at exactly how much of the system we would be unable to use if we had a 62ft boat, and was surprised at what we found. Only a tiny fraction of the network would be unavailable to us.

Bob the boat builder makes the first cut.

And so it begins...
The Watchman is craned out for stretching.

While 62ft boats can fit into the locks on the Leeds & Liverpool Canal and elsewhere, it can be a tight squeeze depending on the state of the lock and the shape of your boat's stern. That's why we decided that 61ft would give us some contingency, and 12 inches wasn't much to sacrifice for the extra peace of mind.

It's eight years since we had *The Watchman* stretched, and we've never regretted it.

The Watchman stretched to 61ft.

*After the stretch –
the hard work begins.*

BEEN THERE, DONE THAT
A NICE BUTTY

ADAM AND HELEN
Nb *Jam Butty*

Adam clearing weed while aboard Jam Butty.

We'd turned our jam-making hobby into a small business aboard our 45ft narrowboat, and before we knew it there was jam everywhere. Every locker, nook and cranny was filled with jars of jam, and we needed to do something about it. We had, in passing, thought about getting a bigger boat, but I was halfway up a flight of locks when the thought occurred to me that a butty would be a rather fine solution.

The more I thought about it the more the idea grew on me. I knew that if I was going to do it I wanted to do it in style, not have some half-dead skiplooking vessel dragged along behind me. The boat would be an attraction and an advertising feature in its own right, and the prospect of calling it the *Jam Butty* was too good to pass up.

Not long after, I was coming down the Shropshire Union and saw the back end of an old historic butty in a boatyard. I knew this was what I was looking for and so, eventually, made a plan with the owner of the boatyard to create the *Jam Butty*. The finished boat cost around £10,000 to restore, plus the paint job. It has no gas, electricity or heating so does not need a BSC. Of course, cruising is slow when you're towing a butty and it can also be challenging to manoeuvre around corners and through bridges, but we're used to it now and I even miss it when I go out cruising in the motorboat without *Jam Butty*.

Would I do things differently if I'd known then what I know now? Possibly, depending on the specific circumstances. Perhaps a bigger boat would be a better solution, but even that option has its downsides. As it stands, we love the *Jam Butty* and so does everyone we run into on the cut and at festivals. Most people come and say Hi – and many of them even buy some jam!

5 BOAT TOILETS

Get any group of boaters together and it won't be long before the conversation turns to toilet talk. Whether ordering a new boat or browsing for second-hand vessels, there are several choices to be made when considering a loo. It's a topic that's certainly worth a chapter of its own.

TOILET CHOICES

Boat toilets aren't like regular land toilets. By their very nature boat toilets can't be fed directly into the sewers and will need to store their contents for disposal at some later time. This invariably means a second encounter with your bodily waste, so it's worth considering which toilet system you prefer. For most boaters the choice of toilet typically comes down to two options: pump-out or cassette. Cassette toilets have a small removable unit in the base where waste is collected and stored. Pump-out toilets rely on a larger immovable storage tank (or 'black-water tank'), often located beneath a bed or integrally in the bathroom. More people on the inland waterways are switching to compost toilets, and incinerator toilets are starting to catch on too.

CASSETTE TOILETS

Cassette toilets are the most popular option for boaters and there are several reasons for this. First, they're often the cheapest to install, with basic models costing around £60 to £70 – although an all-singing, all-dancing model can reach £700. Cheaper cassette loos will usually be of plastic construction with smaller-volume cassettes and water reservoirs, and have lever or plunger pump flush systems. While units in this price range are entirely functional, there are more luxurious models available with features such as swivelling seats, electric flush and large-cassette options.

A typical cassette style toilet. Cassette toilets have a small, removable container to store waste.

The purchase price is not the only cost saving to consider when you choose a cassette toilet. Emptying the contents of your cassette into a sanitary disposal point is usually free, whereas there's almost always a charge to pump out a black water tank.

Another important benefit of a cassette toilet lies in the ease with which they can be emptied. A boat featuring a pump-out toilet needs to be taken to a pump-out facility to be emptied. Sometimes this is not possible, for example if you have broken down or if the weather prevents you from moving your boat. If your tank is full and you're nowhere near a pump-out facility then you're in deep doo-doo! Thankfully, with a cassette toilet you can always take Mohammed to the mountain. Removing the cassette for emptying at the nearest facility is much more convenient if your boat is

BEEN THERE, DONE THAT
TELL US ABOUT YOUR TOILET

JOHN
Nb *Sound of Silence*

When I bought the boat it had a porta potti-style cassette toilet. It would last about a week before it needed emptying. The nearest disposal point is about ten minutes' walk away, which doesn't sound like much, but you try it with a cassette full of… er… waste! I even tried transporting it in the basket on the front of a bike before deciding enough was enough.

I recently fitted a dump-through loo which cost me less than £800 (at the time of writing) for everything I needed to install it, including wood and other materials. I chose a dump-through because they're foolproof, being such a basic design where little can go wrong. It's amazing how many boaters rave about cassette toilets and recommend them as the only way to go, but if you look closely, most of these are weekend boaters who don't use their toilets day in and day out. I daresay they'd change their tune if they had to carry the cassette along the towpath every week of the year.

JUSTINE AND WOODY
Nb *Frog With A Heart*

We decided upon a cassette toilet primarily as a cost-saving exercise. With two cassettes we can fill one and chuck it in the van before replacing it with the spare. We'd empty the full one at the disposal point on the way to work the next day, saving us having to carry the thing along the towpath. Emptying it doesn't worry me too much. You get the occasional splash-back when you're emptying them if you aren't careful, but you only do it a couple of times before you learn your lesson.

The only real problem we had was when visitors used the loo. Often they'd fill the thing with toilet paper, or fill it with water by flushing it repeatedly. Once we had a visitor use the toilet before we had a chance to replace the cassette, thus causing him to essentially pee through the hole directly onto the floor.

immobile for any reason. Many boaters also keep spare cassettes, just in case they're caught short.

On the downside, cassette toilets are sometimes considered a little uncivilised by the uninitiated. The integral storage unit of cassette toilets means their appearance often differs from conventional land loos, leaving guests puzzled and your pan full.

Emptying a cassette is an experience that many find objectionable too, and a full cassette is quite a weighty load to carry if the disposal point is any distance away. Ageing and eroded seals in the unit can also cause problems and allow unpleasant leakage, although all seals are relatively cheap and easy to replace. Most cassettes have a ventilation pressure valve which can stick shut if the seal is worn, and this can cause a build-up of gas pressure and a vaporous release when the toilet is next used and flushed.

PUMP-OUT TOILETS

Those desiring a more conventional-looking toilet will often plump for a pump-out system. These look much more like the toilets you would find in a house and this is often reassuring for those new to boating. Indeed, even some experienced boaters prefer pump-out systems, not only for the aesthetic

A typical pump-out style toilet.

benefits, but because emptying them is far less of a 'hands-on' experience. Emptying your black water storage tank means a visit to a pump-out facility where there's almost always a charge (usually around £15 to £25).

Once paid, emptying involves simply affixing the hose to your storage tank outlet and switching on the machine; the contents are then simply sucked from the tank either into a large tanker unit or directly into the sewers. Many boaters find this to be a much more agreeable process to endure than the emptying of cassettes. Staff in private marinas will sometimes perform the procedure for you (but don't bank on it), whereas CRT provides automated facilities which are credited using a prepayment smart card or token and you perform the task yourself.

Pump-out toilet installation costs vary depending on the type of tank and the type of toilet you choose, and there are many variations to choose from. 'Dump-through' systems sit atop a black water holding tank which is usually made of steel. Prices for toilet pans vary from £170 for the most basic to £1,000+ for the most regal throne. The pedal flushing systems of most brands are universal across the range, so paying more money for your toilet buys you a pretty pan rather than any increased reliability.

Vacuum and compressed-air toilets are popular as they seal off the waste from view once flushed. This disassociation is an attractive benefit for those who prefer a 'home from home' toilet experience.

*Bathrooms are usually
small but functional.*

'Working on this type of toilet isn't too bad either,' says Jo from Snaygill Boats. 'The working bits and moving parts aren't attached to the tank or the pan, so if they do break down they can usually be fixed without getting your hands dirty, so to speak.' As with all toilet system benefits there's a price to pay for convenience and these systems are expensive compared with the other available options. A vacuum loo will cost around £1,500 for the vacuum generator and pan combined, whereas a compressed-air system will knock you back somewhere in the region of £2,000.

As some pump-out toilets can be sited apart from their storage tank it's worth considering that the pipework has the potential to store up to four flushes worth of waste before it arrives at its destination. Michael Punter, from Lee Sanitation, recommends a 'rise and fall' method of routing waste plumbing. 'The waste hose should rise steeply as it leaves the pan before falling gradually into the top of your black water tank. A vacuum or compressed-air flush will easily push waste over the apex of the pipe. It can then flow downhill with gravity into the waste tank, thus avoiding it being stored in the pipework for any period of time. It's also a good idea to keep waste pipes away from hot-water plumbing in order to avoid drying and blockages.'

Costs and convenience aren't the only variables to consider when comparing pump-outs with cassettes. Pump-outs are more prone to blocking than their cassette cousins and this can be a monumental problem. All manner of items can disagree with your pump-out toilet, particularly those fitted with a macerator, and visitors are often the unwitting culprits. Disposable nappies, sanitary towels, tampons, condoms and moist toilet tissues are among the countless objets d'art removed from blocked pump-out loos. It's easier to say what you can put into a pump-out than to list what you can't, and the list is only two items long. The first is anything that has passed through your digestive system, namely faeces and urine.

Case Study: DOWN THE PAN

Unusual items found in the toilet tanks of a hire boat fleet

- Paracetamol plastic blister packs
- Sanitary towels and tampons
- Newspaper sheets
- Disposable nappies
- Disinfectant rim blocks
- Five pairs of ladies' skimpy underwear

💡 Water usage

Toilet type	Average water usage per flush
Dump-through	0.5 to 1.5 litres
Macerator	2.5 litres
Vacuum	0.5 to 1.5 litres
Compressed air	3 litres
Lever-operated sea toilet	4 litres

The second item is common or garden toilet tissue. Boaters with delicate derrières should be aware that luxury and quilted toilet tissue does not break down as readily as the more 'value' brands. Macerator toilets have earned a reputation for being prone to blockages, usually due to overenthusiastic tissue usage or plumbing installation problems.

Blockages can also occur when the contents of your tank harden. This can happen if your tank is left for a period of time or if you forgo the use of toilet fluids. This allows the contents of your tank to dry out, solidify and collect at the bottom, forming layer after layer of hardened sediment until it eventually reaches and blocks the pump-out hose. Good-quality toilet tissues can exacerbate the problem as the lumpy sediment collects and solidifies to such an extent that it can't be sucked by the pump-out machinery. With the tank outlet blocked, remedying the situation can be a truly unpleasant experience. While blockages are rare and mostly avoidable, pump-out owners invariably have a story to tell about their toilet tribulations.

There are several ways to address the blockage problem, none of which can be called a joy. Those with a 'dump-through' facility can use a stick or a length of flexible cable to stir the blockage, the aim being to break it up into pieces small enough to pump out. Another way of doing this is to use a pressure washer, but you need to be sure to take care to avoid any splash-back! Caustic soda and sulphuric acid can be used as a last resort, but you should confer with an expert if you decide to go down this road, particularly if your tank is plastic or has no vent system.

Some pump-out toilets have macerator units fitted which grind up any waste before it's stored, with a view to negating blockage problems. While anything which helps avoid a blocked toilet must be applauded, you must be careful not to block the macerator itself as foreign objects can cause the unit to seize. Bear in mind, also, that it's impossible to access black water tanks through a pan with a macerator unit. Most experts consider a tank with a sealable inspection hatch to be a useful insurance in any pump out set-up.

Finally, eroded seals can be a problem with pump-out toilets too as water from the pan can leak through faulty seals into the storage tank. This can quickly fill a black water tank if the flush water is pumped from the main water supply tank. Again, replacement seals are cheap to buy, and although replacing them on a pump-out system is a little more work, it's entirely doable by anyone with the nose and inclination.

COMPOST CORNER

Composting toilets are becoming more popular on boats too, with a variety of systems being available. With some care they can be wonderfully effective in avoiding both smells and disposal problems, making them an ideal choice for many boaters – myself included. I should point out here that I've been forced to eat my words as, in the first edition of this book, I said that I couldn't see myself installing a composting toilet on my boat. Six years later, I installed a composting loo in the place where my old pump-out bog used to be. Having

used it for almost six years we're rather pleased with it. So pleased, in fact, that we've become almost evangelical about its benefits.

It does seem that composting loo owners are a straight-talking bunch, if the topics of conversation on social media are anything to go by. The Facebook group 'Composting Toilets for Boats and Off-Grid Living' is a veritable mother lode of information, where even the most (ahem) personal questions are answered directly and helpfully.

It's fair to say that composting toilets are, by many people's estimations, a far more agreeable and convenient method than the traditional cassette and pump-out toilet options. You can learn more in the FAQs following.

The author's composting loo.

Compost toilet FAQ
With compost pioneer Colin Ives

Q Can you tell me a little about compost toilets?

A Well, the first thing you should know is that 'compost toilet' is a bit of a misnomer. On boats, very little composting goes on in the actual toilet. Composting takes time and, unless you use the toilet infrequently, it'll probably fill up before it turns to compost. This is why we think the term 'compost toilet' is a bit misleading because most are actually 'humanure-collecting toilets' – that is, solids are collected along with a small amount of carbon to accelerate the composting process. The actual composting is usually done elsewhere.

Q Oh, so what do compost toilets do?

A The simplest toilets divert urine into one container and solids into another. This kind of toilet keeps the pee separate from the poo, which makes them much easier to deal with. It's when pee and poo are mixed together that they make the toxic and smelly gloop we know as sewage.

Separating the liquids and solids can be done in several ways, but one of the most convenient methods is to use a separator, where the front of the separator diverts liquid to one container and the container in the back collects solids. This allows liquids and solids to be managed separately. Keeping pee and poo apart is key to avoiding smells and keeping management to a minimum.

A composting loo separator.

Q Do they smell?

A Hardly, and certainly far less than a cassette or pump-out toilet tank. A well-managed compost toilet should result in no more than a faint damp woody smell, a bit like a forest floor. It's not at all unpleasant and certainly not a bit like the sewage or chemical smell associated with the usual boat-loo options.

Most toilet systems, on boats and on land, mix the pee and poo together to create a sewage gloop. Anaerobic bacteria, which thrive in an airless environment, feed on this gloop and generate gasses, creating that awful sewage smell. Cassette and pump-out toilets suffer from this smelly problem, which is why most boaters use strongly scented chemicals to cover it up. Compost toilets avoid this problem by not mixing the pee and poo and by using a carbon cover material.

Q So what should I do with the contents of my poo container?

A There are fewer options for disposing of poo than there are for disposing of urine, but the options are much better than if you have poo and wee mixed together as sewage. Disposing of sewage is highly regulated and thoroughly unpleasant.

The simplest and most environmentally friendly option is to fully compost the humanure. Poo, by itself, will break down naturally well enough, but it composts much faster if mixed with a carbon-based cover material. Most people use wood shavings or wood-pellet cat litter as their carbon cover, as these materials compost well. The Environment Agency recommends two years of composting, but a well-managed humanure compost mix can get most of the way there in as little as six months. When their primary solids container is full, most boaters empty the contents into another container to undertake the composting. These secondary compost containers are usually larger and can accommodate a surprising amount of material, as it breaks down over time and decreases in volume as composting progresses. Once composted to a decent level the humanure can be buried to finish the process.

In the UK it's legal to bag and bin solid waste – just think about the number of nappies that are disposed of in this way. However, bagging and binning in CRT bins was prohibited 2021 by the Trust. More on this later, but even if you're not using CRT facilities, bagging and binning humanure must still be done responsibly:

- Use bags that are appropriately marked for sanitary use. Compostable bags are available featuring words highlighting that they contain human waste to prevent others, including people at the recycling centres, from opening them. Such bags are available from reputable compost-toilet manufacturers. Never use black bin bags.

- Don't put humanure into dog-poo bins or litter bins. Use only proper domestic refuse containers.

- Don't put humanure into Elsan points.

- Don't overfill bags. They may split and allow the contents to spill out.

The Separett Villa waterless toilet.

The Simploo Nano waterless toilet.

- Double-bag humanure for security against splits. Use two sanitary bags that have the same markings.

Q How often will I need to empty the poo container?

A You'll be surprised at how little poo people actually produce. The average is around 300g per day, and approximately 80 per cent of that volume is water. The remaining 20 per cent is mostly undigested food and bacteria. As poo leaves the body it instantly begins to dry out and pathogens begin to die off straight away.

A 20-litre solids bucket can last one person up to around 40 days in some circumstances, depending on many variables, such as how often you use it, how much time you spend at home and how much food you eat.

Q What do you do with the wee?

A Dealing with liquid containers is much easier. Urine can start to smell after four to five days, so it makes sense to dispose of it well before that time.

In developed countries, urine is relatively benign and doesn't normally contain diseases or parasites, so it can be emptied almost anywhere people don't walk or play – although it's recommended that this be at least six feet from the water's edge. Emptying on grass verges, under hedges or around tree bases are all good options, and some people even use it as a fertiliser. (You'll need to dilute it at a rate of 1:8 to make good fertiliser.) And of course, you can always pour it down toilets or Elsan points.

💡 **Medication considerations**

If you're using strong medications you'll need to be a little more careful about where you dispose of your urine, so don't pour it around fruit bushes or fruit trees.

Q How often do I need to empty the wee container?

A That depends on how many people are using it and how often. On average you can expect up to two litres per person per day, but many people go to a place of work and often pee there. The size of the container you use will also obviously dictate how often it needs emptying, but a 10-litre fluids container will usually last one person a few days before needing to be emptied. Don't leave it any longer than four days, though, as it may start to smell. Many people use a few squirts of white vinegar in their wee bottles and on separators to help keep smells at bay.

💡 Guests

It might be worth allowing guests to throw their tissue in the primary solids container as this occasional amount won't add up to much at all, and it will make the compost-toilet experience a little simpler for your uninitiated guests.

Q What should I do with the toilet paper?

A While toilet paper will compost eventually, it does take a little time. More significantly, adding toilet paper to your primary or secondary containers will make them fill up far more quickly. Instead, you can do what they do in many European countries and throw toilet paper into a bin. And then, as most boats have solid-fuel stoves, you can burn it. It only takes a few seconds, so you can even burn it during the summertime without heating your boat. Alternatively the contents of your loo-roll bin can be disposed of with your general waste, but if you do choose this option it's worth using compostable bin liners so the contents can compost in landfill.

Q Is it really that easy?

A On the whole, yes. Some people have a few smelly teething troubles, but a well-managed compost toilet should produce little more than a faint musty wood smell. And even if a small amount of urine does get in with the solids, the wood shavings will usually soak it up. However, if too much urine gets into the solids it may start to smell and, if this happens, it's usually best to empty the bucket and start again afresh.

Q Getting rid of unpleasant smells sounds like a dream come true

A It's nothing like as bad as a typical pump-out or cassette, but some people find even the musty wood smell unpleasant. In this case, a quiet, low-powered fan will extract these low-level smells along with any moisture that's generated. If you're getting higher levels of smell then it's likely that wee is getting into the solids container. In this case it's infinitely better to deal with the smell at the source, rather than simply moving it outside with a fan. Your neighbours will thank you.

BEEN THERE, DONE THAT
LIFE WITH A COMPOSTING TOILET

TONY AND VICKIE
Nb *The Watchman*

We've been using our compost loo since May 2018 and we couldn't be happier. It's certainly been far more pleasant than the pump-out system we had before. I'd been ignoring and denying the slightly pongy whiff that would sometimes come from the toilet tank, despite my generous use of fluids to mask and negate it. It's also nice to do away with the worry of blocked pipes, worn seals and all the other grotty jobs that sometimes come with other loo systems. Emptying pump outs and cassettes can be gag-inducing and we don't miss that at all, but the real plus for us is the fact that compost toilets don't need flushing, thereby saving precious water. As continuous cruisers who both live and work aboard, we can get through our water tank in less than a week. Having a compost loo means we can go for slightly longer between fills.

The last four years have been quite a journey in terms of composting knowledge. We started out cold composting, using 36-litre containers, which we stored on the boat roof. The slow pace of cold composting meant we very quickly filled the available roof space, so we needed a better solution. After some research, we hit on the idea of hot composting and invested in a 100-litre Hotbin composter. This has been a game changer. Working at temperatures between 40 and 60°C, it composts humanure in as little as three months. The added benefit is that we also compost all of our food scraps, which has greatly reduced the amount of waste we bin.

It's quite hands-on in terms of effort as it requires regular feeds to keep it hot, but the reward is lovely pathogen-free compost that can be gifted back to the land. And we have the satisfaction of being off-grid and self-sufficient. What's not to love?

Hotbin 100litre.

We find that we need to empty the pee container at least every two days, and often after a day and a half. As I say, we both live and work aboard full time so I guess we fill our container quicker than most. We use white vinegar to rinse the pee container and that keeps smells at bay. We also add a few drops of essential oil to the carbon cover, which makes entering the bathroom a pleasure. It certainly beats the eau-de-pong that sometimes greeted us when we had a pump-out system.

It should be noted that our first couple of solids containers didn't go well at all, and this is an issue reported by many of those trying compost toilets for the first time. After about two weeks the smell was pretty unpleasant – which I think was caused by two things. First, I believe there was a lot of overspill of urine into the solids container as we were getting used to using the new loo. Men must sit to pee to ensure it goes into the correct container. Women need to 'sit forward, sit up and aim', which takes a little practice and some getting used to, but most of those who I have spoken to soon get the hang of it. Some women use a 'Shewee' to improve their aim, but most don't seem to need one.

The other issue was caused by not using enough carbon cover. We increased the amount of wood shavings we used at each visit and the problem soon went away. I think the fan we had installed also works wonders and reduces any smells to almost nothing, so I'd highly recommend doing that.

Visitors' reactions vary. We've had those who flat out refuse to use the compost loo, and we've had others who have been thrilled at the idea. We expect a bit of disruption to the system when we have guests, but a little bit of wee in the solids container can usually be compensated for by adding more carbon cover.

All in all we're really pleased with our decision to get a compost loo. It's a well-known fact that conventional toilets aren't particularly good for the environment, and that's probably even truer for the majority of on-board toilets, with their reliance on formaldehyde chemicals. Indeed, the environmental benefits were the most compelling factor in Vickie's decision to try compost loos. For me, it was the convenience, water savings and smell-reduction benefits that stood out.

As far as we're concerned, there's not a downside, as the management of the compost loo is far easier and more agreeable than our previous system in many ways. Indeed, we've become quite evangelical about the whole affair.

INCINERATOR TOILETS

Cinderella Travel diesel incineration toilet.

A relatively recent addition to the boating toilet market is the incinerator toilet. This system uses gas or diesel to incinerate the toilet's contents after each visit and is capable of converting a month's worth of one person's toileting down to just a teacup of ash. It's easy to see the attraction of this when compared with the chore and unpleasantness of dealing with cassettes or pump-outs. But there's a downside, namely the cost.

The gas unit was priced at £3,999 at the time of writing, and the diesel unit at £4,649. The cost of each flush equates to around 60p worth of gas and 37p of diesel. Add to that the cost of bowl liners, at £50 for 500 'flushes', and you can see how the price might be a sticking point for some boaters.

However, if the perceived horrors of a pump-out or cassette are a deal-breaker which you're eager to avoid at any cost, then an incinerator might be just the thing.

SEA TOILETS

Sea toilets were popular on boats before it became illegal to dump sewage directly into the waterways system. These lever-flushing toilets are still available but must now be pumped into a storage tank. Although some older boats still have overboard pumping sea toilets fitted, the Boat Safety Scheme means that alternative toileting facilities must be available.

Sea toilets can't be used on the inland waterways.

LIVEABOARD LOO LOW-DOWN

Smell

Storing any amount of bodily waste for any amount of time will generate some smell. There are several ways of dealing with this problem, with the most common remedy being chemical warfare. There are several brands of chemical liquids available for use in both pump-out and cassette systems, most of which are blue in colour and/or name. These formaldehyde-based fluids can be mixed with the water used to flush or used as a solution added directly into the storage tank, but whether you actually like the resulting chemical smell is a matter of taste and tolerance levels.

Flushing dump-through toilets can release the gases that build up inside sealed black water tanks and the odour can be quite offensive. This can be negated by fitting a breather hose from the top of your tank, venting directly outside your boat, and most new boats are fitted with these as a matter of course.

Breather hoses allow methane to escape gradually from the tank and not build up in the first place. They should be at least equal to the diameter of the inlet pipes as this allows equal displacement volumes of air and waste when flushing and pumping out.

Eco-friendly toilet products

Boat life is often conducted in close synergy with nature so it's unsurprising that chemical-free eco-friendly toilet systems are becoming increasingly popular. The simplest way to achieve this is by replacing formaldehyde solutions with the more environmentally friendly nitrate and oxygen-based products which essentially speed up the natural decomposition process. These eco-friendly fluids are usually green as opposed to the nasty blue formaldehyde version.

Brewer's yeast tablets are also effective in the fight against smells, but be aware that the residues left behind by blue formaldehyde fluids stop both yeast and nitrate fluid systems from working. Boaters wishing to make the transition from formaldehyde to more eco-friendly options usually buy a replacement cassette, although a period of abstention from chemical usage and some vigorous rinsing may do the trick. It's more difficult to rid black water tanks of formaldehyde as they're tough to rinse and cleanse effectively.

Toilet tissue

Recycled toilet tissue is becoming more robust as manufacturers are increasingly using bonding agents. The people at Lee Sanitation recommend a simple test to see how appropriate your brand of tissue is for boat loo use: put two sheets of toilet tissue into a pint glass of water and stir well. If the tissue breaks up easily then it's boat approved. If it stays in sheets then give it a miss.

Breather hoses

Most of us don't notice any smell from the breather hoses which vent outside our boats, but if you would like to spare the noses of delicate passers-by then you may wish to fit an inline carbon filter.

BEEN THERE, DONE THAT
TOILET TROUBLE

BOB, *Leeds & Liverpool Canal, West Yorks*.
A friend of mine was carrying his full cassette to be emptied one summer afternoon when he slipped and fell on the towpath. As the cassette hit the floor it burst open, covering him with the contents, which was unpleasant enough. However, his sympathies lay with the guests on the restaurant boat moored directly next to the incident who were attempting to enjoy an al fresco lunch.

RUBEN, *Erewash Canal, Derbyshire*.
My parents enjoyed occasional days out on my boat in the summer, but my mum was particularly wary of my dump-through pump-out loo. They came to visit one weekend and on arrival my mum rushed to use the loo after the long journey from London. I was a little worried when she called my dad for help, and even more so when I found out why. Somehow my mother had managed to drop her car keys into the pan and flush them into the poo tank. I was left to retrieve them while they retired to a nearby pub for lunch.

Self-pump-out equipment
Self-pump-out kits do exactly what it says on the tin. The kit is either operated manually using a lever or powered electrically and pumps out the contents of a black water tank into the disposal points used by cassette owners. This usually negates the cost of using traditional pump-out facilities but is a more hands-on approach. A few CRT disposal facilities (usually septic tank based) aren't free for self-pump-out users as the volumes being discharged are closely managed.

A LeeSan self-pump-out kit.

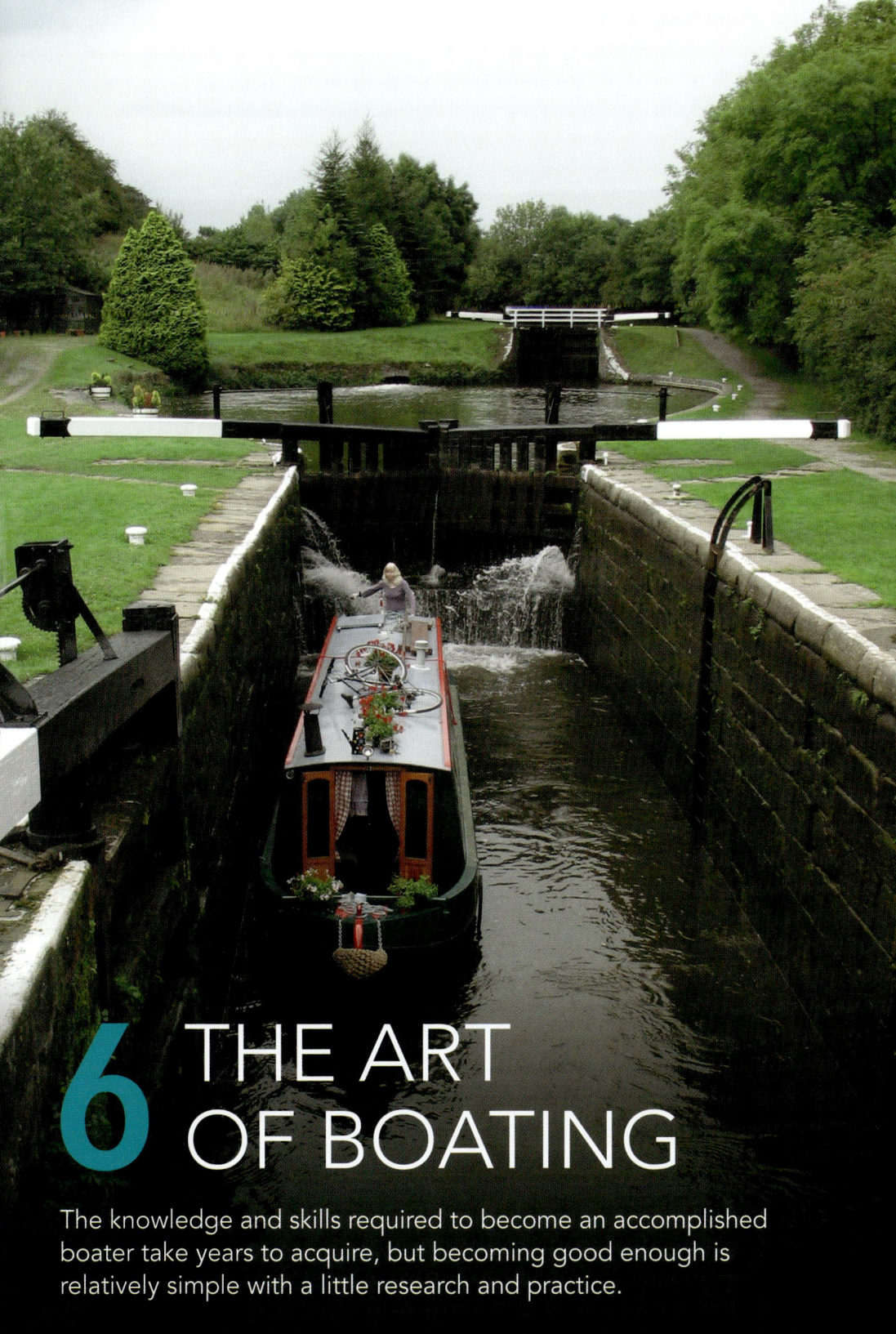

6 THE ART OF BOATING

The knowledge and skills required to become an accomplished boater take years to acquire, but becoming good enough is relatively simple with a little research and practice.

Most of the waterways in England and Wales are managed and maintained by three separate bodies. Most canals are predominantly the responsibility of CRT, several navigable rivers fall under the care of the Environment Agency, and the rivers and lakes of the Norfolk and Suffolk Broads are governed by the Broads Authority. In addition, other waterways are managed by different agencies, some of which can be found on page 67. It's important to familiarise yourself with the rules and licensing conditions of each organisation if you're to be travelling within their jurisdiction as there are some notable variations. However, the guidelines in this chapter will equip you with most of the information you will need for safe and happy boating wherever you may roam.

When you're passing boats coming towards you, they should ideally pass port (left) side to port side, unless conditions dictate otherwise. Basically, you'll need to drive on the right. It's good practice to slow down when you pass too, as excessive speed will cause the boats to veer together, reducing control of your boat and increasing the need to take evasive action. A weaving (or breaking) wash is usually the sign of a poor helmsman. Look out particularly for approaching boats at bridges and blind bends; with a reduced line of sight you need to slow down well in advance. Speeding up in an attempt to beat the other boat through the bridge is a recipe for disaster, especially if the other helmsman has the same idea. The result could be a collision or both boats stuck in the bridge hole, both of which can compromise safety and your bank balance.

SETTING OFF

CHECKLIST

It's easy to get caught up in the excitement when preparing for a day out on your boat. If you're anything like me you'll be itching to cast off those ropes and get going, but like all things boating, it's usually a mistake to rush. Here's a handy checklist of things to remember before setting off. I'm so forgetful I've a copy pinned in the engine room.

- Clear the roof of obstacles such as bicycles, plant pots and the like wherever this is possible. They can be trip hazards when walking on the roof and may also foul low bridges, particularly if water levels are high.

- Ensure all safety equipment, including lifejackets, life rings and throwing ropes, is on board and to hand.

- Raise your fenders to avoid drag and to avoid losing them. They can also be hazardous in locks should they become entangled.

- Have your mooring pins and mallet to hand ready for when you need to moor.

- Check your headlight and horn, particularly if there is a tunnel on your journey.

- Check engine coolant and oil levels before setting off as this can't be done once the engine is hot.

- Is your centreline handy near your tiller, or have you left it coiled nicely at the centre of your boat?

- A pole and hook should be within reach on your roof. An anchor with a rope and chain of appropriate length is necessary if cruising on rivers, and a gangplank is useful too.

- Make sure your tiller and pin are found and affixed before casting off your mooring ropes.

- Make sure you have disconnected your electricity landline cable.

- Tighten the stern gland greaser at the end of each cruise and ensure the bilge pump has been doing its job.

- Stock your larder before setting off; at least have tea- and coffee-making necessities along with the ingredients for tomorrow's breakfast. A disposable barbecue is a canny standby, and powdered milk will tide you over until the next stop.

- Secure any delicate or precarious breakables on board.

- If you have pets on board ensure you have their needs catered for. This may include a doggy lifejacket but will certainly include their food. You may wish to pack their favourite toy too.

As with driving, the safety and consideration of one's passengers are the primary focus of a good helmsman. While there's no substitute for practice and experience, knowing the basics of boating technique and etiquette will give you a head start. From boat handling to best practice, there are plenty of sources of useful information. The Boater's Handbook and its accompanying DVD from CRT and the Environment Agency offer a wealth of safety and handling advice, while www.considerateboater.com talks you through the dos and don'ts of boating etiquette, and many companies offer practical helmsman courses.

💡 Useful items

- Windlass
- Handcuff key
- Waterproofs
- Binoculars
- Snacks/drinks
- First-aid kit
- CRT facilities key
- Waterways map
- Hat/gloves/scarf
- Sunglasses/sunblock
- Umbrella
- Toilet tank/cassette capacity
- Water
- Coal/wood/firelighters
- Gas

'Boating headaches are usually due to a lack of boating experience and know-how, rather than attitude,' says Steve Vaughan from considerateboater.com. 'A little research and reading can help boaters avoid most problems until they get a bit of boating experience under their belt.'

WHEN UNDERWAY

SPEEDING BOATS – THE FAST AND THE FURIOUS

Boating is, by its nature, a leisurely activity and altercations among boaters are relatively rare, but the issue of speeding boaters is a regular cause of discourse on the cut. As with all conflicts, there are invariably two sides to the story, so it makes sense to examine both sides in order to find a solution.

What's the problem?

Most boaters know that the speed limit on almost every canal in the UK is 4mph. Even so, speeding boaters aren't a rare sight. That's a problem, because speeding boats cause a wash which can flood the burrows and nests of any wildlife in residence and damage canal edges, contributing to leaks and breaches. As serious as these issues are, breaking the 4mph limit isn't usually the cause of conflict on the cut. The real arguments start when boaters fail to slow down (or are perceived to be going too fast) when cruising past moored boats. Arguments and shouting are, unfortunately, a common sight.

As with most arguments, there's no silver-bullet solution that will solve the issue. The solution, if it's to be effective,

Canalside bustle.

requires a series of adaptations. It's not as simple as just 'slowing down'. Indeed, it's not entirely accurate to blame speed for the disruption caused by speeding boaters. After all, plastic cruisers, kayaks and canoes can blast past a narrowboat at far greater speeds than 4mph without causing so much as a ripple. Instead, it would be more accurate to say that the issue lies with the amount of water being moved by the passing boat.

> 💡 **Quote**
>
> It's good to have an end to journey towards, but it's the journey that matters in the end.
>
> *Ursula K Le Guin – American author*

The more water being shunted, the more disruption it will cause. Gliding through an almost still canal at 2mph will shift far less water than would occur at 4mph or more. Obviously boats with a deeper draught or a wider beam will move more water than a typical narrowboat, and the issue is also exacerbated where the canal is shallow or narrow. Without the assistance of a speedometer it's difficult to accurately judge our speed when cruising the canals. Even some car drivers with speedometers built into their dashboard seem to have difficulty observing the speed limit, so it's easy to see how boaters might be similarly afflicted. Add in a little daydreaming, inexperience and a wide margin of error in our ability to judge speed, and you can see why the issue of speeding boaters is a common one.

Don't exceed 4mph – even on quiet sections.

Nevertheless, there's no excuse for speeding. Passing moored boats at 4mph or more can be disruptive. A multitude of annoying and dangerous problems can occur when a moored boat violently rocks or bounces off the bank – from spilt tea and items falling off shelves to severe burns when boaters fall onto stoves or cookers. It's also common for moored boats to be set adrift when mooring pins are ripped out. That's why it's recommended to slow down to 2mph or less when you're passing moored boats.

💡 Tech to the rescue

It's now possible to use smartphone app technology to ascertain your speed when boating. However, this is a blunt tool and does not override good judgement as to the best speed to use in any given circumstance.

So, once you've identified the problem and the unwanted consequences, the question is: what can be done about it?

Part 1 – How to avoid speeding

It might seem there's an obvious simple solution to the speeding boat issue, but in reality there's more to it than that. It's likely that these scenarios are familiar to many boaters.

SCENARIO 1

You're sat on your boat, enjoying the peacefully pleasant sounds of the cut, when you hear a boat approaching some distance away. It's always difficult to judge a boat's speed from its engine noise, but you can hear the high-revving motor getting louder, and it's not slowing down. As the bow-wave hits your boat it begins to rock, closely followed by the change of engine note from the passing boat as the skipper drops the revs as their bow comes alongside you. Sure, they 'slowed down' – but the damage was already done.

This is a common experience. Sometimes it's caused by lack of consideration and sometimes it's caused by ignorance. Other times it's caused when the skipper of the passing boat notices that there's someone aboard the moored boat and desperately tries to remedy their speeding and their guilt. The solution in this scenario is to start slowing down way before you reach the moored boat. In a recent discussion on the CRT Facebook page, the common consensus was that cruising boats should slow to tickover at least 2–3 boat lengths before reaching a moored boat. That way, the movement of water will be minimised before you reach the moored boat, allowing you receive a friendly wave and a smile as you cruise past.

SCENARIO 2

After cruising along a quiet stretch of canal for a while, you see a moored boat in the distance. As you approach, you ease back on the revs to slow your boat and cruise past at a significantly slower speed. However, to your dismay, you still receive a shaken fist and an inaudible remonstration from the moored boat owner through their window as you pass. What's their problem? You slowed down!

The problem here is that, sometimes, slowing down a little isn't quite enough. It's an issue of perception. When you've been motoring along for a while, your newly slowed progress as you approach the moored boat seems like a snail's pace compared with your previous speed.

Slow down to tickover speeds when passing moored boats.

However, that might be simply your perception, and your speed might in fact be still causing disruption. The answer is, predictably, to slow your boat well in advance to a tickover. This means dropping your revs until your boat is in neutral and the prop stops turning, before increasing the revs just enough to get the prop turning again. You should reach this point before you get within 2–3 boat lengths of the moored vessel.

When you're cruising past at tickover having slowed well in advance, there's no question that you might be going too fast, as you can go no slower. Perception is a notoriously poor judge of speed so, in the absence of a speedometer, you're better off relying on engineering and physics.

Part 2 – How to avoid disruption from speeding boats

Agreed, speeding boaters are a pain and they can cause significant issues for moored boats. However, there's plenty you can to do when you're moored up to mitigate and minimise the disruption.

Most of the issues caused by speeding boaters can be easily negated by good mooring practices. In almost every circumstance, it's possible for moored boats to be tied up in such a way that even the most irresponsible speeding will cause little or no disruption. This is especially true for liveaboard boaters, who are, statistically, the most likely to be the complainant as they're more likely to be on board when speeders fly past. And I say this as a liveaboard myself, and one who has been a whinging complainant with a sloppy mooring.

There are several means by which boaters can moor up well enough to mitigate the effects of those speeding past. It might seem obvious, but there are so many examples of sloppy moorings to be found on the cut that this list of advisory recommendations might be useful as a gentle reminder.

USE BOLLARDS OR MOORING RINGS WHERE POSSIBLE

Rings and bollards are far more secure than mooring pins. A few passing boats are usually enough to dislodge mooring pins to at least some degree. At best, the pins give you slack mooring lines, so every passing boat will cause disruption. At worst, your pins will become dislodged, leaving you adrift on the cut. It's easy to suspect innocent boaters of speeding when this happens.

USE FENDERS

Inflatable fenders are better than hard rubber or rope fenders when it comes to softening the effects of passing boats. If you want to use rubber or rope, resign yourself to the fact that you've signed up for a less-than-absorbent fender system.

MOOR UP WITH ROPES AT APPROX. 45 DEGREES TO YOUR HULL

That is, with one rope restricting movement forwards, and one restricting moving backwards. If you moor up with your ropes at 90 degrees to the boat and the bank, this allows your boat to swing as the passing boat moves water in one direction or another.

Avoid disruption from passing boats by mooring well.

USE SPRINGS

Sometimes, there's no way to align your mooring ropes to restrict both forward and backward movement because of the position of bollards or rings on the bank. In these circumstances, it's worth having a reserve length of rope available to create a 'spring'. A spring mooring is a good way to reduce movement at your mooring. The term's definition varies with different types of boat, but in narrowboat circles the term generally describes ropes that are secured to a land fixing alongside your boat instead of the more common method of tying ropes to a fixing either in front or behind the vessel.

Springs help to stop movement fore and aft as boats or water currents pass. It's worth having spare ropes to use as springs if you're stopping in high-traffic areas. You can use springs either alone or in addition to the more traditional mooring method, and some boaters use them as their standard operating procedure. Describing how to use them here isn't easy: a quick Google will show you how to do it.

DON'T USE YOUR CENTRELINE FOR MOORING

Tying your centreline to the bank makes your boat unforgiving of even the slightest amount of water movement. The line will snap tight on the roof of the boat, causing the boat to rock more violently. Centrelines are useful for boat manoeuvring, but not at all ideal for mooring.

And finally

Of course, there are many other variables relating to this issue. Some canals have fluctuating levels of water, making tying up tight a risky option. Sometimes the wind is so strong that more speed is necessary. Sometimes hire boaters forget to go slowly, or don't know how slowly to go, or are having too much fun to care enough. And let's not even get into the discussion about passing mile after mile of moored boats on popular stretches of canal, making for painfully slow progress at tickover. These are the vagaries of canal life that make our pastime so interesting. Judgement calls are necessary, and a little understanding, tolerance and kindness will go a long way on the cut.

The ultimate solution to the issue of speeding boaters is to simply let it go. In the vast majority of cases, and especially if you're well moored, speeding boaters don't cause any significant disruption so there's no real reason to get upset. I'll hold my hands up and admit that I've shouted at speeding boats. But afterwards, I felt foolish, as if I'd let myself down. Because really, it wasn't worth the hassle. I'm always tied up well enough not to be significantly troubled by speeding boats, so I was just being self-righteous.

I don't want to be that guy, so nowadays I do my best not to get too wound up. Indeed, just as speeding boaters can have a distorted perception of their speed, moored boaters' perception is similarly fallible and can often make them believe a boat is going too fast when, in fact, it's moving at a perfectly acceptable rate. In most cases, it's not a black-and-white issue, so tolerance and consideration on both sides are necessary. Life is short and canal life is meant to be peaceful and cheery. So let's not shout, eh?

After all, shouting rarely makes any difference to the behaviour of the passing boater. It's rare for a speeding boater to change their behaviour in light of a telling-off. They either know they're doing wrong and don't care, or don't believe they're doing wrong so won't change. Shouting rarely makes any difference, apart from ruining the peace.

In conclusion

As both a cruising boater and a moored boater, I've learned there are things we can all do to avoid altercations about speeding boats. It boils down to three things:

1 Slow down to tickover well in advance of moored boats.

2 Tie up well to mitigate disruption from passing boats.

3 Don't shout at passing boats, whatever happens.

LOCKS, SWING BRIDGES AND TUNNELS

Sharing lock and swing bridge labour is a great way to meet your fellow boaters and is one of the most pleasurable aspects of living aboard. While there are no hard and fast rules, there's a suggested code of conduct which aids safety and encourages goodwill.

Be sure to wait your turn if there's a queue, and be aware that boats that appear to be moored may in fact be waiting in line to navigate a lock, bridge or tunnel. Always check for other approaching boats before moving locks or bridges to make more efficient use of water and reduce waiting time for road traffic. Make sure your boat crew does their fair share of the workload rather than sitting in the cabin drinking tea. Look for approaching boats again before you close the bridge or the lock gates. When sharing locks it's important to err on the side of caution; open paddles slowly and confer with the other boat's crew to let them know what you're doing.

💡 Locks and swing bridges

When you're sharing a lock or a swing bridge with another boat, it might be tempting to get through as quickly as possible to make way for the other boat. However, bear in mind that there are often boaters holding onto their ropes, awaiting their turn. Your speeding out of the lock or through the bridge makes it difficult for them to hold the boat steady. Take your time, go slow and don't cause waves. Nobody is going to mind an extra few seconds' wait.

Slow down when approaching blind corners, tunnels and bridges.

Many boats have been damaged by swing bridges, so be careful.

💡 Hold tight

Keep a tight hold on the windlass when using locks and always use the safety catches. Spinning windlasses can cause serious injury.

Good windlass technique.

Tony's *towpath tales*

Why are they dressed as pirates? I'm sitting aboard my boat writing this chapter, looking out of my window at the boats going past on the Leeds & Liverpool Canal in Kildwick, near Skipton. It's near the end of the boating season, but there's still quite a lot of traffic going by, around half of which comprises hire boat holidaymakers. There are three hire companies within a three-mile radius of here which, coupled with the fabulous rural location, means we see a lot of hire boats in this area.

The hire boat clientele seems to be split into three roughly distinct groups. First are the family holidaymakers: usually husband and wife with a nipper or two in tow, who make their way quietly along the cut. Next come the retired narrowboating stalwarts, who have likely been hiring for years or are ticking off the next line on their bucket list before proceeding to bungee jumping or a trip to Las Vegas.

But my favourites are the stag and hen party hirers. You can hear them coming from quite a distance. In parties of up to a dozen, they're probably stocked up with alcohol and dressed in pirate gear and singing along to the radio. They'll be laid out on the roof and hanging out on the decks and they won't have the slightest idea of what they're doing or where they're going or the faintest idea of waterways etiquette or protocol.

And why should they? They're usually young and excited and enjoying their first experience of boating on one of the most beautiful canals in the world. I've been doing this boating thing for almost two decades, and it still excites me every time I slip from my mooring and head off up the cut. I'm well over fifty now and have long since disposed of my youthful exuberance, but if I were still twenty, I'd be sipping beers and singing along with them all the way to Five Rise Locks.

But I'm not so young or carefree, so I'll wave and tell them that their costumes look fabulous and offer any advice I can to keep them safe and happy. They'll interrupt me for no more than a few minutes at a time, and if that's the extent of the disruption to my day then I have nothing of substance worth complaining about. I'm not quite an old fart yet, but I'm wistful about my youth and there are few things in this world more beautiful and inspiring than watching the next generation doing what they do best – having fun.

Do you know why they're dressed as pirates?

Because they AAAARRRRRRR!!!!!

💡 Boaters and anglers

Although many boaters are also fishermen, some aren't and so may not know best practice or good etiquette to employ when passing anglers. Kevin Wilmot, deputy editor of *Angling Times*, offers this advice: 'From an angling perspective, it's useful if boaters slow down to go as slow as possible when cruising past anglers. Passing boats will, unavoidably, disturb the silt from the bottom of the canal, thereby disrupting the feed and bait the angler has put into the "swim" – the area in which they're fishing. Slower speeds mean less disruption, which is preferable for the angler. Of course, anglers will replenish the swim with more bait when the boat has passed, but the less disruption the better.

'Also, it's good if boaters use the deeper, central channel in the canal when passing anglers. Cruising near the shallower edges of the canal causes more disruption and more silt. The vast majority of boaters know this, and the vast majority of anglers are thankful for boaters who cruise past considerately.'

💡 Running aground

It's common to run aground near the edges of the waterway, particularly when attempting to moor. The best way to get off the ground is by going back the way you came. By attempting to force your way onward you will probably only become more stuck. Reversing off is usually sufficient, but reducing the weight on board by depositing a passenger onto the bank will often help too.

MOORING

Mooring durations and restrictions are discussed in detail in another part of this book, but considerate mooring practices deserve a mention here too. Mooring next to any structure, such as bridges, locks, tunnels, bends, winding holes, water points or sanitary stations, can cause problems and is sometimes dangerous. Stopping at these places should be restricted to the minimum amount of time you need to use the facilities, and in the case of bends and winding holes, not at all. If you decide to moor anywhere near one of these features, be sure to leave more than enough space for boats to use the facilities without needing to make difficult manoeuvres.

Boaters will often choose a mooring on a quiet bit of towpath with a view to avoiding the busy visitor moorings nearby, and while there's no rule that says you can't moor there too, choosing a spot a short distance away is the polite thing to do. Mooring on the non-towpath side (offside) is often impossible and not usually allowed. Offside land is almost always private and a haven to flora and fauna which can be disturbed by mooring boats. Think of other nearby humans too, particularly if mooring in residential areas, and keep noise to a minimum; this includes engine running, music and noisy barbecue parties. CRT rules state that engines must not be running between 8pm and 8am.

RIVER BOATING

Navigating rivers presents more risk than simple canal cruising, particularly if the river is tidal or has a strong current. Seemingly routine manoeuvres such as boating under bridges, entering and leaving locks and even mooring up are much more difficult in a fast-flowing current, and inexperienced boaters should seek guidance. Getting it wrong on a river can have far greater consequences for both your boat and those aboard.

Proper planning is important. Speak to boaters with experience of the river you will be cruising and ask their advice about the specific idiosyncrasies of that river. Local lock keepers are invaluable here too and most can guide you around the major hazards and offer specific navigational advice. The lock keepers will tell you when it's safe to travel, taking into account the currents and tides, and only a fool would ignore their guidance.

Make sure you have the right safety equipment on board and that your crew know what to do and how to use it, should the need arise. In a deep and fast-flowing river, even the strongest swimmer is in danger if they fall overboard. Lifejackets must always be worn and the boat should be equipped with throwing ropes and life rings kept in easy reach.

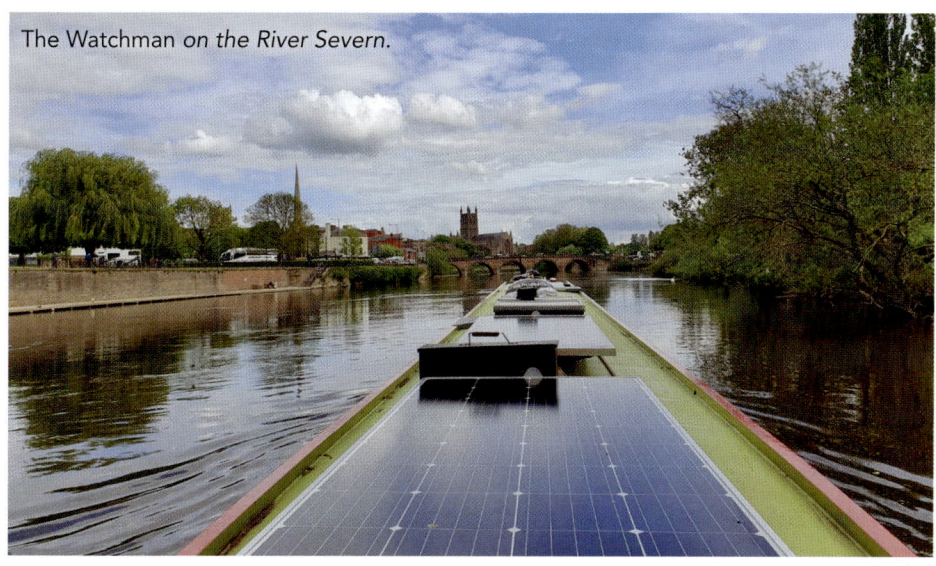

The Watchman *on the River Severn.*

An anchor is another must-have item. Often this is the only way to bring a stricken boat to a safe stop if the engine fails for whatever reason. A VHF radio is invaluable for communication with lock keepers and the large commercial vessels that are commonly found on rivers. Coming across one of these large craft laden with cargo is daunting to say the least, so it's best to be prepared for them and ensure that they're prepared to meet you.

River insurance

Make sure that you and your boat are insured to travel on tidal waterways. Some policies specifically exclude this.

The two-boat rule

It's a good idea to always travel in tandem with another boat when navigating rivers. Most problems are dealt with much more easily if another boat is there to help or tow you to safety.

RIVER MOORING

River moorings need careful consideration as a pleasant high-tide mooring spot can become a steep mudbank with alarming speed. If you're simply passing through as part of your journey you will find floating pontoons at conveniently spaced intervals. These rise and fall with the tide and are usually positioned near road bridges or other branches of the waterways system. The lock keepers stationed at tidal rivers will monitor your position as you cruise through their patch, so it's important to notify them if you intend to stop at a floating pontoon en route.

Mooring at the pontoons on tidal rivers is not as easy as mooring on a canal. The tide and the current must be considered, as each presents a challenge. Approaching a pontoon mooring with a fast-flowing tide or current is a dangerous undertaking. There's a significant risk of losing control of your vessel if the current is strong enough to claim your boat as you attempt to step ashore, not to mention the risk of falling in. The best way is to approach the mooring against the current by continuing slightly past the pontoon before turning your boat around and heading back. This makes for a much slower and more controlled approach as your engine counteracts the direction and force of the current.

It's possible to moor at bankside if the proper facilities are in place, but these aren't usually available for visiting boats. Many permanent riverside moorers use a floating pontoon secured to a hinged metal structure which rises and falls with the tide. These simple contraptions are often made from scaffolding poles and work exceedingly well. Some even have a secure gated access point installed.

The rising and falling water level of both rivers and the canals that are fed from them has caught many boaters unawares. Some seemingly non-tidal waterways can rise and fall alarmingly, leaving a tightly moored boat bound or suspended from its ropes at an unnerving angle. Ask advice from local boaters or lock keepers regarding the eccentricities of the waterway, and be sure to take account of rising and falling water levels.

Dwarfed by a gravel barge on the River Severn.

BEEN THERE, DONE THAT
RIVER CRUISING TIPS

STEVE AND EILEEN
Nb *Rahab*

We were stuck on a flooded river for a couple of weeks when the water level was so high that the locks onto the canal were closed. As the water rose it became clear that we were at risk of being washed onto the bank. In the end we used the bargepole and gangplank to wedge between the boat and the bank to keep us on the river, ready for when the water level dropped. It was quite an adventure wading through 3ft of water to get to the boat.

RIVER LOCKS

Leaving the river via a lock requires careful planning too. A fast-flowing current can thwart an unprepared boater, dashing your boat against the lock wall as you enter, or causing you to overshoot the entrance to the lock. When approaching with the tide you should begin your approach turn into the lock early and be ready to use your engine in short, sharp bursts as you enter the lock. When entering a lock against the tide you should advance slightly past the lock entrance before turning in, since the current will drag you back the way you came as your boat turns broadside. Follow advice from the lock keeper closely as they know their lock and the river flow well and have completed the manoeuvre many times before.

It may seem that river cruising is a risky business and perhaps well avoided but, as with most risky endeavours, there are significant rewards to be had in return. Access to many sections of the waterways network is only possible via a river stretch, and besides, river cruising is exciting and awe-inspiring with its grand scale and new experiences. It might be worth hiring an experienced skipper to coach you as you navigate a river cruise, or perhaps joining another experienced boater on their next river jaunt. There's much to learn and safety should be your first consideration, but river boating is a fantastic experience if it's done correctly.

SINGLE-HANDED CRUISING TIPS

Single handed cruising, without help from a crew, is not just possible, it's imminently enjoyable too – at least for most people. Yes, you'll need to be especially careful and consider some extra precautions, but cruising the cut on your own terms opens a whole new level of the boating experience. It's highly recommended.

LOVELY LOCK LADDERS

Ladders are a relatively recent addition to the historic structures of locks and were introduced as a safety escape feature, rather than as an aid to boating. Although many single-handers find the ladders useful, some consider them unnecessary, preferring instead to haul their boat in and out of the lock using ropes. This bow-hauling method works fine in most cases, although those locks with bridges at their entrance or exit can prove problematic. For boaters with the necessary co-ordination, one answer is to stand atop the bridge and nimbly flick the rope beneath before catching the end at the other side. For those of us lacking in this skill, using the lock ladder is arguably a more efficient method, as long as one is conscious of the ever-present slip hazard.

FRIENDLY FIRE

One of the greatest dangers when negotiating a lock alone comes in the form of friendly help. Despite their best intentions, enthusiastic assistance from inexperienced or distracted windlass wielders can create problems and things can go wrong surprisingly quickly. Don't be afraid to decline help as most boaters will understand that everyone has their own way of doing things. Explain that you have a 'system' and that it's hard to break the habit. Of course, if you're sharing a lock with another boat and their crew, it's everyone's responsibility to stay alert to danger. By all means enjoy the company while you can, but keep a watchful eye on proceedings to ensure everyone stays safe and afloat.

USE YOUR CENTRELINE

A centre rope is your greatest friend when boating alone. Ensure the end of the rope is within reach of your position at the tiller, ready for when you need to step ashore. In most situations you can use the centre rope alone to moor to the bank while preparing a lock, before using a bow rope to haul the boat in when the lock is ready.

Use the centreline again to maintain a good position in the lock, taking in or letting out slack when necessary. Be especially careful when locking down, as boats can easily be hung up if a rope is tied to a bollard. It does also help to have a centreline on each side of the boat if possible as this avoids the need to flick the rope over chimneys and other roof clutter when the need arises.

BRIDGE ISSUES

Lift bridges and swing bridges rely on the use of long ropes, convenient landing points and accurate boat manoeuvring, often supplemented by a little agility and climbing skill. They should always be approached slowly and methodically, and it's useful to practise the process when you have a crew to step in with help should motorists become impatient.

A centreline is vital for single-handed boaters.

BEEN THERE, DONE THAT
SINGLE-HANDED CRUISING TIPS

KEV AND SAFFI
Nb *The Grey Lady*
Preparation is even more essential when you're cruising alone. Everything you need should be within arm's reach while you're underway. Think about everything you do, and then think about it again before executing, and do it slower than you might normally.

Be aware that some electrically operated bridges have a timer to delay over-frequent usage, or a locking period to prohibit being used at peak road traffic times.

It's often asked why most swing bridges leave single-handed skippers on the other side of the cut from their moored boat. It is, in fact, a historical feature left over from the time when boats were pulled by horses along the towpath. An open bridge on the towpath side would ensnare the rope between horse and boat, whereas boat crews could easily negotiate bridges on the offside with no risk of entanglement. It could be argued that bridges should be renovated to accommodate our modern engine-driven boating needs, but the heritage of our waterways should perhaps not be discarded so readily. I find the anomalies and ambiguity to be a rather endearing feature of boating and hope that the heritage of our inland waterways is preserved as closely as possible, even if the resulting tricky swing bridges make me curse occasionally.

BOATING ETIQUETTE

As with every community, canal culture has its own set of unwritten rules. Unlike landlubber life, which seems to be becoming ever more isolated, life on the waterways is often conducted cheek by jowl. We share locks, queue for water taps, moor side by side on visitor moorings, and we're forever forging new friendships with the boaters we meet. We congregate at canalside pubs, share news about the local waterways, and we look after our fellow boaters as if they were kin. Of course boating has many joys but for me, this close-knit community is what makes canal life so very special.

As with any community, canal life has its own ingrained points of etiquette that seasoned boaters will go to great lengths to uphold. These are not boating skills or traditions, but behaviours that help us to happily live together in such close proximity. After all, canal life would be pretty miserable if we didn't look after our friends and neighbours.

So with that in mind, here's my list of boating-etiquette tips to help us all get along nicely.

GENERATOR- AND ENGINE-ETIQUETTE

CRT guidelines state that engines and generators should not be run after 8pm or before 8am, and thankfully most boaters are happy to adhere to this obvious rule out of politeness. But there are occasions when boaters will run their engine or generator for hours on end on a daily basis – a situation that usually occurs when batteries can't hold their charge for long.

Regardless of the hour, constant noise of this type can become annoying. The best way to avoid this potential friction is to address the electrical issues that cause the need for such prolonged engine running, and then to manage and monitor your battery life accordingly.

If you do need to run your engine late at night or for prolonged periods, it's always a good idea to explain the situation to your neighbours, apologise for the disruption and then do what you can to mitigate the noise in future.

HEAD-TORCH ETIQUETTE

Most of us will make use of a torch of some variety when walking on unlit towpaths at night, and for many of us, that will be a head torch. Sadly, sometimes that causes a blindingly obvious problem, namely when someone approaches shining light in your eyes. On a towpath or marina pontoon, this is an accident waiting to happen.

As a young apprentice on jungle expeditions in my youth (don't ask) I was swiftly versed in head-torch etiquette when I failed to direct my beam away from the eyes of one of my campsite comrades. On my way back to my tent one night I crossed paths with the expedition leader. I heard him shout something in his thickly accented English, but I didn't quite catch what he said. I managed to take a few more steps toward him before the light of a thousand suns burned into my retina, stopping me dead in my tracks.

Apparently he'd asked me to angle my head torch away from his eyes and, because I had seemingly ignored him, he switched his own torch to super-bright mode. The experience was not only effective but highly instructional too. It's a lesson I remember to this day and, I must admit, one that I have passed on to several other towpath users that I have met.

MOORING ETIQUETTE

We've all been there. It's nearing the end of the cruising day and you're approaching the visitor moorings you're hoping to tie up at. And there would be plenty of space for you to moor, if only the boats that are already there scooched up together. While this experience is just one of those inevitable frustrations of spending time on the cut, wouldn't it be nice if the boats were moved along to make space for you as you approached?

It's not an easy frustration to fix as boats come and go from visitor moorings throughout the day. However, I've taken to looking at the space around my boat at around 3pm to see if scooching up would make room for another boat. Yes, it's a bit of extra work, and it's not always possible when rings and bollards aren't conveniently spaced, but it can really make someone's day when it all comes together nicely.

And while we're on the subject of mooring, I've mentioned before about marking your mooring pins to make them more visible and tying your mooring ropes to rings and bollards in such a way that doesn't inconvenience the boaters who are already tied up there. It's a nightmare having to untie and unravel ropes when someone ties their lines over yours.

> 💡 **Disabled facilities**
>
> Moorings with facilities for the disabled are rare, so stay off these unless you're entitled. There's usually only a small sign to highlight this type of mooring, so keep a keen eye out when tying up in popular areas.

PARTY ETIQUETTE

We all love a good party. A few drinky-poos, a handful of good friends, a funny story and a singalong is exactly what we need after a hard week at work. Unfortunately, one person's funny story and screeching laughter is another person's frustrating disturbance. Some people just want a bit of peace and quiet.

Don't get me wrong. I'm not saying parties and festivities should be banned. We're not trying to be the fun police here. Good-time frivolities are just what the doctor ordered, every now and again. The problems occur when it's every week or, in some cases, every night. That's just rude.

If you're planning a shindig or a knees-up, let your neighbours know. That way they can either join in, turn a blind eye or cruise off with their boat to someplace that's quieter. But be aware that this type of courtesy only works if you don't disturb the peace too often.

Oh, and be sure to clean up the mess sometime before lunchtime the next day. It's the polite thing to do.

DOG ETIQUETTE

This one shouldn't need to be said, but sadly, it does. As boat folk we are already besieged by the dreaded piles of poop left behind by inconsiderate dog owners. (I even found a fresh pile on the back deck of my boat once!) So please, if you're a boat owner with a dog, I beg you, we all beg you, pick up after your dog when it's done its dirty business.

WEED-HATCH DEBRIS ETIQUETTE

We all hate it when we pick up stuff on our prop and have to go down the dreaded weed hatch to cut the debris away. The socially responsible thing to do is to put the offending jetsam in a bin. Take it with you on your boat if you have to because, if you leave it on

Debris recovered from the author's prop.

the towpath, the likelihood is that it'll end up back in the water and around someone else's prop sometime in the not too distant future.

You've already done the hard work. Surely finishing the job and saving someone else the hardship you've just endured is the nice thing to do.

LOCKING ETIQUETTE

As with all aspects of life, some people like to do things differently. Maybe the other way of doing things is better, maybe it's worse. Maybe they know something you don't or maybe there's a good reason why they do it differently to your tried and tested method.

Locking is a great example of this principle in motion. I'm always happy to adjust my technique to suit the other person's wants and needs. Okay, so it might take a second or two longer, but we're not in a hurry here, are we? It's good etiquette to ask the person on the boat how fast or slow they'd like you to go – especially if it's not your boat in the lock. After all, we're not all seasoned boaters and some of us are a bit nervous.

And one more thing; it's always nice to help other boats through the lock that you're waiting for, even if you're boating solo. And if they don't need your help, that's quite alright. At least you were kind enough to ask, and there are plenty of boaters who'd appreciate a helping hand.

BUMPING ETIQUETTE

Show me someone who claims to have never bumped another boat and I'll show you a humongous fibber. We've all done it, through incompetence or because the weather conspired against our otherwise expert-level tillering.

While it's unlikely these collisions will cause any damage, they're invariably quite a shock for the people inside the boat you've hit. The best thing to do, whatever the circumstances behind the bump, is to apologise profusely, explain that you made a mess of it and that you're entirely embarrassed. In fact, you probably shouldn't be allowed on the tiller ever again.

But whatever you do, take responsibility and say sorry. In my experience, most boaters will laugh it off and wave you on your way. (Not that I bump other boats often, you understand!)

STEPPING-ABOARD ETIQUETTE

While it's unlikely you'll cause an accident simply by stepping aboard a boat, there's an outside chance that the people inside are standing on one leg while holding a full cup of coffee next to a red-hot stove. Sure, such accidents are unlikely, but it's possible.

That's why stepping aboard someone's boat without being asked is a bit of a no-no in the canal world. Think of it as a bit like being a vampire who can't enter a premises unless they're invited. It's the same thing, albeit rather less risky.

ASH-PAN ETIQUETTE

I've lost count of the number of times I've seen piles of ash under hedges on the towpath, and some of those ash piles have been so hot as to burn the surrounding undergrowth. It's simply unacceptable.

And yes, I realise that wood ash is considered a fertiliser, but most boaters use coal, which produces ash that is not at all good for plant life. And even wood ash needs to be dug in to be of any fertilising use. So why not avoid the problems and fire risks entirely by getting a 'tippy' receptacle to collect your hot ash, and then deposit it in a bin when it's cooled.

Or better still, donate your ash to the nearest dry dock to help seal up the gaps in the planks that hold back the water. The boatyard will happily take it off your hands and thank you for it.

> 💡 **Collecting deadwood**
> Fallen deadwood is a valuable ecological commodity, since it's home or food for a wealth of flora and fauna. Localised collecting near marinas or popular mooring spots can rapidly desecrate an area of its deadwood resources. I have a rule where I consider it acceptable to collect deadwood that can be reached from the towpath. Everything else belongs to Mother Nature.

ICE ETIQUETTE

Yes, it is possible to cruise the cut when it's iced over. And yes, there are likely to be those rare occasions when it's necessary to do so. But spare a thought for your fellow boaters' blacking before you start pushing sheets of ice along the waterline, not to mention those scarily delicate GRP cruisers that will surely sink if pierced by a shard of ice.

But what about if staying put means you'll overstay on a visitor mooring? Matthew Symonds, CRT's National Boating Manager says, 'Boating when the canal is frozen can be dangerous and cause damage to other boats. If a boater finds themselves in that situation, rather than risk causing damage or be unsafe we'd rather they stayed put. We'd ask you to please contact the local licence support officer to let them know so that a temporary overstay can be agreed until the ice has cleared. If boaters don't let us know they could get an overstay notice.'

SETTING-OFF ETIQUETTE

It's always exciting to be setting off. If you're anything like me you'll be running through the checklist of things you have to do before you untie your lines and push the throttle – taking up fenders, attaching the tiller arm, bringing your coiled centre rope to be nearer the tiller, all of which I have forgotten to do on more than one occasion.

Another thing I often forget to do is to check if another boat is approaching. More than once I've pushed the front of my boat right into the path of another vessel. It's so embarrassing because it seems to be something I mess up frequently. I don't know why I forget to look sometimes, but if you're one of the people I've done this to, I'm so sorry.

WAVING ETIQUETTE

Whether it be boaters, cyclists, runners, anglers or canoeists, the ever-widening rift between canal-using camps is a sad and sorry state of affairs. Although I've never been fishing, I have a couple of theories as to why anglers so rarely interact with us boaters.

As a boater, when I approach an angler I routinely slow to tickover. Having done this unselfishly nice thing, it would be nice if the anglers gave us a cheery wave and said thanks. Sadly, that seems to happen only rarely, and I always wondered why.

Recently, I was chatting with my fisherman friend (who is a bloke and not the cough lozenge) and he offered another perspective. Perhaps fishermen and fisherwomen feel the same way. Having spent all morning feeding the swim of water where they're fishing, they've stopped what they were doing, reeled in their rod and let our boat past without obstruction. Surely the least they can expect is a thank you? So, that's what I started doing and, lo and behold, fisherfolk suddenly became a lot more friendly! (Well, most of them anyway.)

On the other hand, I still think the reason some of them seem a bit narky is because we've ruined their meditative state. After all, staring at a small red dot on the water's surface for hours on end is nothing short of zen-level meditation if you ask me. I'm sure I'd be annoyed if a big lumbering lump of metal with a thudding great diesel engine interrupted my higher state of consciousness.

What I'm trying to say, in a roundabout way, is that waving, saying hello and being nice to our fellow canal users is the ultimate level of waterways-etiquette expertise. I might be getting a bit John Lennon here with all this peace, love and harmony on the waterways stuff, but those cheery interactions we have so frequently on the cut are what makes the waterways culture so special. And if we want the waterways to be the nice place we all wish it would be, we need to think about how we treat our fellow canal-loving comrades.

As Mr Lennon himself once said, 'Peace is not something you wish for. It's something you make, something you do, something you are, and something you give away.' Sounds as if John would have been a jolly nice boater.

BOAT HIRERS

💡 Hire state of consciousness
Jo, Snaygill Boats

It usually takes a few days for our boat hirers to settle in to the boating mindset. If we are going to get calls about running out of water or battery life problems, we know it will be in the first week of the hire period. After that time they start to regulate their usage and consumption and generally ease back and start enjoying boat life. After the hire is over they're so relaxed that we often see them pull out of the car park at an amusingly sedate pace.

Hirers aren't pirates, but some private boat owners have a holier-than-thou attitude toward them. While it's true that most hirers will not have the experience and expertise of a seasoned boater, it's worth remembering that we were in exactly the same position once upon a time and many of us were bitten by the boating bug through hiring. 'If it wasn't for hire boats then the waterways as we know them would not exist,' Steve Vaughan of considerateboater.com reminds us.

Hire companies work hard to ensure that their customers have enough tuition to manage the boat, but an hour of coaching cannot make an expert boater. Few hirers will be purposely discourteous, but novices are going to make mistakes.

Often a hirer will welcome some considered and friendly advice, but don't be put out if they don't want it. Few of us enjoy our errors being highlighted.

Hire boat tuition.

Hire boat fleet.

Tony's *towpath tales*

Single-handed boating

It was still pleasantly warm as I rocked gently in my hammock after a long day on the cut. The claret-red backdrop of sky was gatecrashed by occasional swooping bats as they hunted for their supper, while fat silver carp jumped and flipped in the water. The sun was finally dipping below the horizon of hills and I grinned again as I looked around, pleased with myself for finding such a beautiful and serene mooring. My journey would begin again tomorrow and this place would become another memory of a great day on the cut. But for a few hours it was mine to enjoy selfishly, all to myself.

I've explored a fair chunk of the network, and while I'll often have at least one crew on board to help with locks and tea-making duties, I always look forward to those days when I can cruise alone. Perhaps it's because our modern world is so full of continual chatter and communication that we don't often get a chance to enjoy being by ourselves.

Summertime

During the summer months there are plenty of other boaters, fishermen and pedestrians around to punctuate my day, and for the most part these are a welcome distraction. While I am perfectly able to negotiate locks and moving bridges single-handed, the opportunity to shoot the breeze with other boaters is one of the greatest pleasures of life on the cut, despite our conversations being executed in series, and cut short when the lock gates open to let us out.

I always make a point of hopping ashore with a windlass so that I can do my fair share of the work, but more often than not there are enough hands ashore and I'm encouraged to stay aboard. I must admit I do feel quite lazy, chatting with the other skipper while their industrious crew scurry across the locks.

Locks and moving bridges

Locks and moving bridges can be wearisome when cruising alone. As a remedy I've found the best approach is to dispense with the idea of speed and efficiency, and instead embrace the slow and methodical nature of the process. Indeed, I find that almost every part of boat life is more pleasurable if one adopts this philosophy. At locks I use my binoculars on the approach to select a suitable mooring point before sauntering up to the towpath at a slow tickover. I'll moor loosely, take a leisurely look around and perhaps collect some unsightly litter before preparing the lock and bringing the boat in at a crawling pace.

It seems that the deeper the lock, the more nervous I become, particularly if using the lock ladder to board and alight. My boat always seems a little forlorn and vulnerable when left on its own at the bottom of a lock, and I'm always eager to get back aboard. Despite this impatience, I feel more comfortable and confident if I use only the paddles on one side of the lock, dispensing entirely with the need to rush across the gate. Admittedly this is a time-consuming option, but I'm happy to compromise speed for serenity. As I step aboard and pull away I say a little thank you to the waterways gods for allowing me safe passage through another lock, single-handed.

Executing swing bridges is an exercise in science, skill and luck in equal proportion. There are many variables to consider and even a simple moment of distraction can prove troublesome. I am wary of windows and cratch covers becoming impaled on the corner of the bridge as the boat passes through. The wind is no friend of mine either and seems to conspire against me. But I always feel a little smug and accomplished when I'm safely back on board and the sight of the bridge is fading into the distance behind me.

Safety

Sir Francis Younghusband once said, 'Experience teaches much, and teaches it sharply,' and thankfully my experiences of mishaps have been few and the consequences minor. Relishing the carefree, idyllic life on the waterways alone must be contrasted with a strict and concentrated approach to safety. It's foolish to risk personal injury in an attempt to save a window or 'cilled' stern gear, particularly as incidents involving single-handed boaters may go unnoticed for hours.

Despite my own cautiously focused approach, there have been occasional near misses where only my strong grip on the boat or lock ladder has saved me after a slip. I'm convinced enough of the risks to always wear a self-inflating lifejacket when locking single-handed. Despite having not yet fallen into a lock I can't help calculating the increasing odds of doing so each time I repeat the process. Perhaps one day my luck will fail and my number will come up.

Winter

If pushed to make a choice I'd grudgingly admit that I prefer boating in the warm summer months, but grudgingly for sure, as winter cruising has its own magical charm. I love frosty mornings with branches sleeved in a silver sheen, smoke unfolding from my chimney and not a soul to be seen. True connoisseurs of solitude will relish these cold, crisp months when one can cruise for days without passing another moving boat, enjoying the fantasy that the waterways were yours to own.

During the winter, boating comes into sharp focus as every activity and manoeuvre becomes more acute. My fingers are crossed, with prayers and curses each morning, as I attempt to start my decrepit old engine that should have been serviced during the comfortable summer months. I cling to the hope of finding a coal merchant to replenish my dwindling supplies. Icy lock beams and ladders concentrate my attention, as do the freezing cold hand rails of my boat. I'm always amused when my wet ropes from yesterday are frozen in coils or straight like dowelling rods by last night's freeze. All of these musings trip through my mind during the day, and without a crew to confer with the responsibility of dealing with them is entirely mine. They're tests which give me a sense of accomplishment and pride once each is safely overcome.

Single-handed cruising isn't easy and requires adaptations in both technique and attitude. But for those with sufficient supplies of brains and brawn, cruising the waterways alone can be a rewarding and meditative enterprise. Repetition is the mother of all skill and many single-handed boaters will claim to be at least as efficient as crewed vessels.

The real joy of single-handed cruising lies not in the speed at which one can negotiate a lock, or ease with which one masters a swing bridge, but in the uninterrupted and serene enjoyment of the waterways and one's boat. I don't think I can say with any sincerity that I've ever truly cruised alone. In reality, it has always been a team effort: me, and my boat. We make a great team and she's never let me down.

Boating during the winter is tough but rewarding.

7 WORKING NINE TO FIVE

While working and liveaboard boating aren't mutually exclusive, they sometimes don't seem to fit together neatly. For those of us who still need to work for a living, here are some of the things you need to know.

The transient nature of boating can be difficult for those who work in one place. Even those who work for themselves can encounter communication and logistical challenges. However, most of the problems can be overcome with a little ingenuity, planning, hard work and good luck. The solution may be a radical one, but boaters are generally a resourceful bunch and most would not allow a small inconvenience such as a job to stand in the way of their liveaboard dream.

CONTINUOUS CRUISERS

Juggling a regular job with continuous cruising is difficult so most employed liveaboards have a permanent mooring. Waterways regulations state that continuous cruisers must move to a new district at least every two weeks, and hopping back and forth to stay near your workplace will soon attract the attention of the local moorings officer and disapproving fellow boaters.

There are many other inconveniences too. Retrieving your car each time you cruise to a new location can be a logistical nightmare, and commuting by public transport is complicated or impossible under continuous-cruising conditions. It can also be difficult to find enough time to run the engine to charge leisure batteries, so power consumption often becomes critical and rationed.

Recruitment agencies offer a limited and intermittent solution for some liveaboard continuous cruisers. Offering your services to the agencies in each new district you moor can secure a temporary income until you move on, but most available agency work assignments are poorly paid unless you have a valuable skill that is in demand, and the proximity of your boat will still depend on mooring duration regulations. Consider, too, that this type of itinerant employment is unlikely to deliver a constant flow of work, particularly during times of economic downturn, although intermittent work is often all the liveaboard needs if their lifestyle is sufficiently frugal.

While intermittent employment is an option, this type of lifestyle is hardly convenient or stress-free. Many continuous cruisers are self-employed or have another means of income, and most of those who start off as salaried nine-to-five workers soon tire of it, eventually giving up either their job, their boat or their continuous-cruising attempts.

PERMANENT MOORERS

Finding a mooring that is near enough to your place of work will often mean making a compromise. Your daily commute is the most likely sacrifice as you will probably need to balance the mooring location and facilities against the proximity to your work. That said, the availability of local moorings are likely to dictate your options to you. Be sure to read the moorings chapter of this book closely.

Having a permanent mooring need not inhibit the boater's tendency to roam, but having a regular job certainly seems to.

The convenience of a permanent mooring, particularly one with good facilities, is hard to give up, and once again the boater must balance the desire to use their boat as it was intended against the necessity of earning a living.

Determined liveaboard boaters will often make radical changes in order to live the lifestyle to which they aspire, and the method of earning a living is usually high on the list of changes to be made. Many new liveaboards seem to undergo a career change as they covet a less stressful life or because their current employment does not accommodate a boating lifestyle. Necessity being the mother of all invention, boaters with enough courage and determination will usually find a means to achieve their goal and find a happy compromise.

Harriet McAtee, Nourish Yoga Training, offers online yoga classes from her boat.

The usual boating-specific challenges can complicate matters for liveaboards who work from home or work for themselves. Phone signal, address issues, internet connection, mail and courier deliveries and even the limited space on board can each be a headache, but innovative and determined boaters always find a solution.

RENTING OUT YOUR BOAT

While on a frugality and downsizing mission, people often make radical changes to their lifestyle. For new boaters looking for innovative ways to save and earn more money, hiring and renting out their boat may appear to be a good way to capitalise on their asset. It might seem like a good idea, but in reality this type of commerce only makes sense for those running a fleet of boats.

Increased licence costs, insurance costs and Boat Safety Scheme requirements are the main factors to consider and are imperative, of course, since the safety of your boat and that of the hirers or tenants is vitally important. Supplying proper training and instruction on boat handling and facilities is an art, and ongoing support when things go wrong is vital. Breakages, wear and tear and theft must all be factored in to any business plan involving boat hire, making the venture viable only for larger-scale operations. Unofficial hiring and renting does happen, but the potential for it turning into a nightmare is enormous. There's a whole section about this topic in the chapter discussing mooring options. It's well worth a read if you're considering renting out your boat.

BEEN THERE, DONE THAT
EARNING A LIVEABOARD LIVING

DARREN AND DEBBIE
Nb *Dunster*
Occupation – musician

When I lived in a house I had a much bigger studio and more equipment and more instruments. Most of these were sold when I moved aboard as there wasn't enough space. I did stash some of my kit at a friend's recording studio and inevitably these got used by other artists recording there. In return I get to use the studio equipment for free, so I haven't lost out at all, and it's nice to share resources around within our profession.

Being on a boat hasn't stopped me from making music for a living, despite the constraints. I think that if you have the right attitude you can find a way around most things if you really want to, and the pros definitely outweigh the cons. Sometimes we move the boat closer to where we are playing a gig if the venue is near a nice place on the canal. Boat life is also a great way for a musician to live: all that outdoors and travel and relaxation is exactly the right environment for creativity to flourish.

Darren, Nb Dunster.

BEEN THERE, DONE THAT
EARNING A LIVEABOARD LIVING

STEVE AND EILEEN
Nb *Rahab*
Occupation – photographer and teacher, respectively

Living on a boat has not had much impact on our work lives at all. We both earn a living teaching part-time and Steve also runs a photography business. We both bring work back home to the boat, but it's the type of work that can easily be done on a laptop while sat on the sofa. We both have a car, so commuting is easy, and when we are out and about on the boat it's not much of a problem to use public transport.

We both chose to work part-time because we didn't want to sell our souls to a lifestyle that revolved around work and money. We earn less but we have more fun and free time, which fits in nicely with our relaxed boating lifestyle and ethos. In fact, Steve turned down some lucrative work recently as it would have meant long days and a long commute. It just didn't seem worth the stress. In an ideal world we would like to do more boating and see more of the network, but we have found a happy balance between that ideal and the need to earn a living.

TONY AND VICKIE
Nb *The Watchman*

We work from home running our own company – an international membership organisation for people who keep reptiles, believe it or not!

We can do our jobs from anywhere with an internet connection, which means we can move around the network more or less as we like. We have a small office aboard, just 8x6ft, in which we have a couple of standing desks and some storage space.

The most important consideration for us is the internet connection – we simply can't do business without it. There have been a couple of occasions where we have had such a rubbish internet speed that we have had to move the boat to a better location. It's usually most apparent when we have online meetings, because it's just not acceptable to be dropping in and out while we're trying to communicate. That's why we spent a bit of money on signal-boosting technology, and it was well worth it.

8 HOME COMFORTS

Living on a boat is wonderful, as long as you're prepared to trade convenience for a more hands-on way of life. Boat life makes you deeply aware of your resources and how you impact the world around you. And that's part of the magic.

Imagine the scene… it's January and the evenings are cold and dark by six o'clock. You arrive home late from work, and after taking off your wet coat and muddy boots you start to build a fire, only to find that your coal scuttle is empty. Thankfully you have adequate supplies stacked neatly beside your boat, but to refill your scuttle means going outside again, into the wind and the rain.

Ten minutes later you remove your coat and boots for the second time and begin to build the fire. In half an hour your boat should be comfortably warm, but until then, only a steaming mug of tea will help. You fill the kettle and light the hob before filling the sink with soapy water. It's time to tackle last night's dishes, but halfway through filling, the tap begins to splutter – a sure sign that your water tank is about to run dry. Now you have a dilemma. Do you postpone the dishes and tomorrow morning's shower, or do you brave the weather once again and fill your tank? Resignedly, you don your boots and coat once again and head out into the rain with your hosepipe.

By the time you get back inside the roaring stove has warmed your boat nicely and you look forward to a well-earned cup of tea. But surely the kettle should be boiling by now? With a glance towards the hob you realise that your gas bottle has run out. It's small consolation that it did so now and not in the morning when you were in the shower covered in soap and running late for work. And at least your batteries aren't flat… yet.

Welcome to boat life, albeit in a condensed form. You would have be pretty unlucky (or disorganised) for all of these frustrations to afflict you in a single night, but afflict you they will, at almost predictably regular intervals. This is the major difference between life afloat and living in a house. In a house, your home comforts and utilities are available at the flick of a switch – on tap and seemingly infinite. On a boat, your supply of these consumable resources will run out eventually.

Perhaps this is why green living is so popular in the boating community, as the lifestyle lends itself easily to the environmentalist's cause. Peter Underwood writes about living aboard for the popular waterways newspaper *Towpath Talk*. 'When people move aboard they're confronted with the resources it takes to keep them in the style to which they have become accustomed and exactly how much waste they produce,' says Peter. 'Every resource – coal, diesel, wood, gas, food and water – must be brought onto the boat by you, and every piece of waste you produce must be disposed of by you too. Suddenly you have a personal relationship with your means of creating heat and power.'

Everything you rely on for heat, power, hygiene and cooking will run out or break eventually, often at the most inopportune moment. Murphy's Law reigns supreme on the cut. Electrical systems will fail, leaving you without power unless you can fix them or pay someone else to do so. Your toilet tank will be full when you badly need to go or when you have guests arriving.

It may even break down completely. Everything on a boat takes time to fix and usually costs more than you expect. The simple and idyllic boat life that you aspire to must be earned. Those who are well suited to it will not only be prepared for these eventualities, they'll also have a smooth system in place for dealing with them, a backup plan for when things go wrong, while being resigned to the fact that they probably will. Welcome to boat life.

WATER

There's not much science involved in the provision of water on a boat. Somewhere aboard you likely have a tank which, when empty, must be refilled. Ideally the tank will be situated centrally so that the constant filling and emptying does not cause your boat to list.

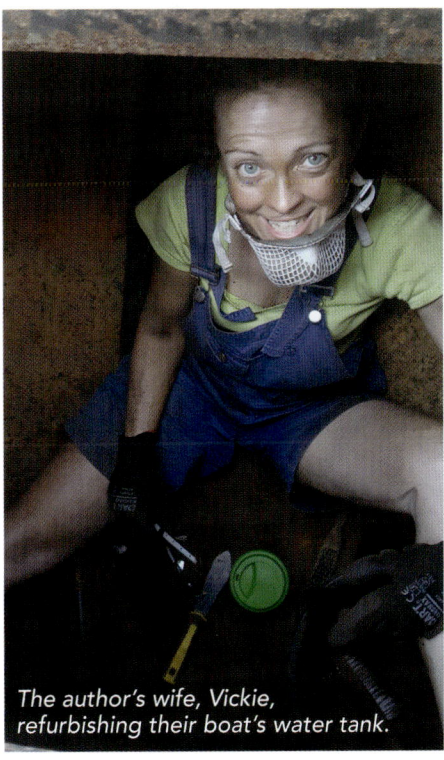

The author's wife, Vickie, refurbishing their boat's water tank.

Steel tanks will invariably rust and eventually need treating with specialist coating every few years. As a result, these steel tanks will feature a large inspection hatch for access as you will need to get inside to treat the rust and paint the interior. Plastic water tanks are often translucent which allows you to view the water level easily, but there may not be enough visibility to allow you to inspect the contents in detail, so some kind of removable inspection hatch is highly recommended.

Even the mains-fed water that you use to fill your tank will contain small particles of dirt, dust and other debris, and in a vessel as large as a boat's

water tank these will eventually settle to form a layer of brown 'silt' on the bottom of the tank. Over time this layer can become significant enough to be visible when you run the tap, causing brown or murky water to run as the tank is approaching empty. If your tank has easy access, this problem can be solved by using a pump to suck out the bottom few inches of water, running the suction hose or pipe along the bottom of your tank to suck out the debris settled there. In steel tanks you'll likely want to strip and clean the tank at regular enough intervals to negate the problem – probably coinciding with the timing of a new interior coat of water-tank paint.

💡 Newly painted water tanks

Remember to allow a newly painted tank to dry fully before filling and emptying the tank a couple of times prior to its first proper use. This should remove any residual paint aftertaste from the water.

💡 Water, water everywhere

It's possible to fit a water filtration system that can convert canal water into drinking water. They're not cheap, and the less expensive options are often less safe or reliable, but the technology exists.

The systems can be retro-fitted to existing boats, and many boat builders will be happy to include such a kit in a new-build boat.

It may be advisable to use water-purifying tablets in your water tank, but these often impart an unpleasant taste and seemingly few boaters use them. More often than not, those who are concerned with water purity are leisure boaters who use their water tanks infrequently and therefore should worry about bacterial build-up. Often they either use bottled water or fill containers from their tap at home and transport them to use aboard their boat during their stay. Again, few liveaboard boaters have the patience for this and perhaps develop a stronger immune system as a result. Perhaps.

ELECTRICITY

Boats with a permanent mooring have most of the convenience of a land-based home as far as electricity supply is concerned. Marinas, boatyards and boat club moorings usually have a metered electricity point for each boat.

Most boats still use lead-acid batteries, although some are now switching to lithium. Regardless, an on-board battery charger is standard on most boats and your batteries are kept topped up for as long as you're hooked up to the mains. Most modern chargers will regulate the supply, backing off when the batteries are fully charged. However, this constant charging over a long period can apparently fry the batteries to the point where they're useless – an issue you will become aware of only when you leave your mooring and the luxury of its electrical supply. The real test of any boat's electrical system will happen when you're away from your mains supply and rely on your engine, the alternator and the fitness of your batteries. This is the time when any fault in your system becomes evident. Once the life of a full charge drops to an intolerably short length of time, you know you need to get a new bank of batteries.

It's tempting to think that installing extra batteries is a good idea and that ten batteries can give you longer life between charges. While this sounds sensible it's not that simple as you'll need to fully recharge the batteries in order to maintain their efficacy. Unless you have solar or a generator you'll need to run your engine, and a few hours of engine running can fully charge only two or three leisure batteries. To charge six or more would take most of the day and constitutes a false economy. Of course, using solar and generators – as opposed to running your boat engine – can help to keep leisure batteries topped up, and this is a cheaper and more reliable than an old diesel engine during the wintertime.

On the downside, generators are noisy contraptions to a greater or lesser degree and therefore often found running outside the boat on the towpath, to spare the boater's ears. Beware, though, that any generator on view can become a target for thieves, who can be guaranteed a booty if they wait until you leave your boat unattended. The additional risk of having petrol on board must also be seriously considered.

Battery maintenance is a dark art which requires your batteries to be used and somewhat discharged at regular intervals. However, they should not be run down too far too often, for fear of damaging them so badly that they no longer retain a charge.

It's often recommended that your battery bank not be depleted beyond 50 per cent of their capacity, although it's impossible to determine when this point is reached without a suitable meter or battery management system. While flattening your batteries beyond this point doesn't mean instant death, do it too often and you'll start to experience problems – specifically with the length of time your batteries will last between charges.

The Watchman *receives an electrical upgrade.*

Most boats have a 12V electrical system installed, with appliances such as water pumps, lights and even some fridges running directly from this 12V supply. However, most modern battery-dependent appliances such as laptops, mobile phones, MP3 players and the like use a 230V supply to charge their batteries. This is not a problem when moored at a venue with mains electricity supplied, as the 230V three-pin sockets aboard will be fed directly. The issue arises when your boat is away from its mooring and mains supply, but there are a couple of ways to deal with this issue. The most common is to install an inverter which converts 12V supply to 230V, thereby bringing the three-pin sockets back into action. The downside here is that the inverter itself uses power to do its job and therefore essentially 'wastes' more of your batteries' power.

A cosy Dutch barge interior.

A more efficient solution is to use a 12V transformer, charger or adapter for the appliance you wish to use. 12V chargers are available for all mobile phones, and most laptops can be powered by a 12V transformer which can be bought separately. Travel irons and hairdryers run directly from 12V, as do mini dustbuster-type vacuum cleaners.

A major stumbling block for many liveaboards is the compromise that must be made regarding white goods such as refrigerators, freezers, washing machines and tumble dryers. All these appliances can be found installed aboard boats, however, and even dishwashers are occasionally seen, but the compromises of power usage, water usage and space are significant factors to consider. For those moored permanently, power and water are less of an issue, the only inconvenience being a more regular water tank top-up. But all take up space and most are impractical or impossible to use when you're cruising, depending on your electrical system.

Refrigerators are an exception, and if you have the right fridge, most boats can enjoy refrigeration while cruising. The best choice for the liveaboard boater with cruising aspirations nowadays is a 12V fridge which runs without needing an inverter. Unfortunately, 12V fridges are considerably more expensive. 12V washing machines and 12V dishwashers don't exist yet – at least not to my knowledge.

Washing machines used to be a rare sight aboard boats, and particularly rare

> 💡 **Frugal fridge-free winter**
> During the cold months you can switch off your fridge and keep food in your cratch area. This is most practical for those with a canvas cratch cover in order to hide their food from scavengers, but those without a cover might use a box with a sealable lid. Be careful when telling non-boating visitors where to put the butter when they have finished with it.

with those who would regularly cruise. This seems to have changed over the last few years, likely as a result of the influx of new liveaboards who view the lack of a washing machine as a deal-breaker. There are a couple of good solutions, both of which are a better option than using the local launderette.

The first is the increasingly popular twin-tub machines which have been enthusiastically endorsed by liveaboard boaters. Although they look as if they're made by Fisher-Price, and weigh only a few kilograms, these washers are pretty amazing. They save on power usage by not heating water inside the machine, relying instead on being filled with hot water from your tap. The best models have a pump to expel water once it's been used and, although not as convenient or time-efficient as automatics, they're a great way to do your laundry aboard.

Other boaters employ an even more ingenious method, using a conventional automatic washing machine. Again, instead of relying upon the machine heating the water, these are filled with hot water from the boat's hot-water supply, thereby negating the machine's heater entirely. If the supply is plumbed with a thermostatic mixer tap, the temperature of the water can be controlled before it enters the machine. Although these machines use more energy than the aforementioned twin tubs, this option may be a solution for those liveaboards who simply won't compromise away from an automatic.

STARTER BATTERIES

It's important that your starter battery is somehow kept charged and separate from your leisure batteries. (If you run down your starter battery you won't be able to start your engine to recharge your leisures.) The simplest solution is to fit what is known as a split-charge relay device. This ensures that once the starter battery is fully charged it's isolated from the leisures to ensure it's available for starting the engine, even if the leisures are run flat.

There are apparently many varieties of more efficient and intelligent battery management systems available, and if you understand 'electrickery', these might be worth investigating. However, many boaters stick by the philosophy that simplicity rules supreme, and many unreliable battery management systems are removed and replaced with a split-charge relay system. This seems to be a most common adaptation made to boats intended for liveaboard purposes, not least because the cost of maintaining and replacing management systems can be high.

SOLAR FOR LIVEABOARDS

Solar power has become more affordable and efficient over the last few years, so installing solar is a bit of a no-brainer for liveaboards nowadays. While it's entirely possible to live aboard without solar power – and, indeed, many boaters do – it's difficult to imagine a circumstance where additional solar power wouldn't be of significant benefit. It would be easy to end this section right there, just saying solar is great for liveaboards – but it's worth spending some time thinking a about your energy needs and the way you use your boat if you're to get the most from a solar installation.

PROS
- You can charge your batteries without needing a nearby electricity supply.
- You can avoid running your engine or generator for long periods of time just to generate power.
- They don't use fossil fuels.
- Batteries last longer when they're kept topped up.
- Once installed, the power is free.

CONS
- There's an initial installation cost.
- They take up space on your roof.
- Errr, that's it.

POWER IN – POWER OUT

It's useful to think about solar power in the same way we think about saving money. In order to grow our bank balance it's important not only to put money in, but also to avoid taking money out wherever that is possible. Planning a solar installation works in much the same way, in that we need not only consider the power being added into our batteries by the panels, but also limit the power being taken out of our batteries by the appliances we use on board. Essentially, we're aiming to deposit as much power as possible into our batteries and to withdraw as little as possible.

ENERGY OUT– REDUCING YOUR USAGE

The energy expenditure side of the equation is a good place to start when you're considering a solar installation because you will need a smaller and cheaper solar installation to supply your needs if you're using less energy.

There are some quick and easy wins, such as swapping halogen and fluorescent lamps to LEDs, which makes a surprisingly big difference. You might be surprised to learn that you can run as many as ten LED lamps on the same energy used by one halogen bulb. Avoiding the use of immersion heaters to produce hot water is essential if you want to be self-sufficient when you're away from your mooring and, thankfully, most boats have alternative options for heating water, such as diesel or gas-powered heaters.

But the big gains start to happen when you stop relying on your inverter. Inverters convert the 12V power from your batteries to the 230V power needed by many electrical appliances. Unfortunately, inverters are relatively power-hungry devices, particularly the larger units required to run 230V appliances which need lots of power – most notably your fridge.

It's a good idea indeed to change as many appliances as possible to 12V supply in the bid to eliminate your need for the inverter. Desk fans, hairdryers, chargers for phones, tablets and even laptops are available in 12V options. Music lovers can be easily satisfied: many boats already have 12V car audio systems installed, while others use mobile phones or tablets connected via Bluetooth to 12V speakers.

Even 12V televisions are available. Indeed, you'll likely find perfectly serviceable 12V versions of all of your 230V appliances. It all adds up, and the less you use your inverter the more efficient and effective your solar installation will be.

Of course, to do this you'll need a good number of 12V sockets located in convenient places along the length of your boat – something to consider if you're planning a solar installation for a new-build boat.

💡 **Tim Davis – Onboard Solar**

My advice to anyone considering a solar installation is to ensure you have a 12V fridge. It's a game-changer. Despite the fact that many modern 230V fridges use relatively little power, the need to run a chunky inverter all day every day means they'll quickly run down your batteries. Swapping to a 12V fridge makes all the difference.

ENERGY IN – YOUR SOLAR INSTALLATION

There's no getting away from the fact that running your engine for hours on end while moored just to generate power is annoying, and this is the most common reason boaters consider solar. It's certainly true that solar will reduce the amount of engine running significantly, sometimes even negating the need entirely. But in order to achieve the best results you'll need to install the most suitable system. The type of solar system you'll need will depend on the type of boater you are, so let's look at a few different boating profiles.

Profile 1 – the marina dweller

With your boat hooked up to the mains all day every day, there's not much need to compromise your energy usage or the type of appliances you use. Washing machines, dishwashers, big-screen TVs, fridges and even freezers are all yours to enjoy. And why not!?

What type of solar system do you need?

If you never leave your marina's electrical supply there's little, if any, need for you to think about installing solar – as long as you never leave the marina and you're happy to pay for your electricity.

Profile 2 – the intermittent cruiser

You're moored in a marina for most of the time, venturing away from your landline power supply only occasionally. It might be for a weekend, or it might be for a few months. While you're out and about you'll probably move every few days, because visiting a new location is the whole point of a leisure cruise. As such, you'll be running your engine regularly, and this will charge your batteries enough to provide most of your energy requirements.

What type of solar system do you need?

A relatively small solar system will help to top up your batteries enough to ensure you don't need to run your engine when you're not on the move. A 165W system will do the trick, assuming your boat is 12V-friendly and you can do without your 230V appliances for a while.

Profile 3 – the continuous cruiser

You'll move your boat regularly, but you might be moored for up to two weeks in one spot. Your cruising alone won't supply your batteries with enough power for a two-week mooring stay, so you'll need a bigger solar system if you don't want to be running your engine every day or so.

What type of solar system do you need?

A 330W or 495W system will get the job done for most of the year, depending on your load. If you have a 230V fridge,

The Watchman's power requirements are fulfilled by the solar panels during the summer months.

the 495W system is probably best. If your fridge is a 12V appliance, the 330W will probably do.

Profile 4 – the towpath moorer

You'll probably cruise occasionally, but most of the time you're moored in a place with no shoreline power. You might be a well kitted-out narrowboat, wide beam or barge with many of the same 230V appliances you'd find in a regular house, which presents a significant challenge if you don't want to run your engine while you're moored for long periods of time.

What type of solar system do you need?
A 660W or 990W system is the way to go.

The 990W system will give you the kind of power you would get from a plugged-in charger system. It's a big system and you'll need plenty of suitable roof space to accommodate it.

THE POWER HOUR

Sometimes there's no getting away from 230V appliances. Washing machines, vacuum cleaners, power tools and even hairdryers are devices that some of us would rather not have to live without. These high-drain appliances will all need you to run your inverter, so why not arrange to use them all at the same time while you're running your engine? Many solar-powered boaters go in for what has become known as the 'power hour' where they use the vacuum, washing machine or angle grinder while running their engine, thereby replacing the power they're using through their inverter. And, while you're at it, why not shower while the engine is running too? It's another good way to limit the amount of engine time, leaving you to enjoy the peace and quiet for longer, later.

💡 **Tilt**

Mounting your solar panels on a bracket that allows them to tilt will make an enormous difference. The extra power you generate by tilting them to face the sun is surprisingly significant. Plus angled brackets keep the panels away from the hot roof, thereby keeping them cooler and working more efficiently for longer.

Solar panels FAQ

Tim Davis from Onboard Solar answers some frequently asked questions

Q Our 230V sockets also have USB sockets alongside them, so I don't need my 3-pin plug to charge my phone. That's good, right?

A No, I'm afraid not. These sockets are a bit of an optical illusion on boats as you'll still need a 230V supply from your inverter to power them. They don't have a dedicated 12V supply.

Q Most 12V TVs are tiny, so I'll need a 230V wide-screen monster. Is it still worth getting solar installed?

A First of all, it's worth noting that 12V TVs have come a long way in the last few years. You can get some quite impressive 12V televisions nowadays, so there's probably one big enough to suit you. But even if you want to run a 230V set, it's certainly still worth getting solar. Most TVs are low-powered these days, and you'll probably not be watching all day. The problem with 230V appliances and inverters is mainly caused by using them all day and all night, such as when you run a 230V fridge. Watching TV for a few hours a night won't be a major issue, even if you binge-watch *Game of Thrones*.

Q Why don't we simply install loads of solar panels? Then we can use whatever electricity we like.

A Good idea! The more solar panels you install, the quicker they'll charge up your batteries. And you can never have too much solar because the systems controller will back off when your batteries are full. On the subject of batteries, if you're generating lots of energy with your panels, you'll need a means to store that power, so it makes sense to have enough batteries to do that. The only consideration is cost and the space available for panels and batteries, but if those constraints aren't a problem then go for it. It's always a good idea to over-spec.

Q I have only two leisure batteries aboard. Is that enough?

A Probably not, but it does depend on how many appliances you're using. If your energy usage is particularly low then a small bank of batteries will be fine. But as soon as you start adding fridges, freezers, televisions and the like, you'll need more batteries. Remember, solar simply acts to charge your batteries, and two leisure batteries can store only so much power. Three or four leisure batteries is a more workable number for most circumstances. Solar will charge the batteries and give you enough power during the day, and that energy is available to be used overnight.

Monitoring your solar doesn't need to be complicated.

Q I'd like to install solar panels, but I'm worried the system will be complicated to manage with all those meter readings and switches. Is there a system that is easy to work with?

A Absolutely. A good solar installation will work entirely automatically and require no intervention or management from the user. Of course, it's interesting to understand some of the read-outs on your meter, but it's not necessary by any means.

Q Are solar systems useless during the winter?

A No, not useless, but the output is greatly reduced. This is especially true during the shortest, darkest and most misty days of December and January when the sun is low in the sky. You'll be lucky to get enough power to run a 12V fridge on those days. But they're rare, and most decent solar installations will provide enough to power a well-configured 12V boat for most of the year. You'll probably need somewhere between 450W and 700W to get by on the worst winter days and you'll be producing a miserable 1–2 amps. You'll need to be frugal with your power usage too, of course.

On the other hand, on those bright and clear crisp winter days your solar panels will be producing almost as much power as they do during the summer, so it's not all bad news. The bigger your system, the more likely you are to get by during the winter. You'll always be producing something, and something is worth having. With a well-configured 12V-friendly boat and a decent solar installation like those listed above you'll get by on all but the worst winter's day.

Some days, our solar doesn't cut it.

Flexible solar panels look neat but have their drawbacks.

Q I'm worried my solar panels will be stolen. Is that something that happens often?

A No, not at all. I've fitted around 2,000 boats with solar installations all over the network and only ever heard of three incidences of theft. All of these happened when boats had been left unattended in vulnerable places for a few weeks. Opportunist theft can be discouraged by securing the panel structures to the angled brackets they're mounted on. These brackets are stuck to the boat with adhesive that's extremely difficult to remove, so all but the most determined and well tooled-up crooks will have trouble getting them off.

Q Are walk-on adhesive gel-covered solar panels an option?

A Yes, they're an option, but they have their drawbacks. They're more expensive than framed panels and less effective too. They're also easily damaged, are slippery to walk on and often need replacing when subjected to the extreme summertime temperatures on the roof of a boat. On the plus side, they look great and keep the roof of your boat looking tidy.

WIND POWER

Wind turbines can also be installed on a boat. Some liveaboards are deterred by the constant background hum these turbines produce, but most who actually own one say they soon became accustomed to it.

Liveaboards often use solar and wind power together.

HEATING

The most common question to be asked by non-boaters is 'Is it cold in the winter?' In fact, quite the opposite is true. There's so much to consider when choosing an on-board heating system that it can be difficult to know where to start. Whether you're fitting out a new boat or renovating an old one, you'll need to consider the pros and cons of each option if you're going to make an informed choice.

GAS

Propane gas is used for cooking by the majority of liveaboards and many use gas to produce hot water too. The size of the bottle you buy will be dictated by the size of your gas locker, but most boats have lockers to accommodate 13kg bottles. Some boats do have smaller lockers, but for liveaboard purposes the smaller bottles are inconveniently small and unnecessarily expensive by unit price.

SOLID-FUEL STOVES

PROS
- Eminently reliable.
- Attractive.
- Easy to use.

CONS
- Can take 30–60 minutes to heat a cold boat.
- Creates ash, which will invariably coat the surfaces inside a boat.
- Coal is heavy to handle and sometimes difficult to store.
- Statistically the most likely to be the cause of dangerous carbon monoxide-related incidents on boats.

Be sure to a keep a spare gas bottle.

💡 **Common brands**
- Morso
- Bubble
- Portway
- Hungry Penguin
- Clearview

Ah, the old faithful solid-fuel stoves. Most boats have them, and for good reason. They're eminently reliable and easy to service, and they look great too. The stove might seem like a back-to-basics heating option, but modern stoves do feature some progressive technologies. Improved insulation reduces fire risks, insulated flues improve efficiency and safety, and some even feature cooking compartments.

When used in a bricks-and mortar home, the heat a stove can kick out is enough to warm entire rooms, or even a whole house. Imagine, then, these same appliances being used in a narrowboat. It's no wonder you often see boats with all the doors and windows open during the bleakest of winter weather. There's a knack to managing your stove, and no two stoves are alike. It will take a few months of practice for you to get the hang of lighting yours, maintaining an even temperature and, most crucially, keeping the fire going overnight. Practice makes perfect, but it would be more realistic to accept the relationship with your stove as a truce rather than aspiring to master it.

But keeping the boat warm is simple compared with keeping the boat cool. During wintertime it's easy to take your eye off the ball and allow the stove to get so hot that the cabin is unbearable or the stove becomes a dangerous fire hazard.

David Hull is a respected boat engineer and surveyor who has maintained and restored almost every type of heater in his 26 years in the boating business.

'Stove efficiency is all about flue temperature,' says David. 'When new regulations insisted on insulated flues it had nothing to do with preventing people burning their hands on the flue. It was all to do with temperature controllability. A hotter flue means more draw, which in turn makes the stove more controllable.'

Many boaters use a stove with a back boiler fitted to supply heated water to radiators elsewhere on the boat. Most back boiler systems use a pump to circulate the water around the system but it's possible to run a system without a pump, using convection instead.

Which coal?

Most boaters with solid-fuel stoves use coal-type fuels of some variety. Once again, storage can be a problem, particularly for continuous cruisers. Even in some marinas a limit is applied to the amount of coal you can pile up next to your boat, for reasons of safety and aesthetics. Some even insist that nothing is stored on pontoons or jetties.

Kindling is often easy to acquire cheaply or for free but be considerate when collecting deadwood from the canalside as this has ecological consequences (see Chapter 6).

💡 Condensation

Warm air that manages to find cold steel creates condensation, and all but the most perfectly insulated boats will endure occasional drips.

Asking a boater which coal they prefer is a bit like asking which beer they like best, because at the end of the day, it rather comes down to personal preference. The decision essentially boils down to balancing the amount of ash that is produced with the burning temperature and price per kilo.

💡 Cold feet

The bottom of your boat is under water and, as a result, it can be terribly cold, even when the rest of the boat is warm. A good pair of slippers really help.

BEEN THERE, DONE THAT
BACK BOILERS AND RADIATORS

TONY AND VICKIE
Nb *The Watchman*

We recently fitted a stove with a back boiler on our boat, thereby providing the opportunity to use the stove to heat radiators. It's an ingenious system which relies on the rising hot water pushing its way through the copper pipes towards a series of three radiators, which run along the length of the boat. As the water heats it's pushed up to the highest length of pipework and through the radiators, and as it cools it returns through the lower pipes back to the stove's boiler to be reheated and sent on its way again.

There's some mathematics involved in ensuring the size of the radiators can accommodate the heat provided by the stove's boiler, so be sure to get the advice or help of someone who knows what they're doing. Where necessary, it's possible to install a pump to move the water, instead of relying on the system's hot and cold gravity feed. To my mind, this is free central heating, which could negate the need for diesel-powered heaters.

Tony's *towpath tales*

In my opinion, a stove-top fan should be standard equipment on every boat with a stove. These wonderful contraptions sit atop your stove and the heat makes the blades of the fan turn, thus wafting warm air to the nether regions of your boat. Be careful not to drop your fan as they're prone to develop an annoying rattle as the fans rotate – which is why we tend to stash the thing safely when setting off on a cruise.

Stove maintenance

Maintaining solid-fuel stoves is something most boaters can do as there's not much that can go wrong, but when things do go wrong it can sometimes be expensive to rectify. Areas of likely damage include:

- **Broken glass** – Cheaply and easily replaced as long as the screws holding the glass retainer in place don't shear off as you attempt to remove them.

- **Riddler** – A seized or warped riddler is usually the consequence of using unsuitable fuel and running the stove at too high a temperature. Most of the coals available for boaters are suitable and can be easily managed, but the products available from petrol stations usually burns too hot and causes damage. The convenience of a bag of petrol station coal to tide you over seems worth the extra expense until you realise the damage it causes to your stove. A new riddler will solve the problem if the grate is not warped too, otherwise replacing both is necessary.

- **Firebricks** – These sometimes break, particularly in fires that have been running too hot or when bashed about during spring cleaning maintenance. They're not expensive, but make sure you get the right product for your model of stove. There are countless different types of stove so it's usually best to ring ahead to ensure the store has the ones you need in stock before setting off.

- **Flue collar** – Water drips, trickles and stains are all the result of a leaky flue. Removing and resealing the collar attachment between the roof and the flue is the only solution. Look out for rust holes too, remembering to check around the back of your flue pipe. Carbon-monoxide poisoning is a real risk.

- **Stove door rope seal** – These are cheap and easy to replace. Take a sample of the rope from your stove to ensure you buy the correct thickness.

- **Flue/stove union** – The seal between the stove and the flue can perish quite rapidly as the cement seal crumbles away. Be sure to check and reseal the union regularly. Along with cement, some boaters use stove door rope and copious amounts of glue to make a seal around the flue.

COMPACT DIESEL HEATERS

PROS
- Near instantaneous heat and water.
- Efficient and controllable temperature regulation.
- Reliable when fitted correctly.

CONS
- Temperamental if installed badly.
- Noisy when running, although insulation can dull the noise inside the boat.
- Hot exhaust fumes can create a fire hazard. Some marinas insist on protecting their pontoons with fire-retardant baffles.

💡 **Common brands**
- Eberspacher
- Webasto

These heaters have become almost ubiquitous on new-build boats over the last ten years and it's easy to see why. They're most often used to heat radiators, thereby providing warmth throughout the vessel – unlike a typical solid-fuel stove, which can often struggle to heat the nether regions of some longer boats. In addition, some Eberspacher and Webasto diesel heaters can also provide instantaneous hot water, making them eminently useful for residential boats.

The units work by dripping fuel under low pressure, which is then vapourised and ignited to create a flame. The flame then burns continuously to heat water that can feed radiators and supply hot water for taps.

'These units had a bad reputation a few years ago,' David explains. 'Boaters would complain of frequent breakdowns and expensive repairs, which would last only a few weeks before breaking down again. However, it wasn't the unit that was at fault.'

David went on to explain that the breakdowns were entirely due to poor installation – a finding uncovered through extensive research conducted by the Eberspacher company. 'The boating market is but a tiny fraction of Eberspacher's business,' said David. 'But they were troubled by the large number of complaints they were receiving, so they decided to research the issue. They found the problems were invariably caused by poor installation, so the company embarked upon a training and education campaign to ensure the equipment was installed correctly.' Within a few years the new boats with correctly fitted Eberspachers were operating admirably and diesel heaters became the go-to option for many boat builders.

The faulty installation issues included using the wrong size of pipework or purchasing the wrong spec and model for the boat. Some were even naively purchasing automotive units instead of marinised ones, but these have the wrong ECU 'brain' programmed with the wrong temperatures and power thresholds. 'Automotive units simply won't work reliably on boats,' says David.

Boaters looking for a cheaper option should be cautious of some of the Chinese-manufactured units you can buy online, though. While some good ones are supplied and fitted by distributors in the UK, many of them will ultimately suffer from the poor installation issues we discussed earlier.

DIESEL STOVES

💡 Common brands

- Refleks
- Bubble
- Kabola
- Dickinson

Refleks diesel stove.

PROS
- No need to buy or haul bags of coal.
- Greatly reduced stove cleaning.
- No more ash covering surfaces inside the boat.

CONS
- Fuel costs can be higher than coal costs by some reports, although this may vary.
- No more dancing flames to watch.
- A separate fuel tank may need to be installed.

These should more accurately be called oil stoves because they can be fuelled using heating oil too. They work by dripping fuel into a bowl at a constant rate, with the drip rate being controllable to enable temperature adjustments. A faster drip rate equals more fuel being burned, which produces more heat, and vice versa.

'Aboard a boat you'll probably only need to keep the drip rate on its minimum setting, and many boaters simply leave the stove running 24/7,' says David. 'Be sure to switch it off and clean it as directed by the manufacturer's instructions, though, usually every six weeks.'

Again, all of the commonly-sold brands are reliable and safe with the only real discerning feature being how they look. The Kabola and Bubble stoves look much like a typical solid-fuel stove, usually black with a front-opening door, while the Refleks are tall, cylindrical metal units, available in stainless steel, copper or brass. 'If you want to be fussy you could say the Refleks is more fussy to light and clean because it's accessed from above, but it's not difficult really and makes hardly any difference,' says David.

Some people complain about a diesel smell being emitted when using this type of heater, but if you're getting a smell then you're using it wrong. Get a qualified engineer to check the system and demonstrate how to use it effectively and I guarantee the smell will go away.

There's also the issue of strong winds to consider, although this isn't exclusive to diesel stoves – solid-fuel stoves will experience the same problem. During high winds a strong gust can blow down the flue and extinguish the flame, thereby emitting a puff of smoke. The stove will immediately re-ignite and there's no safety risk or damage to worry about. One way to prevent this is to install an insulated flue and a longer chimney as this will create higher flue temperatures and a stronger draft that's resilient to gusts of wind.

OTHER HEATERS
Ranges
Boaters looking for a country-cottage aesthetic might opt for a traditional range. The Rayburn and Aga units can be fuelled by solid fuel or diesel, with the diesel-fuelled option working in much the same way as the diesel stoves listed above. While these units certainly look good, it's important to consider the pros and cons.

Diesel air-heaters
You can also use diesel heaters to heat air, rather than using them to heat water in radiators as described above. Intake air is passed over a heated core before being expelled as warm air into the room. The expelled air can also be ducted to deliver heat to different parts of the boat. However, this system only works well on relatively small boats because the air will often cool en route through a long run of ducting – and nobody wants cold air blown at them. It's worth knowing that these systems can also be used to heat water supplied to taps.

Gas air-heater
Similar to the diesel-powered air heaters listed above, these units operate identically, only this time using gas as a fuel source. They're also best suited to smaller boats, and they're similarly rare to find on the waterways. Indeed, these units are more often installed in camper vans where the blown air is more likely to service the smaller space. Some manufacturers supply units that can heat a small amount of hot water, likely sufficient for washing up but not enough for a decent shower.

Diesel hob and air heater

It's unusual to see a diesel-fuelled galley appliance aboard a boat, but there is a two-in-one diesel-fuelled hob that also has a hot-air blower installed. These are, again, best suited to small boats or motorhomes.

Central-heating boilers

There are many boats with heaters such as this that use diesel to heat water to supply radiators. Unlike the Eberspacher and Webasto heaters which can be 'brightened' or 'dimmed' to produce more or less heat, these use a thermostat, programmed with preferred high and low temperatures, to turn the system off and on.

'Some of the older Kabola boilers were fussy to light and temperamental to use,' David reminisces. 'If you didn't get the hang of lighting them properly the fuel wouldn't vapourise and they would run with a yellow flame, producing lots of sooty carbon deposits.

The new Kabolas are much easier to operate, being ignited by an electric switch and a pressure jet of fuel, making them far more reliable.' The Hurricane brand also features wi-fi controls, making it user friendly and efficient to operate.

Gas central-heating boiler

This type of boiler was common aboard boats a few decades ago, and while the older models had their issues, the newer versions are pretty good all considered. 'The Ellis brand isn't around anymore as far as I am aware, but I'll still occasionally see an old Alde 2921 or a 2828,' says David. 'When I see them I do my best to recommend a new heating system.' These old boilers were designed for park homes and caravans and they drank gas. 'I remember it would not be unusual to get through four 13kg bottles of gas during a two-week hire period.'

Today, the new Alde units are no bigger than a small suitcase. They're designed to fit into small spaces, they're quiet, and they're vastly more efficient. One of the other advantages is that they're virtually service free. 'They were designed for off-grid and inaccessible applications, such as in Arctic research centres, so they needed to have a long and trouble-free service life,' says David.

HOT WATER

Hot-water needs for leisure boaters are easily provided by using a calorifier set-up, as this system uses the engine to heat a tank of water. This is efficient while cruising as hot water is created for free – essentially a bonus side effect of your cruise. Even when moored it's not too inconvenient to occasionally run your engine to get enough water

BEEN THERE, DONE THAT
DOUBLE GLAZING

CHARLIE AND WENDY
Nb *Philip George*

I can't recommend double glazing windows highly enough. It's made a massive difference to the warmth inside our boat, eliminating those cold draughts you sometimes get near single-glazed windows, and there's zero condensation. We once had ice on the outside of the window during a particularly cold winter a few years ago. The temperature inside the boat was toasty warm, but the ice on the outside stayed frozen – a good demonstration of how effective these double-glazed windows are. Thankfully you can get purpose-built double-glazed units for boats which are far more pleasing to look at than the clunky household double-glazed frames you see on some boats. Our installation cost £3,500 for six large windows and four large portholes.

BEEN THERE, DONE THAT
WHAT TIPS DO YOU HAVE FOR NEW BOATERS?

JOHN
Nb *Sound of Silence*
Water tanks can get a little yucky if they're left unused for any length of time. Water tank purifying tablets are available, but they leave a slight after-taste. This can be almost eliminated by installing an in-line filter to your cold water line, and it will filter out any small particles that might be in there too.

TONY AND VICKIE
Nb *The Watchman*
Don't forget to boil your kettle on the top of your stove during winter – it's free hot water and helps to preserve gas supplies.

STEVE AND EILEEN
Nb *Rahab*
Reduce the amount of gas you buy by switching off the pilot light when you aren't using the boiler. The saving is quite remarkable and cuts down the number of times you need to change the bottle significantly.

CHARLIE AND WENDY
Nb *Philip George*
Clean your toilet plumbing at least every year. A build-up of limescale will cause blockages which could easily be avoided through regular maintenance.

for showers and to boil a kettle for washing dishes and the like. However, this can become a chore for some liveaboards, others are happy with this type of set-up.

One of the most convenient arrangements is to have a gas-fuelled boiler to provide an almost instant supply of constantly hot water. This type of boiler has many benefits for the liveaboard compared with a calorifier set-up, which can only supply one tank of hot water before needing another hour or two of engine running to replenish it. The costs are difficult to compare as applications differ. For those who cruise regularly enough the calorifier system can be said to provide free hot water, but in reality few boaters cruise every day, or even every week. While using a gas-powered boiler does mean using more gas, this costs far less than the equivalent cost of running the engine for two hours while moored, simply to get hot water.

Some boats use a back boiler attached to their stove to generate free hot water. While these work well during the wintertime when the stove is lit, it's not practical to light the fire during the summer months, so an alternative option, such as running the engine to heat a calorifier, must be installed alongside. Having two hot-water systems might seem like overkill to some, but it's a sensible belt and braces precaution, while others simply can't resist the lure of occasional free hot water.

INTERNET ACCESS

The internet is essential to my very existence and without it I simply wouldn't be able to do my job. Online research, countless emails, sharing files and online video meetings are work-a-day occurrences for me, and living and working aboard a boat adds a whole bunch of extra challenges. I must admit to being a bit of a Luddite when it comes to technology, but my wife, Vickie, revels in such challenges. After many years of trial and error, I think she has our internet needs sussed – at least to the point where an internet idiot like me can use the system reliably. So if you're looking for simple solutions for your internet needs and woes, this section should shed some light on your options.

OPTION 1 – USE A SMARTPHONE

Many boaters only need the internet for occasional low-data access while they're aboard – emailing, checking websites and the occasional video call perhaps.

After all, the non-liveaboard leisure-cruising types probably appreciate a break from the internet.

For some low-tech liveaboards with this type of low-use profile, a smartphone's internet access will sometimes suffice. As long as your phone contract has enough data allowance and there's a sufficiently strong phone signal wherever you are, you'll do just fine.

The strength of the signal in any given area will depend on which phone provider you're with. Word on the towpath says EE provides the most reliable service, and in my own experience, EE seems to work well in most areas of the network. You can also find out in advance if a planned mooring spot has a good internet data signal. We downloaded a mobile app called Open Signal, which you can use to search any location to ascertain the signal strength of any particular network. Some apps and websites will show mobile mast locations too. (Try www.OpenCellid.org)

💡 Network options

Vickie and I have consciously chosen different phone service providers in the hope that if my EE-network signal isn't strong in any given area, then her Three-network phone will work instead.

OPTION 2 – SMARTPHONE TETHERING AND HOTSPOTS

Relying solely on a smartphone isn't an option for me. I need to use a laptop so I can type quickly using a full-size keyboard, but that doesn't mean you need a separate contract, because the cheapest and easiest way to get internet access on your laptop or tablet is to 'tether' the device to your smartphone's internet data allowance.

You can do this by opening the settings on your phone (look for a gear or cog icon), and then select 'personal hotspot' or 'mobile hotspot', depending on whether you're Apple or Android. Once there you can activate a 'hotspot' which allows your phone's internet signal to be accessed by nearby devices. You should then be able to find your phone's internet signal on your laptop or tablet, and you'll be granted access using the password generated by your phone. It sounds complicated when written here, but your phone and laptop will walk you through the reasonably intuitive process. And when you've linked the devices once they will recognise each other without a password thereafter.

There are a few potential minor downsides to accessing the internet this way, the first potentially being the amount of data you have purchased as part of your phone contract. If you want to watch films or transfer large files then you'll need a beefy mobile phone contract with plenty of data allowance.

Secondly, being inside a steel tube might block the signal to your phone,

and while propping your phone in a window will often help, it can be a frustrating rigmarole to find the sweet spot. Finally, and I honestly don't know why, accessing the internet on my laptop via tethering has never been quite as fast or reliable as using a separate dongle or a modem. There's more on these devices below.

💡 Marina wi-fi

Some marinas have wi-fi services available for boaters to use, and sometimes these marina-based wi-fi services even work! Most times there will be a charge for using the service and it's usually pretty good value. So, if the marina's service works and you have a good signal in whichever spot you're moored, this can be a great way to get online while afloat.

OPTION 3 – GET A MOBILE BROADBAND DONGLE

You might have seen these small devices dangling by a cable in the window of some boats, which is why I would hilariously refer to ours as the dangle-dongle. A dongle works in much the same way as tethering to your mobile phone except, and don't ask me why, they seem to supply a much stronger, more reliable signal. Having a dongle also alleviates the need to go into your phone's settings every time you want to connect your laptop to the internet.

A wi-fi 'dangle-dongle'.

You'll need to buy a dedicated mobile-broadband contract which will come with a sim card and a dongle device. These start at around £10 pcm for 5GB, which is enough for occasional web browsing and emailing. Or you can get more data if you're happy to pay more – a 150 GB contract will cost more like £25 pcm, which is enough data for moderately heavy internet use, such as watching films online, and an unlimited-data deal is currently around £50 pcm.

It's useful and cost-effective to know that, once your contract is over, you can then shop around for a cheaper sim-only

mobile phone contract with sufficient data for your needs. Simply replace the dongle's old contract SIM card with your new one. Remember it's worth checking for cheaper deals as often as your contract allows and negotiating one service provider's prices against another's is a good ploy. Make sure your chosen supplier provides good coverage, though.

OPTION 4 – USE A ROUTER

If you're permanently moored in a marina, or if you only use the internet while you're there, then it makes sense to get a conventional router like the one you'd use at home. The only downside to these is that they need 230V power when in use, so if you're cruising or off grid you'd need a power-hungry inverter switched on the whole time you're online. However, if you're moored up with a landline power supply then this won't be a worry because you won't need an inverter.

Interestingly, though, these 230V routers can often be converted to run on a 12V system, alleviating the need for landlines and inverters, because most routers only need a 5–12V supply. Indeed, this is what we did aboard our boat, although I should more accurately say, 'this is what Vickie did.' I asked Vickie to explain the conversion process for the benefit of this section but I failed to understand half of what she said, which probably means it's a job for someone with more knowledge and expertise than me. What I do know is that you'll need a 'buck converter', which will adjust the voltage and maintain it at a constant level regardless of your leisure batteries' level of charge.

💡 12V win

Another consideration that makes mobile-broadband dongles a good option for boaters is that they can be run from a 12V cigarette-lighter-type connection. This alleviates the need for cruising boaters to run an inverter the whole time while you're online as you might need to do if you were to use a regular, home-style router.

A wi-fi router.

The benefit of these heavyweight routers is that they seem to supply a far stronger signal, so you're much more likely to get a good connection than you otherwise might using a dongle or mobile hotspot. You'll pay the same contract fees commensurate with your data usage as you would with a dongle, so you can pick a package that suits you best.

OPTION 5 – SPLASH OUT ON STARLINK

I met a boater at the Braunston Historic Boat Rally last summer who extolled the virtues of Elon Musk's Starlink internet service. Having looked into it in detail, it does seem to be the gold-standard internet connection option, with super-fast download and upload speeds and almost zero connectivity issues. Starlink works well because, instead of using land-based mobile masts it relies on satellite links – thereby eliminating the line-of-sight issues between masts and routers. Being directly overhead, there is rarely anything between you and a satellite to block the signal, so the connection is imminently fast and reliable.

As for the downside, I'll give you one guess. A residential connection with unlimited data costs £75pcm last time I looked, and a roaming connection that can be used in various locations (such as you might need aboard a cruising boat) costs £85 to £450 plus to purchase the necessary hardware. Compared with the £10 to £30 costs of a typical wi-fi mobile broadband contract, that's a huge leap in cost, so you'd need a really good reason to splash out on Starlink.

That said, Vickie and I have seriously contemplated biting the bullet and going for it – compelled by the far too numerous episodes of me swearing at my laptop as the internet drops again out during an important video call. Apparently, £85 a month is a bargain if it puts an end to my tantrums. In calmer moments we concluded that, while it would be nice to have a bomb-proof internet service, the occasional value of such a luxury would not justify the cost. Instead, I have promised to curb the swearing.

OPTION 6 – CALL THE PROFESSIONALS

Thankfully there are a handful of companies out there in canal land that will provide signal-boosting equipment or install internet service aboard your boat, thereby taking away much of the headache. If like me you find the internet and technology rather frustrating or you don't have time to invest in learning about it then this could be your best solution. A quick Google will turn up several options, and some companies also advertise in canal magazines such as *Waterways World*.

OPTION 7 – UNPLUG

I'm of the opinion that computers, the internet and wi-fi signals are far too unreliable, complex and frustrating for most people to use, so it's only a matter of time before people get annoyed and forego using them altogether. Personally, I don't think this internet thing is going to catch on, so perhaps we should all simply wait until the fad dies out.

OTHER WAYS TO BOOST YOUR SIGNAL

It used to be common to see internet dongles encased in plastic bottles to guard against the weather and then taped to a pole standing high above the boat in a bid to improve the line of sight to the mobile mast. Today there are more sophisticated ways to boost your internet signal depending on the type of dongle or router you have.

External antennae

Most dongles and routers have the option to add an antenna that can be positioned outside the boat – usually stuck to the roof with a magnet. The one we plumped for was an 'omnidirectional' antenna, which means it can pick up a signal coming from any direction – as opposed to 'directional' or 'yagi' antennae, which will often receive a stronger signal as long as they have a clear line of sight to a mobile mast. We decided that the directional antenna wasn't a good option for us as we would need to swivel it to point at a particular mast every time we moved our boat. We simply don't have time for that.

Hardwired router connections

It's also possible to hardwire a laptop to the router using an ethernet cable connection, thus eliminating the vagaries of a wi-fi signal. This is ideal for when I need a good connection in my boat-office to attend a video meeting, but less useful when I'm lounging on the sofa watching *Game of Thrones*.

Line of sight

You'll get a much better wi-fi signal if you can set up your router or dongle in a location where there's a clear line of sight between it and the laptop, so try to avoid having a bulkhead between you and the signal. Interestingly, bodies are apparently good at blocking wi-fi signals too.

Avoid cuttings

Moorings with steep embankments between your boat and a mobile mast are to be avoided if you want a good signal, assuming of course that you're reliant on masts and not the Starlink service.

9 STAYIN' ALIVE

Boating is no more hazardous than living in a house. Each has its inherent risks. But with a little care and common sense, these can be reduced to a minimum.

As with every part of our lives, knowing the risks and taking sensible precautions are the keys to staying safe. This chapter looks at the dangers and their consequences specific to the liveaboard boating lifestyle, while aiming to equip the reader with the necessary information to negate them.

While several people die or are seriously injured every year while boating it's important to put this in perspective, because boating would appear a long way down the list of dangerous leisure activities. Nevertheless, there are still plenty of ways you could come a cropper if you don't take proper precautions.

Here's a list of things to consider to ensure you stay safe afloat.

CARBON MONOXIDE POISONING

This so-called 'silent killer' was once the most common cause of death aboard boats on the inland waterways, but awareness campaigns by the Boat Safety Scheme, along with their mandatory carbon monoxide alarm requirements, have reduced the numbers of deaths significantly.

But installing a detector alarm is not the only precaution, though. A proactive approach to prevention is essential too: annual checking of gas appliances and a regular inspection of your stove and flue should be noted in your diary and observed religiously.

WHAT IS CARBON MONOXIDE?

Carbon monoxide is created through the incomplete combustion of any carbon-containing fuel and is a by-product of any appliance that burns these fuels. Solid-fuel stoves, gas boilers, diesel heaters, cooking appliances and engine exhausts are all potential sources of carbon monoxide gas in varying amounts, and if these appliances aren't properly used and maintained, the risk of poisoning is significant.

SOLID-FUEL STOVES

Boat surveyor David Hull is a former Boat Safety Scheme examiner and his experience and advice has likely saved the lives of countless boaters during his 26 years of service. 'I've often met people who leave the door of their stove open when it's alight, usually to let more heat out, but sometimes just because they like to look at the flames,' says David. 'What this does is create an exit with a larger surface area than the draw from the chimney flue, causing smoke and poisonous carbon monoxide to enter the boat instead. Please never do this!'

Carbon monoxide can also leak into the boat through much smaller holes too. Cracks in the stove's main unit, holes rusted in the flue and leaking seals and joints can create pathways through which carbon monoxide can enter the boat. In these circumstances your boat acts like a bucket, gradually filling with carbon monoxide until it concentrates to a lethal level.

Using a hob for heat is extremely dangerous.

💡 Stay cool

Burning unsuitable fuels or letting your stove get too hot can cause cracks and faults in the stove's construction.

GENERATORS

Generators are another high-risk appliance when it comes to carbon monoxide poisoning. 'Running a portable generator aboard a boat is a massive risk. It shouldn't need to be said, but it's something I see happening far too regularly. One of the big mistakes is to run the generator on the deck with the exhaust being aimed overboard or through a flap in the canvas cover. It only takes the wind to change direction and you'll have carbon monoxide being pushed back onto the boat.'

APPLIANCES

Gas-powered hobs, grills and ovens are less often the cause of carbon monoxide poisoning, but issues do still occur. 'It's an especially bad idea to run these appliances as a way to heat the boat but it's something we see happening surprisingly often. It's usually the owners of smaller boats, such as GRP cruisers, who tend to do this, and it can be deadly,' says David. 'And while we're on the subject, be sure to get your gas and diesel appliances checked regularly by a qualified specialist.'

VENTILATION

And finally never, under any circumstances, block the ventilation aboard your boat, as this prevents poisonous gases from escaping. It can also stop your appliances from burning correctly by depriving them of sufficient oxygen. This makes them burn with a yellow flame and produces more carbon deposits – all of which increase the likelihood of carbon monoxide poisoning.

Boat safety advice

Gary Smales is a boat safety examiner at boatsafeteyexaminer.com.

He is based in Colne, Lancashire.

The greatest proportion of safety on a boat comes down to simply using common sense. Unfortunately we see far too many incidences where this has not been applied.

One of the most common safety issues we see is blocked ventilation. Vents in doors get blocked to prevent draughts, despite the fact that ventilation is there to provide sufficient air flow for the interior of a vessel and help protect against carbon monoxide poisoning. I've seen vents blocked with obvious covers, but I've also seen vents that have clingfilm inside them. An examiner wouldn't notice these were blocked without purposely probing with a blade or screwdriver, so that's what we have to do. I've even seen newly-built boats with inadequate ventilation. It's usually where the large, decorative ventilation cover hides an inadequately small hole drilled in the wood.

Another problem we see regularly on liveaboard boats is poorly maintained wood-burning stoves with flues that are almost blocked by a build-up of soot. I think it's because some people treat a boat in the same way they treat a house, where everything is available at the flick of a switch. Boats require a little more maintenance. It can become dangerous if you don't keep on top of it and there have been several fatalities on boats recently for exactly this reason.

A lot of people don't realise the risks of carbon monoxide poisoning. Carbon monoxide is heavier than air and boats are generally watertight, which means carbon monoxide can build up in great concentrations. Carbon monoxide is produced anywhere where there's combustion – so in a solid-fuel stove, a cooker, a heater or a generator.

Solid-fuel stoves, which many boats have aboard, create the highest risks inside a vessel – but generators come a close second. These are a particular problem because they're commonly seen on boats' decks, which is extremely dangerous. Even when generators are used on the bank they can be a hazard if the wind is blowing in the wrong direction.

Never block air vents.

CARBON MONOXIDE SAFETY CHECKLIST

- Install at least one carbon monoxide alarm aboard your boat, following the manufacturer's instructions.

- A carbon monoxide alarm in the engine room is also useful to warn against leaks in your engine's exhaust system or diesel heater.

- Make sure all carbon monoxide alarms are suitable for use aboard, displaying the correct BS service and safety accreditation. Look for an alarm showing it was manufactured to BS EN 50291. BS EN 50291-2 are best for marine use.

- The alarm aspect of the detector is important as it's vital to be made aware of the hazard in order to take necessary action to avoid disaster. The old-fashioned colour-changing dots are essentially useless.

- Burn suitable fuels that do not create excessive heat that can damage your stove.

- Keep all vents clear and don't block them for any reason.

- Have your appliances checked annually by a professional – don't wait for your Boat Safety Scheme examination.

- Solid-fuel stoves are particularly hazardous, so inspect the following parts regularly:

  - Check your stove and flue for holes caused by rust and damage.

  - Check the door seal and replace the rope if necessary.

  - Check the corners of your stove for holes caused by overheating expansion.

  - Check the union between the stove and the flue, and also at the roof.

  - Clean inside the chimney and flue at least annually, preferably more often.

  - Check the flue is not blocked by ash collecting on the baffle plate inside your stove.

  - Check that no on-board vents are blocked.

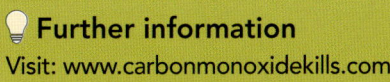
💡 **Further information**
Visit: www.carbonmonoxidekills.com

Tony's *towpath tales*

I woke up with a headache again, for the third day in a row. I didn't worry about it too much and put it down to the fact that I often fail to drink enough water. Besides, the headache had usually gone by the time I got to work, so I took an aspirin, drank some water and carried on with my day. My first job was to check my emails.

A few days before I had posted a question on a boating forum about my stove. It had been acting up, not getting hot enough despite a generous load of coal and wood. It was also belching out smoke each time I opened the door and my boat seemed continually full of smoke. One of the girls at work even thought something was on fire in the office before we realised that the smell of smoke and burning was coming from me.

At my desk with a cup of coffee I clicked on the boating forum page and found my question had a few replies. I paraphrase here, but basically the replies went something like this:

'Your flue is blocked and needs cleaning.'

'If you don't do it you will die of carbon monoxide poisoning.'

'You're going to die if you don't clean your chimney.
That's "die", you understand.
Dead.'

I got the message.

I took the morning off work and set about fixing the problem. A layer of soot, rust and ash had settled on top of the baffle plate and was blocking the flue so that air couldn't get in and smoke couldn't escape. Three hard and dirty hours later I had a clean chimney, ash an inch thick on every surface in my boat and coal ground deep into my hands. Then I spent another couple of hours doing the same job on my friend's boat. I was exhausted and black to my elbows, but at least we weren't going to die.

I really should have seen a doctor, and I'd recommend that you do the same if you ever find yourself in a similar situation.

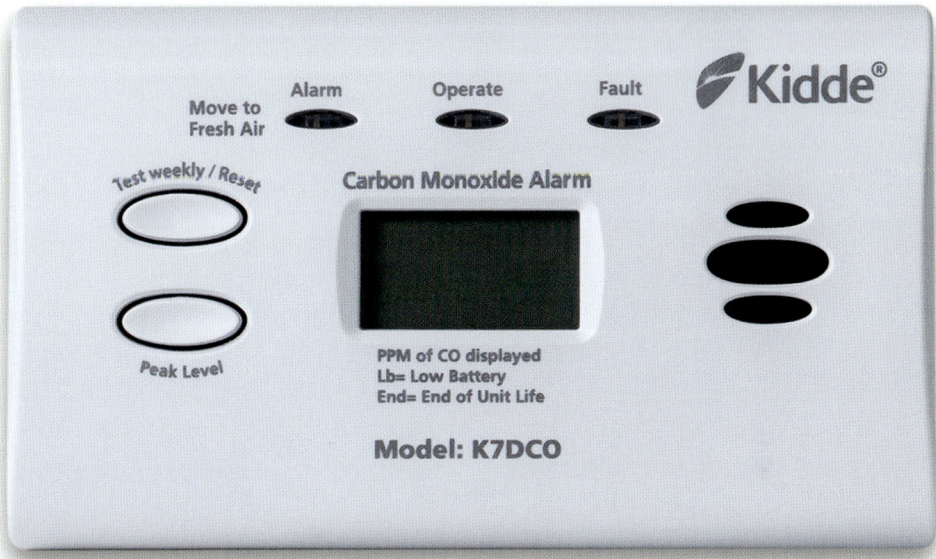

Thankfully, carbon monoxide alarms are a requirement of the Boat Safety Scheme. Be sure to check yours regularly.

BEEN THERE, (ALMOST) DONE THAT
HOT ASHES

HANNAH, ANT AND MABEL
Nb *The Corridor*

When we were just starting out aboard we were collecting our hot ash from the stove in a bucket that we kept inside the cabin until it was full. Most people will be shaking their heads, because most people know that this is a serious carbon monoxide poisoning risk. We simply didn't know, and we only found out when our carbon monoxide alarm kept going off and we put two and two together. It could have ended in disaster!

💡 **Deadly smoke**

Just two breaths inside a boat filled with toxic fumes and smoke could be enough to render you unconscious.

The remains of a GRP boat after a fire. Thankfully, the occupant escaped unharmed.

FIRES

Fires have killed 30 boaters in the last 20 years. Until recently, carbon monoxide poisoning was the most common cause of death aboard boats on the inland waterways. But following a campaign of education by the Boat Safety Scheme, along with the now mandatory requirement to install CO alarms, carbon monoxide poisoning has been relegated to second place on the list. That successful campaign means that boat fires are now the most common cause of death aboard, and the Boat Safety Scheme has this challenge in its sights.

Thankfully, boat fires are relatively rare and most are preventable if your boat is well maintained and compliant with the standards required by the Boat Safety Scheme, and there's plenty

more you can do in addition to keep you and your crew safe. Here are some of the most common causes of fires afloat, some information on how to prevent them, and what to do should the worst happen.

SOLID-FUEL STOVES

According to the Boat Safety Scheme website there have been at least 24 boaters hurt and several more have been killed when using solid-fuel stoves in recent years. In addition, there were dozens more incidents where nobody was hurt but where boats have been damaged or destroyed. The lessons learnt from these incidents can help you to prevent the same from happening aboard your boat, so let's take a look at what can go wrong.

Overfiring

This is a common cause of solid-fuel-stove-induced fires and it occurs when stoves are supplied with too much air or too much fuel. Leaving stove vents open too far for too long is a common mistake. This introduced too much oxygen, causing fuel to burn quickly and fiercely, subsequently heating the stove until it becomes hot enough to ignite nearby flammable materials.

The overfiring problem can also be caused when boaters make the mistake of leaving the main door of the stove open, either as a means to get the fire going quickly or because they simply want to watch the flames.

Overfiring can also occur if the stove is loaded with too much fuel, even if vents are open as normal and doors are kept closed. And it's always a bad idea to leave your boat unattended after banking the stove with lots of fuel, even for short periods.

Finally, it's worth remembering that the risk of overfiring is increased when using a new stove or a different fuel, as it inevitably requires practice and experience to predict how each will react. Be watchful and cautious until you know how your stove behaves.

💡 Flue and chimney fires

Overfiring can also cause flue gases to reach dangerous temperatures, which can ignite tar or soot that has accumulated in the chimney or flue.

Avoiding overfiring

- Always check that the stove's vent or air controls are set to prevent overfiring, especially before leaving the boat, going to bed or travelling through a tunnel.

- Don't leave the lower ash-pan door open, even for short periods. Many boaters do this and it's a dangerous habit to get into.

- Check your stove for damage that could allow air to enter the fire box and thereby cause overfiring.

- Be aware that high winds whipping across the chimney top can cause flue gases to be sucked out and the draw to be two or three times the normal strength.

- Bituminous coal (also known as house coal or Polish coal) is more difficult to control and should be avoided. Smokeless fuel is best.

- Sweep your flue and chimney regularly to prevent tar and soot from building up there.

- Be aware that overfiring can ignite flammable materials near well-installed stoves and the risk is multiplied if the stove has been installed poorly. Identify and fix poor-installation problems by asking the advice of a qualified surveyor when purchasing a new boat, or by heeding the advice of a Boat Safety Scheme examiner. It's also wise to choose fire-resistant furniture and fabrics, which can be identified by an appropriate label.

💡 If your stove overfires

- Close all of the stove's vents if you can get near it.

- If a fire cannot be tackled safely, or if there is a flue or chimney fire, evacuate everyone from the boat and call emergency services.

- Alert those in nearby boats and buildings and move nearby boats if it's safe to do so.

Pyrolysis

Hopefully the name of this hazard is unusual enough to stick in your mind because it's another relatively common cause of stove-related boat fires. Pyrolysis is a chemical reaction caused by heat that breaks down wood into a kind of charcoal, and this charcoal can catch fire surprisingly easily. It doesn't need a direct flame or even an extreme amount of heat to cause this material to ignite and, worryingly, the issue will likely be occurring out of sight, behind tiles or other materials that cover the wood around your stove.

You might have a pyrolysis problem if you can smell charring or hot materials, or if something just doesn't smell right. You might also notice discolouring around your stove or see wisps of smoke that you don't expect. If it's possible to check the materials around your stove for charring you should do so but you should seek expert advice if you're at all concerned. You could significantly improve safety by refitting the area around your stove.

And while we're on the subject, it should be common sense to keep furniture, soft furnishings, books, waste paper baskets, dog beds, logs, pictures, blinds, swags and paraffin lamps well away from the stove – but we're going to say it anyway.

IN THE GALLEY

Any naked flame presents a fire risk aboard a boat. It's so easy to forget to switch off hobs, especially if you're called away to do other things or get distracted by television, books or telephone calls while you're cooking a meal.

Case Study: BOAT-FIRE TRAGEDY IN STONE

In 2018 a woman and her dog died aboard their boat when it caught fire during the early hours of the morning near The Star public house in Stone, Staffordshire. Firefighters managed to rescue the woman from the boat and administered CPR but she was pronounced dead at the scene. The dog also died as a result of the fire. An investigation found that the main door of the boat's solid-fuel stove was left open and burning fuel had fallen onto a nearby carpet.

It's obviously important to keep flammables such as oven gloves and tea towels away from naked flames in the galley, but you might also want to think about blinds and curtains that could sway into the flame when the boat rocks. And if the gas bottle runs out or the flame dies for any other reason, be sure to turn the appliance off before re-igniting.

While we're talking about cooking, boaters should be extremely wary of portable cooking appliances such as camping stoves and the like. While the Boat Safety Scheme does not specifically ban gas canisters or camping stoves, using them aboard a boat is asking for trouble, and it's particularly unwise to change gas canisters inside the cabin or even under canvas covers. Use these appliances on the towpath if you must, but they have no place aboard a boat.

And finally don't use barbecues aboard or under canvas covers. Not only is this an obvious and significant fire hazard but there's also the catastrophic risk of carbon monoxide poisoning because charcoal gives off dangerous amounts of this deadly gas.

MINI FIRES

Although candles and gas lamps might enhance the snug atmosphere aboard your boat, many would say that the risk simply isn't worth the reward. Using these items in a house presents risk enough, but the confined spaces and unstable nature of boats make candles and gas lamps a far more serious hazard. There are some great LED-based alternatives, so maybe these are a safer compromise.

💡 Gas canister storage

Gas canisters for camping stoves and the like should be stored in the same way we store gas cylinders, ie outside the cabin in a self-draining and fire-resistant locker. This also goes for spent cylinders as these can contain sufficient gas to cause a significant explosion.

Burning incense is less of a risk but still needs to be undertaken with care and common sense. Incense cones are safer than incense sticks as the burnt ash is less likely to fall somewhere you don't want it to, and oil-reed diffusers are safer still.

Cigarettes are another common cause of fires in houses and boats alike. If you must smoke aboard then the big advice here is to never smoke in bed or when you're tired. It's worth remembering that some medications can make you drowsy too, so take extra care if you're smoking while medicated or tipsy. You should also empty ashtrays regularly as these can catch fire if hot ash is allowed to build up, and you should always make sure your cigarette is completely out.

💡 Alcohol

Many incidences of fires aboard have happened when the occupant has been drinking. Extra care should always be observed if you're enjoying a tipple.

ELECTRICAL FIRES

Modern canal boats will often feature complex electrical systems – so much so that understanding and maintaining the system is way beyond most boaters' abilities. And electrical complexity isn't the only hazard to consider. Electrical systems aboard boats are, by their very nature, subject to increased risks due to their exposure to water and severe weather, vibrations and rough usage.

💡 Electrocution

While it's not a significant risk aboard boats, poorly installed AC electrical systems can cause deaths aboard. The most frequent causes are using improper fusing and cables, coupled with poor or absent earthing. Again, professional installation is recommended.

Ensuring all electrical maintenance, installations and repairs are done by a competent person is without doubt the best way to improve your safety

EXPLOSIONS

The presence of gas or petrol aboard your boat presents a fire risk, but the risk is minimised by safe handling procedures and protocols.

Petrol

Although petrol-fuelled appliances are rarely installed as an integral part of a narrowboat's system the use of petrol for such things as generators and chainsaws is relatively common. Petrol is also often used to fuel the outboard motors aboard GRP cruisers so it makes sense for boaters to understand the risks inherent in using this highly flammable liquid because simple mistakes can cause devastating boat fires.

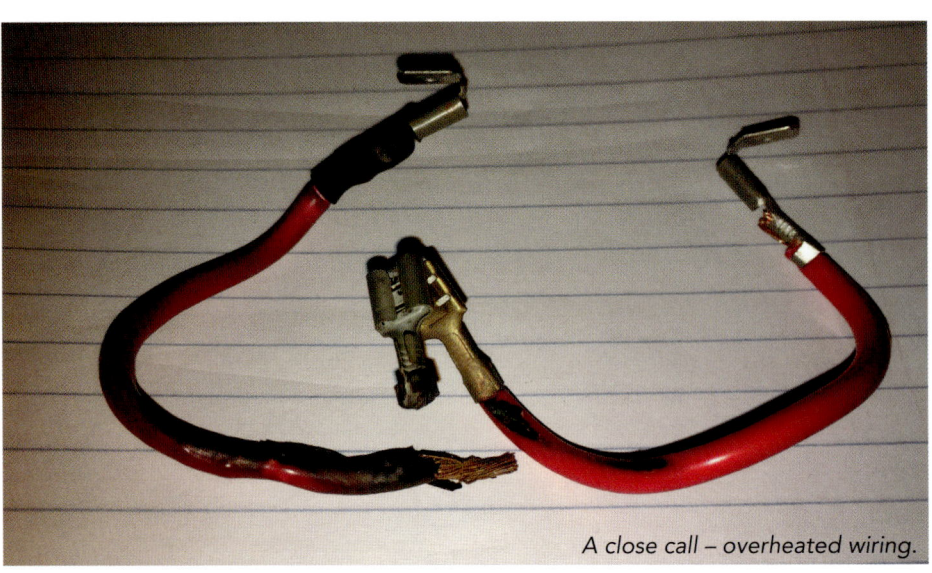

A close call – overheated wiring.

The main point to remember is that petrol that is spilt or exposed to air can create a deadly vapour that can be easily ignited, and this is especially dangerous when the heavier-than-air vapour collects inside the hull of a boat. Even a small amount of spilt petrol will create a disproportionately large volume of explosive vapour.

Petrol-handling tips

- Prevent petrol vapour from entering the boat when refuelling by closing the doors, windows or hatches and closing the awning.

- Only undo the petrol container cap when you're well away from the boat.

- Refuel generators well away from the boat.

- Leaks, spills and vapour can ignite easily. Clean them up straight away and make sure filler caps are secure after refuelling.

- Only carry spare petrol if necessary and store it in suitable containers and a self-draining locker or on an open deck.

- Stow generators in a self-draining locker, or on an open deck where the heavier-than-air petrol vapours can't flow into the boat's cabin or engine bay. Store spare fuel in the same way.

'Improper use and storage of petrol is the most frequent cause of boat fires and explosions,' explains David. 'If stored aboard it should be treated in the same way you would store a gas bottle because the explosive risks are identical.'

No smoking

Do not smoke when filling your boat with fuel or changing a gas cylinder. It might seem like common sense, but it's easy to forget these things as smoking is such a subconscious habit.

Gas Safety

An on-board gas supply is no more hazardous on a boat than it is in a home, but given that many boaters have a propensity for DIY it's important to be extra careful. When working around gas pipes or appliances the usual common-sense precautions apply and a qualified person is usually necessary when working on a gas appliance.

Remember that propane gas is heavier than air and therefore may not be smell-able at head height. Most gas alarms sold for use in houses have instructions stipulating that they should be installed in a high position, as domestic gas is lighter than air; in the case of propane gas used on boats, however, these alarms should be installed near the floor.

It's becoming increasingly common to see entirely gas-free vessels entering the new boat market, but gas installations are still pretty common among both new and used boats. A correctly fitted and well-maintained gas system should present no problems but, sadly, many boaters consider gas to be a 'fit-it-and-forget-it' system. It's not.

Gas systems should be checked regularly to ensure their safety, and a four-yearly examination for a Boat Safety Scheme certificate is unlikely to suffice. Most examiners will recommend a gas check by a qualified professional at least annually, and this is especially important for liveaboard boats.

💡 Last check before lights out

Check your boat before you go to bed. Make sure cooking and heating appliances are off, the stove door and vents are set correctly, and candles and cigarettes are fully extinguished.

GAS SAFETY TIPS

- Make sure gas cylinders are stored upright and are secure after they've been changed.

- Fit a bubble-type gas leak indicator in the LPG cylinder locker and test for leaks with proprietary leak detection fluid.

- Whenever possible, turn gas valves off before you go to bed or leave the boat.

- Replace gas hoses showing signs of cracking, brittleness or discolouration.

- Store gas cylinders outside the cabin in a self-draining and fire-resistant locker.

- If you can smell gas, turn the supply off and get it checked out straight away.

HOW TO SURVIVE A BOAT FIRE

Observing the rules and protocols above will greatly minimise the risk of a fire occurring on your boat. But, if the worst were to happen, there's plenty you can do to maximise your chances of getting out of there alive.

Get a smoke alarm – or better still, several

Anyone who has ever witnessed a boat ablaze will have the horrific image etched into their brain. It's frightening how quickly a fire can spread and engulf a boat, so every second counts if occupants are to escape safely.

That's why it's almost certain that fitting a smoke alarm will become a mandatory requirement of the Boat Safety Scheme in the near future. While the exact detail of the new rule is yet to be announced fitting at least one alarm looks likely, and it would make sense for boaters to fit additional alarms anywhere there's a risk of fire. This might include near solid-fuel stoves, gas-fuelled cooking appliances, battery banks, engine rooms and diesel heaters.

The most deadly time for any hazard to occur aboard is while the occupant is asleep, and reading online news reports about boat fire incidents would seem to confirm this. A smoke alarm can provide vital seconds' warning, and those seconds can mean the difference between life and death.

Alarm advice

- Optical sensor alarms with hush buttons and 'sealed for life' batteries are best for boats. See www.boatsafetyscheme.org/fire for more information on the alarm choices and a list of industry-recommended models.

- Fit alarms in places where you will hear them clearly if they go off.

- Consider installing linked alarms that will go off at the same time.

- Test the alarm when you board after some time away, and at least monthly.

- Never disconnect it or remove working batteries.

Optical sensor smoke alarm.

Use fire blankets and extinguishers safely

The fire extinguishers required by the Boat Safety Scheme examination are of a size that can be used to either extinguish small fires or to create a safe escape past flames. Larger extinguishers are, of course, more effective, but safely escaping the vessel should be your primary concern.

💡**Be prepared for powder**
Dry powder extinguishers create a dense powder-cloud which reduces visibility and impairs breathing.

Firefighting-kit tips

- The Boat Safety Scheme requires a minimum rating of 8A 34B for fire extinguishers. It's worth Googling 'fire extinguisher ratings' for an enlightening explanation of what different fire extinguishers can be used for.

- Regularly check the pin and firing mechanism of every extinguisher for problems or signs of weaknesses.

- Check the dates on extinguishers and fire blankets, although not all extinguishers display an expiry date.

- Have extinguishers serviced by a competent person, or replace them as recommended by the instructions.

- Give powder extinguishers a shake now and again to prevent the contents from clumping.

- Only choose extinguishers that carry recognised approval marks, and choose units marked with at least an 'A' and 'B' fire rating.

- Keep fire blankets and extinguishers within easy reach, close to exits and risk points, such as the galley and engine area. Don't store them in cupboards.

- Check extinguishers regularly for dents, leaks and loss of pressure.

Be prepared

Here's a handy list of dos and don'ts that could save your life:

- Make sure everyone aboard knows how to close emergency valves and switches in case of fire.

- Keep a torch easily available to help you escape at night.

- Keep exits clear and keys to hand.

- Don't lock or bolt doors and hatches from the outside.

- Know your location so you can tell the emergency services where you are. Tell them where nearby road access points are if you can.

- Consider having a 'grab bag' of vital possessions ready for an emergency, as this can prevent the urge to remain aboard searching for these things.

💡**Magnifying glass effect**
Domed-decklights (sometimes called 'bullseyes') can focus light rays and cause fires in strong sunlight, so be vigilant while aboard and cover the unit when you're away from the boat.

What to do if there's a fire

- If in doubt, don't fight a fire yourself. Get out, stay out, call 999 for help and wait for the fire and rescue services.

- Don't enter a smoke-filled space.

- If you're already in a smoke-filled space, keep low down where the air is clearer.

- Starve the fire of air. Don't open engine hatches or doors unless you have to.

💡 **Note**

This chapter features content from the Boat Safety Scheme

For more information about all aspects of boat safety visit their website: **https://www.boatsafetyscheme.org/ stay-safe-advice.**

You can also use the website to contact the BSS team about any boat safety topic or if you have an incident or near incident you would like to discuss with them.

FALLING IN

Falling in the cut is usually funny rather than dangerous, but there are plenty of occasions where falling in has been deadly. There are several hazards to look out for and plenty that we boaters can do to prevent tragedies from happening.

THE TILLER ARC

'Anyone steering the boat should always stand in front of the tiller, rather than at the side,' says boat surveyor David Hull. 'Plenty of people have been knocked into the water by the tiller – either because the rudder struck something in the water that caused it to lurch, or because the skipper didn't see someone and pushed the tiller into them. It happens a lot.'

This is why the safety standards for hire boats has a requirement for the arc of the tiller to be designated or marked on the back deck as a means to highlight the tiller-swing danger zone. It's worth remembering that falling in while the boat is underway is particularly dangerous, especially when falling from the stern. There have been numerous tragedies where boaters have tangled with the propeller. 'If you do fall in off the back of a moving boat, make your way to the bank rather than instinctively attempting to get back onto the boat, because that's where the propeller is,' recommends David. 'And similarly, if you're the skipper and someone falls in, don't reverse the boat and the propeller towards them. Instead, switch off the engine if possible.'

Suicide seats

'While we're on the subject of tiller-arc safety we should discuss suicide seats,' says David. These are the perching seats fixed on the stern within the tiller-arm's arc, which are without doubt a risky place to sit when the boat is underway. 'These seats are so common and there are plenty of cases where people have been knocked off them into the water by the tiller – and some were near fatal.'

ICY CONDITIONS

Notwithstanding the circumstances already described, falling off a boat in the summer months is largely an inconvenience. Falling in during the winter, however, is a very different thing. Again, there have been numerous tragedies where boaters have ended up in icy water and been unable to get out. This could be because the shock of hitting cold water saps their strength or takes their breath away, causing them to panic and struggle. Other times the boater wasn't physically able to get out before hypothermia set in.

'The waterways are particularly hazardous during the winter months,' says David. 'There are far fewer people around to help if you find yourself incapacitated in the water, and you have less time to get out before things turn deadly. I recommend everyone has a whistle or a waterproofed mobile phone to hand, just in case.'

Suicide seats are really common.

'And it goes without saying that extreme care should be exercised when stepping aboard, navigating locks or even walking on towpaths or pontoons,' he adds.

SINKING

The risk of sinking as a result of a hole in your steel hull is remote. I have canvassed many experienced boaters and they recount few incidents of battleship-style hull breaches. Sinking is more likely to be due to a boating incident in a lock or on a river where water is somehow allowed into the boat. Hanging the boat on a lock cill, trapping fenders and bow buttons or opening gate paddles too early are the main offenders, but the list of possible causes is long.

Barry Whitelock MBE is renowned and vastly experienced, having been the resident lock keeper of the famous Five Rise staircase locks on the Leeds & Liverpool Canal for over 20 years. 'Take your time with locks. There's no rush,' says Barry. 'Have a signal that everyone understands to alert for any problems. If there's a lock keeper in service there then follow their advice exactly and wait for their instruction. It's their job to get you through the lock safely and efficiently.'

Mooring is another risky activity where sinking is a risk. Mooring too tightly on a waterway with variable water levels can create problems, causing your boat to tip as it rises or falls with the water. Allowing a hull skin fitting (such as an exhaust or vent) to fall below the waterline can easily cause the unthinkable to happen.

Barry Whitelock MBE.

Gongoozlers.

GONGOOZLERS

A 'gongoozler' is someone who enjoys watching boats and boating activity. Most gongoozlers are passive observers and essentially harmless, but others will interact with boaters, sometimes to detrimental effect. Abusive gongoozlers are easily ignored, but those who attempt to help out or otherwise get involved can be dangerous. Some gongoozlers even carry lock keys and windlasses and will take it upon themselves to assist with locks and bridges uninvited. Clearly there's a significant risk of sinking or damage from this type of 'help', and great care must be exercised by the boater to negate the hazard. A useful tip is to announce that you 'have a system' and that you thank them for their kind offer of help, but your process is so ingrained and habitual that it's difficult to deviate from it.

CLEAN-WATER SINKING

The contents of a ruptured water tank won't be enough sink a boat by itself. But if you're filling the tank from the mains and it's cracked or split, you could unintentionally add enough water to flood the boat. Always watch tanks while filling. Ignoring a leak can quickly turn into a serious hazard.

SLIPS AND TRIPS

Slips and trips are the most frequent and likely accidents for boaters, and particularly for liveaboards. Friction is your friend on a boat and extreme care should be taken if friction is compromised. Boats and pontoons are equally hazardous and it's easy to be careless. Water is the most common lubricating culprit, particularly if frozen as snow or ice, but diesel and oil spills are also common slip hazards.

💡 Anti-slip safety tips

- Many liveaboards have a whistle attached to their boat keys in the hope that if they were to slip and need help, the whistle would be available to attract attention.

- Locks and bridges are particularly hazardous and it goes without saying that extreme care should be exercised.

- Spilt diesel and oil are severe slip hazards and should be cleaned up immediately.

- Never jump onto or off a boat. Step aboard or ashore comfortably, and if this is not possible, move the boat closer.

- Never jump onto the roof of a boat from a lock or from another boat.

- Highlight mooring pins with hi-vis material or white plastic bags.

- Clean the roof regularly as leaves, mud, soot and slime will increase the risk of slips.

- Step squarely onto wet boats and pontoons as sideways momentum can cause your foot to slip from under you in wet or slippery conditions.

- Never get blasé about the risk of slips and falls. Falling onto a steel boat can break bones and cause head injuries, and the risk of falling into the water while unconscious is very real.

Always step onto a wet surface squarely as it's surprising how fast your foot can slide sideways from under you. Bumps, breaks and bruises are painful, but not often deadly. The main concern is the risk of head injury and drowning, particularly if you're alone when it happens, as most generally are.

Rooftop equipment can be a trip hazard.

Keep ropes coiled and tidy.

VANDALISM AND BREAK-INS

Even in the most salubrious of neighbourhoods, it's impossible to eradicate the risk of vandalism or burglary completely, so it's wise to take sensible precautions to deter perpetrators. The most obvious method is to select your mooring places carefully. The prevalence of litter and graffiti is a reasonably reliable indicator that there may mischief-makers in the vicinity, and it's worth speaking with local boaters and lock keepers in the bid to avoid notorious trouble hotspots. Town centres often suffer antisocial problems caused by late-night revellers. Noise, litter and people peeing in your plant pots are unpleasant nuisances to bear; actual vandalism and burglary are thankfully uncommon.

Burglar alarms for boats are available, but few boaters find them necessary. Some of these alarms have motion sensors that emit an electronic beep as you near the boat – highly irritating for those moored nearby. Canvas covers at the bow or stern provide nominal protection for items stored within, but also provide cover for intruders to work unseen on your security. Good padlocks seem to deter all but the most determined burglar, but it must be accepted that it's easy to get into any boat if the intruder is determined enough. Given that there's little space or inclination to collect high value possessions, most boaters are more fearful of vandalism than of burglary, but remember neither experience is common on the waterways.

Boaters occasionally experience antisocial behaviour while cruising or when stopped at a lock or a bridge, often from youths or children. Good interpersonal skills will usually deter bad behaviour, and briefly engaging with the local youth can stop problems before they start. If bad behaviour does occur, the best advice is to use your mobile phone, first to call the police and then to photograph or record the perpetrators. This usually brings an end to the episode swiftly.

There are also several 'canal watch' schemes of various descriptions running in numerous parts of the country. Liveaboards in London have formed regular patrol groups to monitor towpath crime hotspots, conscious of the fact that police, local authorities and CRT need local help to address canal crime. Boaters patrol in groups of four, with a remit simply to act both as a deterrent and as extra eyes and ears for the police service. Vigilante action is thoroughly discouraged. The happy spin-off is that the patrol serves as an opportunity to meet other boaters and make new friends. For more information email canalwatchlondon@gmail.com.

Other, less hands-on canal watch schemes are active in different parts of the country, so it's worth speaking to local boaters to check what's happening in your area. Facebook groups also provide a good insight into the safety status in any particular area, often giving up-to-the-minute information about recent issues.

195

BEEN THERE, DONE THAT
TOP SAFETY TIPS

STEVE AND EILEEN
Nb *Rahab*

Unless your dog is perfectly behaved, don't allow them on deck when you're cruising. We have seen dogs launch themselves off boats to try to get at another on the towpath, we have seen them trip people up as they're stepping ashore, and we even once saw a dog fall overboard while tied to the boat by its lead.

TONY AND VICKIE
Nb *The Watchman*

Carbon monoxide is one of the greatest risks for boaters. Installing an alarm is a Boat Safety Scheme test requirement, and we were advised to have at least two on board.

The one in our bedroom, which is fitted at the same height as our heads when we sleep, is most reassuring. This will warn us if carbon monoxide is entering our boat from the exhaust of another boat moored nearby. Apparently this has happened causing the death of the sleeping inhabitants, and it's a likely enough risk for us to want to take precautions.

DARREN
Nb *Dunster*

If I am cruising or working on the boat I always empty my pockets of vulnerable valuables, just in case I fall in.

Similarly, I never hold my keys in my hand as I step on or off the boat as I'd hate to slip and fling them into the water. At least if they're in my pocket when I fall in I will still have them when I get out.

WOODY
Nb *Frog With A Heart*

As one qualified to work with LPG boating gas I've come across some truly shocking DIY gas installations. They aren't common, but for the sake of safety it makes sense to get your gas system inspected by someone who knows what they're looking for and has the right equipment to find and fix any faults that might exist.

JOHN
Nb *Sound of Silence*

If someone falls overboard while you're underway, cut the engine immediately. Once in the water most people are compelled to swim back towards the stern because this is the lowest part of the boat. Unfortunately that is where the propeller is.

ILLNESS AND DISEASE

Canal water is home to some rather unsavoury stuff. While much of it will result only in mild stomach upsets, Weil's disease (also known as leptospirosis) is potentially fatal. Incidents of Weil's disease are rare and deaths are rarer still. But as with all risks, it's worth knowing how to avoid Weil's and what to do if you suspect you may have contracted it.

Weil's disease is transmitted through contact with animal urine which, most notably for canal users, will usually be from rats. It's found in stagnant, still or slow-moving water and also on canal and river banks. It's contracted through contact with the mouth, eyes, ears, nose or open wounds on the body. Falling into the water, handling wet ropes and even wet or muddy shoes can pose a risk.

Cleanliness is the best precaution – washing hands thoroughly before eating and drinking and taking care to avoid other contaminations via the mouth. All contact with the water should be considered a risk and procedures such as working in the weed hatch could cause a problem, particularly if you have scratches or other open wounds on your hands and arms. Boat life being what it is, open wounds and scratches are a common, so understanding the risks is important. Be careful, too, when clearing debris from around your prop through the weed hatch as fishing twine and hooks are sometimes found there.

Of course, the possibility of contracting Weil's increases should you fall into the water. It's recommended that you shower immediately and see a doctor as soon as possible as a precautionary measure, explaining what has happened and your concern about Weil's.

💡 **Weil's disease symptoms**

- Headaches
- Fever
- Chills
- Vomiting
- Muscle pain, particularly calf muscles
- Malaise
- Bruising and bleeding beneath the skin

Knowing the symptoms of Weil's is important should you contract the disease unwittingly. Most of the symptoms are similar to those you get when you have a cold or flu, and the odds are that if you have these symptoms you probably do have just that. But be aware and be prepared to act accordingly if you experience these symptoms, and be sure to stress your concerns about Weil's disease to your doctor.

Canal towpaths and riversides are popular venues for dog walkers too. Unfortunately, some dog owners aren't as conscientious as they should be and dog poo is a frequent waterside hazard. Inadvertently walking dog poo into the boat and grabbing ropes that have been similarly fouled is enormously annoying. Boaters with first-hand experience of this will understand the restraint that has been exercised when writing this section, as the desire to use more industrial language is overwhelming.

DRINKING AND BOATING

Relaxation is often accompanied by a glass of wine or a cold beer, so it would appear that boating and drinking could be lots of fun. Unlike when driving a car, there's no law against boating and drinking, but rest assured that if an accident were to occur as a result of intoxication it's likely that someone would be found to be at fault and made liable. Careful alcohol consumption is recommended while aboard.

*Bingley Five Rise Locks, West Yorkshire –
one of the Seven Wonders of the Waterways.*

💡 Stayin' alive round-up

- Don't leave boat doors padlocked on the outside while you're in the boat and make sure any locks are easy to open in a hurry from the inside. On hire boats, doors must open from the inside without the need for a key or tool and this is a good principle for all boats.

- Don't keep lead-acid batteries in sealed boxes. While the gasses that escape from lead-acid batteries will normally rise and disperse naturally, they can explode if contained in a sealed unit, and even a small amount is explosive.

- Single-handing boaters should wear a self-inflating life jacket and have some means of signalling alarm, such as a whistle or a waterproof mobile phone.

- A rope ladder can be a real help if someone falls in and isn't physically able to haul themselves out of the water. Even if you think you're strong enough to exit the water after a dunking, you'll be surprised how much weight is added by wet clothing and how much strength is sapped in icy conditions. Getting out at the bank is usually the easiest and safest option.

- When locking, if there's someone less able in your crew, always ensure there's also someone able bodied inside the cabin to help them escape should something go wrong. Better still, have them exit the boat onto the bank during locking to negate the risk almost entirely. Remember, side hatches are often unusable while in a lock.

Tony's *towpath tales*

I was once moored up at a boatyard abreast a boat with a cruiser stern. In order to get onto my boat from the bank I had to walk across other boat's the back deck – which was fine during the light of day, but one evening as I left my boat in the dark I didn't notice that someone had removed the deck boards to work on the engine. Stepping off my boat I fell into the cruiser's engine bay, ending up at the bottom in a crumpled mess and in terrible pain. Thankfully it was nothing that a few stitches couldn't put right, but from that day on I'll never leave my boat without my head torch if it's dark. Few mooring places have adequate lighting and boat life seems to be littered with trip hazards, so I cite a head torch among the most useful items of boating safety equipment.

10 DIRTY FINGERNAILS

If you own a boat you should be prepared to get your hands dirty.
Even a brand-new boat in A1 condition will require a hands-on
approach to keep it afloat and fully functional.

Living aboard is a dirty-fingernails kind of lifestyle and your boat will require constant attention. Although generic boat maintenance and management has been discussed elsewhere in this book, it's important to look at this issue from a purely liveaboard perspective.

One of the major reasons for liveaboard boaters returning to dry land is that they have been unprepared to deal with the consequences of bad boat maintenance and equipment breakdowns. Malfunctions can sometimes be costly and are always frustrating, and while they can't be avoided completely, regular boat maintenance, a good toolbox and a 'can do' attitude are certainly required. Unlike for weekend boaters, going home and leaving it to be fixed another day is not an option.

A good rule of thumb is to never half-do a job. A quick fix should only be considered a temporary measure, as a collection of bodge jobs and workarounds will quickly make boat life unbearable. Each time something goes wrong with anything on the boat, think 'How can I fix this so it does not happen again?' Often this will mean replacing whatever is in place with a more suitable system or product, usually one that is easy to maintain and repair. Boat life seems to attract people with the requisite handy skills so it's often possible to tackle small jobs yourself or with the help of a friendly neighbour. However, sometimes the only answer is to dig deep and hire a professional.

ELECTRICS

'Electrical problems are by far the most frequent cause of breakdowns,' says Jo from Snaygill Boats. 'Alternator, starter motor, battery management and charging problems can close down a boat.' Most often the problem has been hidden while the boat is moored up with shore power, only becoming apparent when cruising makes the boater reliant on the battery system.

The problem almost invariably originates from poor battery maintenance where the batteries have not been sufficiently recharged after use. Of course, the boater only finds out that their batteries are dead when they set off on a cruise and find that they have no power. For most boaters, battery management is a poorly understood science that will regularly lead to frustration and electrical issues. And I count myself among these naïve liveaboards, having cursed my boat's electrical system for more than a decade before my wife taught me where I was going wrong. It's certainly a lesson worth learning.

TOILETS

Toilet problems come a close second in the frustration and inconvenience stakes. Pump-out toilet owners will know that a full toilet tank that will not pump out is an urgent and unpleasant problem to fix. Poking around with sticks inside the tank can often solve the issue temporarily, but eventually a permanent solution will be required.

BEEN THERE, DONE THAT
LOOK OUT FOR LIMESCALE

CHARLIE
Nb *Philip George*

I work at a boatyard so I see a fair few toilet issues, and by far the biggest cause of toilet malfunction we see is the build-up of limescale. It occurs over time and can cause macerators to malfunction and can also cause blockages in the pipework. The resulting cost and inconvenience are rather unnecessary, because the problem is so easy to avoid with a little routine maintenance. Cleaning the pumps and treating the limescale in the pipework every 12 months or so will stop the vast majority of toilet troubles. I wish people would do this, because I don't particularly enjoy the job when they bring their toilets to us to fix.

Making sure foreign bodies that can cause a blockage aren't put into your black water tank is common sense, but in addition you should ensure that the usual contents don't solidify (see page 103). Don't scrimp on toilet fluids as generous use will usually prevent the problem, but an occasional blast with a jet wash device will help too. Cassette toilet owners are advised to have a spare cassette to use should one fail or be unexpectedly full, and pump-out users are advised to have a cassette toilet in reserve in readiness for the same problems.

💡 **Fair warning**

Macerator toilets will often die slowly, giving you plenty of warning that they're about to fail. Be ready to tackle the issue before it becomes a major problem.

WATER

Water systems often fail during the wintertime when cold weather and thaws can cause burst pipes. Although this is more of a problem for weekend boaters who don't keep their boats warm while they aren't aboard, it can affect liveaboards too. Hiding plumbing behind the fit-out joinery might be aesthetically pleasing but this makes it more susceptible to cold weather problems. Pipes that can be kept warm while the boat is being heated will solve the issue for most liveaboards, but a vigilant watch for leaks is still advisable. Even during the summer, leaks are possible because of vibrations and the increased usage a liveaboard boat system gets. Water pumps and shower drain gulpers break down frequently for this reason and it's worth having a spare on hand as a quick replacement.

Water tanks can also develop leaks and faults, most commonly being caused by collisions and bumps when boating. A poorly secured tank containing hundreds of litres of water can shift significantly in a collision, causing fixings, pipes and filler inlets to fracture.

Leaky window frames are the bane of many liveaboards, particularly those with older boats. The constant heating and cooling of the steel and woodwork and the deterioration of ageing sealant can cause formerly sound window frame seals to leak and subsequently rust. The only definitive solution is to remove the window, treat the rust and then properly replace and reseal the window. However, this can ruin the look of a nice paint job, so it's easy to see why boaters might be reluctant to bite this particular bullet. A temporary fix by applying silicone or another similar sealant to the edges of the frame might stop it for a short while, but the problem will return eventually.

it will speed up the job considerably. Wire-cutters, bolt croppers, pliers, mole grips, a sharp knife and lots of colourful language will usually suffice. Listen out for rattles and keep an eye on the engine temperature and the revs-to-speed ratio.

A stern gland is the threshold between the interior of your boat and the water outside and is packed with grease and a specialist filler rope to seal against leaks. A tap attached to a cylinder of grease is turned after each cruise to force grease into the gland to keep it packed and waterproof. However, the whole gland will deteriorate over time and will require removing and repacking occasionally, usually once every couple of years. The need for this job to be done becomes evident when your engine bay and bilges begin to collect water even after you have applied grease by turning the tap after each cruise. The bilge pump, which removes the inevitable water collecting

A conventional stern gland.

> 💡 **Free quick fix**
> If your window frame leaks from the top edge, then those with hopper-style windows can open the top flap to catch the drip so that it runs outside the boat.

WEED HATCH AND STERN GLAND

A common problem when cruising is for debris to collect around the boat prop, so having the right tools to remove

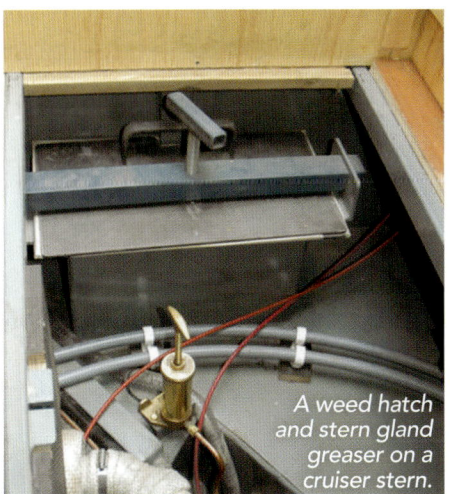

A weed hatch and stern gland greaser on a cruiser stern.

there, will solve the job temporarily as the condition worsens, but you will soon need to tackle the problem. It's a fiddly job that requires careful execution to ensure it's done correctly, but it's well within the scope of most boaters. Those with trad boats might find access difficult.

CLEANING UP A LEAK

A good piece of advice is to never let a drip turn into a leak, but if a leak does occur you will need some means of removing the water from your boat. Most boats have an inspection hatch in the floor somewhere near the stern of the boat. Regular checks here will reassure you that all is well with your water system, but if you discover water here then you need to find out where the problem is. Thankfully the water in the inspection hatch is usually clean water rather than canal water, indicating that the problem lies in the boat's plumbing system, not a hole in the hull.

Once the problem is located and fixed, your next job is to remove the water from the bilges. A spare bilge pump that can be wired up to a battery will do the job in most cases, but if you have a lot of water there it's quicker to use a toilet pump-out system. Be aware that water will have gathered in all of the nooks and crannies of ballast under the floor of your boat and will probably take a few days to make its way to the inspection hatch before you can pump it out. This is a good reason to never use gravel or sand as ballast, although it's not uncommon to find it used in old boats.

Once most of the water has been removed using pumps, the easiest way to collect the last remaining mess is with disposable nappies. Nappies soak up large amounts of water in just a few minutes and are then easily removed and disposed of. Be sure not to leave them in place for more than a few hours as they quickly deteriorate and fall apart, becoming another difficult clean-up job in themselves. Another option is to use an aquavac and empty it regularly, or to scatter cat litter and use a dustpan and brush to remove it when the water has been absorbed.

STOVE LEAKS

The union between the stove flue and the stove collar fitting on the roof is an occasional source of leaks. Although this looks to be a complicated job it's actually quite simple, if a little time-consuming.

Removing the brass dressing from around the flue inside the boat will grant access to the fibreglass packing between the flue and the collar. Remove this before going outside the boat to tackle the roof collar. Remove the bolts holding the collar in place before checking that

💡 Chimney tips

- A double-skin chimney will stop tar from burnt wood leaking into your boat.

- Beware that chimney coolie hats can drip this tar onto your exterior paintwork.

- Removing and storing your chimney inside your boat during the summer months will extend its life considerably.

- Secure your chimney to the boat with a thin chain so that it will not fall into the water if kicked or fouled on a tree or low bridge.

- Keep your chimney collar clean, painted and rust free. Rusty collars cause iridescent smears on the paintwork down the side of your boat. These are sometimes blamed on tar from the smoke, on the lack of a double-skin chimney, or on having a coolie hat dripping tar down the side of your boat. More often, though, it's rusty collars that are the culprit.

Regular checks on the flue collar fitting are important.

the collar is not sealed to the flue by cement or sealant. If so, you might need to use a drill or hacksaw blade to break it. You might also need to employ stern persuasion in order to remove the collar as lots of sealant is generally used to install them. Once removed, clean all sealant and rust from both the collar and the roof before applying a rust treatment to the affected areas.

Use a flexible heat-resistant sealant to reinstall the collar, being sure to add a bead around the interior and the exterior edges as well as around the securing bolt holes. Replace new fibreglass packing to fill the hole between collar and flue from inside the boat, and use stove cement or more sealant to fill the remaining space between from outside. Finally, ensure that the union between the stove top and the flue is secure, and refurbish it if required.

ENGINE MAINTENANCE

Engine maintenance is important for all boaters, but liveaboards who rely on their engine to charge their batteries have an added incentive. Annual servicing is recommended, but be sure you can do the job fully and efficiently before tackling it yourself. Jo from Snaygill Boats explains why: 'We get lots of boats brought to us with problems caused by self-servicing. Either the job has been abandoned once the owner realised it was more than they could handle or we end up repairing the consequences of poor servicing attempts. Learning how to service your own boat is great if you

learn how to do it properly, but a badly maintained boat is just going to cause problems at some point in the future.'

DIESEL BUG

Diesel bug issues are becoming more prevalent for a whole range of vehicles, not just narrowboats, and the problem is getting worse. The bug is a microbial organism that lives and breeds in the fuel tank, specifically in the interface between your fuel and any water that has contaminated it.

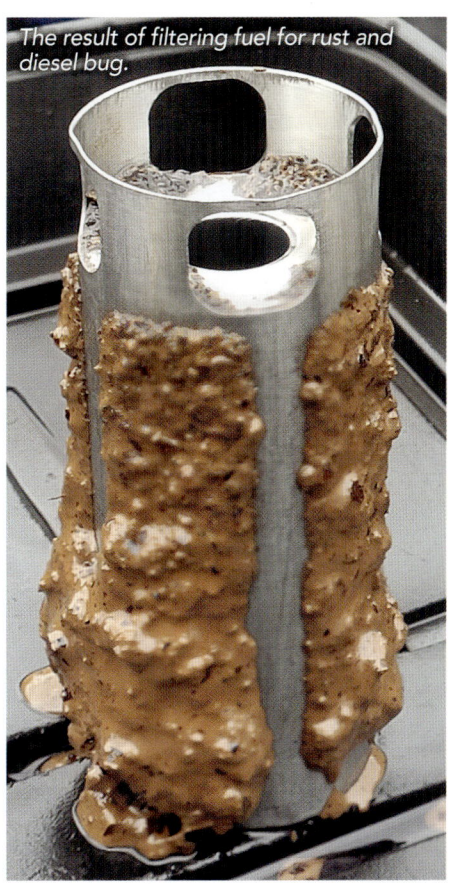
The result of filtering fuel for rust and diesel bug.

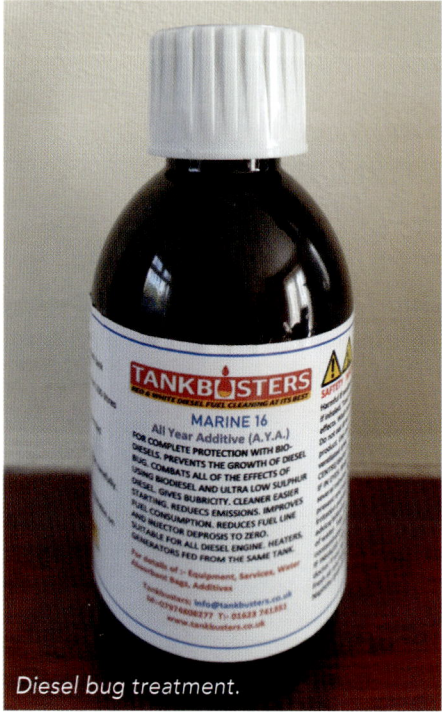

Diesel bug treatment.

Water is present in all diesel we buy, believe it or not, but it can also get into your tank either by accidental contamination or when condensation forms as the internal tank temperature changes. Contaminations can be seen as a black sludge that affects the fuel line, particularly the filters. The bug breeds best at temperatures of 30–40 degrees Celsius, making narrowboat fuel tanks an ideal environment given the proximity to the engine bay and the heat produced there.

The European legislation for all diesels to have at least a 5 per cent content of biofuel has exacerbated the problem as the organic material it contains is an ideal substrate for diesel bug. The problem may become worse still as the mandatory proportion of biofuel in the mix is likely to increase further as new legislation is imposed over time.

Prevention of diesel bug is difficult, if not impossible. Keeping your fuel tank full, particularly during winter, will reduce the amount of condensation created within the tank, but it's thought that most diesel is contaminated with water to some degree in the supply chain during normal handling and storage. There are also several treatments available to combat the problem, such as chemicals and magnetised units to fit to the fuel line, and there are several companies who will come to your boat to clean both the diesel and the tank. This is a particularly good idea if you're planning a river cruise, as the rocking and rolling of river cruising will disturb the silt and diesel bug contamination in your tank, making it more likely to enter your fuel line and starve your engine of fuel – not a good situation if you're on a tidal waterway.

One glimmer of hope is that the problem also affects the road haulage industry and therefore a reliable and cost-effective solution will hopefully soon become available to protect this enormous industry from losses.

💡 **Top DIY tip**

A spirit level is of no use whatsoever on a boat.

LIVEABOARD BOATER'S TOOL KIT

- Adjustable spanner
- Angle grinder
- Bailing device – jug or similar
- Bilge pump
- Bolt croppers
- Bow saw
- Cable ties
- Chainsaw
- Cordless drill and driver
- Disposable nappies
- Dustpan and brush
- Electrical screwdriver
- Electrical tape
- Funnels
- Gaffer tape
- Goggles and mask
- Hammer
- Hatchet or hand axe

- Head torch
- Jigsaw
- Jubilee clips
- Latex gloves
- Mole grips
- Pliers
- Ratchet screwdriver with various bits
- Selection of nuts, bolts, screws and tacks
- Silicone sealant and gun
- Socket set
- Spanners in metric and imperial sizes
- Stanley knife and replacement blades
- Tape measure
- Wire-cutters
- Wiring-locator device
- Wood saw

11 EVERYDAY MATTERS

Once you introduce ambiguity to your residential status by moving aboard a boat, you often slip through the gaps in the network of modern society. Most offices of officialdom will ask for your name and address, and unless you can give an answer that is acceptable to their computer system you'll probably experience problems.

Everything from your driving licence to your access to health care and financial services can be affected, and unless you want to hide from the world entirely you need to be prepared to find a solution.

Submitting a tax return, registering to vote, claiming benefits and even getting an OAP bus pass is complicated for those without a recognised conventional permanent address, but there are ways to deal with the issue. Continuous cruisers are most vulnerable to the problems that living aboard can cause, and sometimes the only answer is to rely on the safety net provided for those who are homeless.

One solution is to use an address that is accepted as your official residence, such as that of an agreeable friend or member of your family. While this may seem the most simple and suitable answer, the location of that address and its proximity to your current mooring defines how effective a solution it actually is. Postal services, couriers and registering with doctors and onto the electoral roll are all problematic if your official address is nowhere near your mooring spot.

DOCTORS AND MEDICAL SERVICES

I dread being ill. Not because I'm a terrible patient who whines and moans at the slightest discomfort, but because I know that getting to see a GP is sometimes a whole heap of hassle.

After almost 20 years of living aboard I've had several frustrating experiences when trying to see a doctor. Sometimes the surgery simply hasn't known how to deal with my liveaboard situation. Other times the reception has been almost hostile, with the surgery refusing to let me see a doctor unless I can prove I have a permanent address in the area. Over the years I've learned to be patient when dealing with GP surgeries, but I've also armed myself with the necessary information so I can get the treatment I need.

SICK AND TIRED

My first experience of GP problems occurred on the Grand Union at Hemel Hempstead, just a few months after I bought my boat. I was still a bit giddy about my new liveaboard life and would often seize the opportunity to talk about it with anyone who would listen. The surgery receptionist was at least somewhat interested, but her demeanour changed dramatically when she heard that I would only be in the area temporarily.

Apparently the receptionist could only register patients with a permanent address in their catchment area. While I endeavoured to explain that I did indeed live in their catchment area, albeit temporarily and aboard a narrowboat, the receptionist couldn't be convinced.

'How long are you going to be in Hemel Hempstead?' she asked.

'I'm not sure,' I replied. 'A few weeks maybe?'

'Unless you're going to be resident here for a significant length of time it's just not worth us registering you.'

After some debate about the definition of a 'permanent resident', the only solution the receptionist could offer was for me to visit my current doctor, who was located two hours away in Epsom. Eventually exasperated to the point of despair, I told her I had just that moment decided that I was staying in Hemel Hempstead for the rest of my life and would like to register with the doctor there and stay in the area forever. We looked at each other for a moment, and then filled in the necessary paperwork. We both knew I was lying, but if that's what it took to get a doctor, then that's what I was prepared to do. To be quite honest, I felt so wretched at the time I simply didn't have the energy to debate the issue anymore.

Another time I found myself denied care by a GP surgery because, as a boater, I was considered a traveller and therefore couldn't legitimately prove I was resident in their catchment area. In response, I asked that they put their position in writing, specifically that they would not provide care because I was a traveller. The receptionist paused, before retracting the statement and making an appointment for me.

Since then I've had several similar experiences, with GP surgeries telling me I couldn't see a doctor unless I registered, and that I couldn't register unless I could prove I was resident in their catchment area. As you'll soon see, both of these statements are incorrect.

Case Study: A GP'S PERSPECTIVE

'Continuity of treatment is an important part of our job,' says Kathy Tedcastle, a GP based in Grange-over-Sands in Cumbria. 'This is especially true when patients have complex medical histories which require ongoing treatment or regular medications. We need to keep track of their treatments, review their progress and adjust their prescriptions accordingly. And, to do that safely, we need as much information as possible.'

So, how does that work for boaters who get sick as they travel around the system, I asked.

'If you don't have an existing condition there's usually no problem. Any GP can treat you symptomatically,' explained Kathy. 'However, if you have an existing condition and are taking medications, things can be a bit more complicated. Before we can treat you, we need to know about any existing conditions and what medications you're taking, and the doctor you're visiting won't have access to your records that contain this information if you're registered at another surgery.

'Sadly, some patients aren't able to tell us everything we need to know. That's why accessing your medical records is so important and why visiting the GP you're registered with is preferable. Of course, that may not always be possible, so the GP will usually endeavour to register you at their surgery so they can gain access to the notes. In an ideal world your notes can be transferred electronically in just a few days, but sometimes it takes a little longer. Occasionally we have to wait for paper records to be posted by snail mail, and this can often take weeks and sometimes months.'

So what happens if the patient needs urgent care and can't wait days, weeks or months?

'On the rare occasion when the situation is so urgent and complex that we can't wait, we can contact the patient's registered GP and ask them to fax or email a summary. This will usually be a shortened account of the patient's conditions and a list of their medication. The summary will invariably be brief, but it's at least something for us to go on until we can get the patient's full records. It's not ideal, though, as the summary won't likely show the treatments and medications the patient has tried before or how they were affected by them. We'd need to ask the patient to fill in the gaps, but that's not always an option we can rely on.

'Above all, our greatest concern is patient safety. When GPs and reception staff recommend visiting your own GP, they're invariably focusing on safety and continuity of care, rather than trying to make life difficult. Receptionists should be equipped with enough knowledge to deal with unusual situations that don't quite fit the standard operational procedures, such as boaters. Sadly, that's not always the case, and some receptionists perhaps aren't as knowledgeable or as helpful as they could be. But do rest assured, the vast majority will have your best interests and care at heart and their advice is usually well meaning. In the majority of circumstances, visiting your own registered GP will be the most effective and safest option, and when it isn't we'll do our best to help as much as we can.'

BEST PRACTICE

So, what should you do if you need a GP but aren't near the surgery where you're registered? First, it's important to know that you're legally entitled to get treatment at any NHS GP surgery in the UK as a temporary resident, regardless of your residential status or where you're currently registered as a patient.

That said, it's always worth considering if it might be better to visit the surgery where you're currently registered. This is usually the best course of action for those who have ongoing treatment for chronic conditions. The continuity benefits of your doctor having access to your medical records are significant. However, if visiting your regular surgery isn't practical you should of course seek treatment at a local surgery.

If you're a boater without a permanent home address, the NHS allows you to register with a GP surgery using a temporary address or even the GP surgery's own address. This flexibility ensures that transient individuals, such as boaters, can access essential healthcare services without the need for traditional proof of address. When registering, you'll be asked for basic information such as your name, date of birth, and address. While an NHS number can be helpful, it's not required for registration. Some surgeries may request additional details to help transfer medical records or verify your status as a parent or guardian.

It's important to note that registering with a GP surgery outside your local area may limit access to certain NHS services, such as home visits and out-of-hours care. Therefore, it's advisable to discuss these potential limitations with the GP surgery before registering. If you encounter difficulties during the registration process, you can seek assistance from your local Integrated Care Board (ICB), Citizens Advice, or your local Healthwatch. These organisations can provide guidance and support to ensure you receive the healthcare services you need.

> ### 💡 How to register with a GP
>
> For more detailed information on registering with a GP surgery, visit the official NHS guidance here: www.nhs.uk/nhs-services/gps/how-to-register-with-a-gp-surgery/

ALTERNATIVE OPTIONS FOR TREATMENT

We're not referring to herbal remedies, healing crystals and homoeopathy here, but there are several alternative treatment options available on the NHS. Perhaps one of these could be an efficient way to get treatment without visiting a GP.

Phone call or video consultations: It's often possible to arrange a phone or video call with your registered GP. Since the Covid pandemic, this has become an increasingly common option at many surgeries.

Urgent treatment centres: Many towns and cities have urgent treatment centres (UTC) often referred to as walk-in centres. You can go to an urgent treatment centre

if you need urgent medical attention, but it's not a life-threatening situation. UTCs are open at least 12 hours a day, every day. To find one simply Google 'Urgent Treatment Centres'.

Conditions that can be treated at an urgent treatment centre include sprains and strains, suspected broken limbs, minor head injuries, cuts and grazes, bites and stings, minor scalds and burns, ear and throat infections, skin infections and rashes, eye problems, coughs and colds, high temperatures in both children and adults, stomach pain, vomiting and diarrhoea, as well as the need for emergency contraception.

NHS 111: If you're unsure of the best source of treatment you can ring the NHS information line by dialling 111 or by visiting 111.nhs.uk. This useful service is there to help if you need urgent medical help or you're not sure about what to do

or where to go. They will ask questions about your symptoms and recommend the best way to get the help you need. It's available 24 hours a day, 7 days a week. If you need to go to A&E, NHS 111 can even book an arrival time, which might mean you spend less time in A&E.

REPEAT PRESCRIPTIONS

Thankfully you don't need to visit your GP if all you need is a repeat prescription. Richard Holdsworth is a liveaboard boater and continuous cruiser who requires regular repeat prescriptions for an ongoing condition. 'I'm registered with a GP in Leeds, but I regularly travel around the waterways network. This means I could be anywhere in the country when I need a new prescription. Thankfully, it's really easy to do this remotely and arrange to pick up my medication at a local pharmacy, wherever I may be. Here's how I do it.

1 Open the NHS app and click 'Order a prescription'. (Some GP surgeries use other apps, such as Patient Access, but the NHS app should work for everyone.)

2 Click 'Your nominated pharmacy' and change it to a pharmacy of your choice.

3 Click 'Order a prescription' to request a repeat prescription from your GP. They will then send your repeat prescription to your newly nominated pharmacy.

4 Drop into the nominated local pharmacy to pick up your prescription. You may need to provide some proof of ID, such as a driving licence or date of birth.

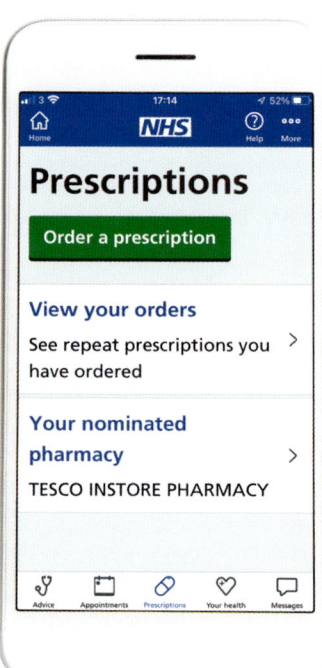

'I tend to always use big pharmacies, such as Boots, and I have never had any problems, but I know people who have used small independent pharmacies and they seem to work just as well. Regardless, the system has been a godsend to me and I have picked up prescriptions all over the country. I wouldn't be able to continuously cruise without it.'

CONCLUSION

The last thing you need when you're under the weather is to have to fight for your right to see a doctor, and it would be wonderful if all GP surgeries were familiar with the rules as they apply to many boaters' circumstances. Unfortunately, that's unlikely to happen. So what are we to do?

In my experience, it's always preferable to avoid the glitches that are seemingly inherent in the system. If I have the option to use an address within the surgery's catchment area then that's always the path of least resistance.

If that's not an option there's always a provision for you to use the surgery's address on your patient records, which means you'll need to collect any medical correspondence from the surgery in person.

But the best course of action, if at all possible, is to visit or contact the surgery where you're registered. That way you can be sure they have access to your medical records and avoid the headaches completely. Unfortunately for us, that's not always practical, but getting treatment is the primary goal. Who said boating was a low stress, carefree pastime?

MAIL AND DELIVERIES

Although many mooring providers don't offer residential moorings, some have provision to receive mail for those with boats moored there. The risk here is that by receiving mail at a mooring address it can be perceived as evidence that the mooring provider is breaking their planning terms by accommodating residential boaters, so many marinas draw the line at providing this service. Some still do, though, and a little detective work can help you to spot when mail services are available at a prospective mooring provider site.

The best option for receiving post is to have it delivered to a friend or relative who lives nearby, but if that's not an option, there are others. In many places it's possible to use a poste restante (French for 'post remaining') service. This is a free service that was popular historically and is intended for those without a specific address. It enables itinerants to collect mail from a post office or sorting office near to their current location. Finding a post office or sorting office that still remembers, understands and offers this service is rather a pot-luck process, and some will simply bluster or refuse to accommodate it. Usually the mail is addressed to the recipient using the address of the collection office or sorting office and marked 'POSTE RESTANTE', but others use the address of the recipient's mooring, knowing that the letter can go no further than the most local sorting office. In either case it's imperative to establish an understanding with the local staff at the office to ensure it all goes smoothly. Some marinas have had this system in place for many years, with boaters and office staff being on first-name terms.

💡 Lockers

When ordering products online there's often the option to have the item delivered to a local locker. These are located outside supermarkets, petrol stations or stores and you'll be offered a choice of those local to you when placing your order for delivery.

You'll be provided with a code in your order confirmation email, and you simply punch this code in at the keypad when you go to collect your parcel from the locker. A door will spring open and voila! There's your parcel. It really is as easy as that.

These lockers aren't an option for regular post and letters, but thankfully there are a handful of companies that will provide a postal address service for boaters. Some are created specifically for boaters, while others are aimed at small business owners running their company from home. Mail can be sent to the company's address, whereupon it will be either scanned and emailed to you or re-delivered to an alternative location. Of course, these services cost money, but where there's no other option they're a great solution. The scope and cost of these services vary to some degree, so it's worth comparing them.

Courier deliveries for those without a specific address can be hit and miss. Often couriers will arrive at a postcode looking for a house with an interesting name having mistaken your boat name for a house. Unless the recipient is on constant watch for the puzzled courier the parcel will go back to the depot, and with nowhere to leave a calling card, you'll never know that they have been. Occasionally a long-serving delivery driver will keep the same patch for years and get to know the contact details for local boaters, but this is a rare occurrence and can't be relied upon. There are a couple of solutions, the first being to request that the sender lists a mobile phone number on the address label of the package. This is a reasonably reliable workaround, but occasionally the sender manages to omit the number from the label, or the delivery driver misses the number or doesn't want to call it from his own mobile phone. A more reliable option is to have the parcel delivered to your place of work or to a local friend if these options exist. While it would not be acceptable to use such addresses for official address purposes, most employers (and friends) are happy to receive the occasional package.

PROOF OF ADDRESS

Not being able to get mail delivered to your mooring can cause significant problems when being asked for proof of your address. The requirements of banks and other service providers such as mobile phone services vary greatly.

Some require proof in triplicate of a registered address that they have listed on their database, whereas others have a more flexible approach. As a general rule it can be much more hassle to set up a new account with a new organisation than it is to change an address with an existing one. This can force boaters to stick with a company not through loyalty or because they offer the best product or service, but because the prospect of changing supplier is so fraught with difficulty.

Again, the easiest solution is to have one single registered land address where all formal correspondence is delivered. The problems of proximity are negated in most cases, as statements, bills and invoices can be viewed online. Internet banking is fast becoming the norm too, and most bills and transfers are easily done on the web.

The matter gets complicated when companies require several different proofs of address. If you use different addresses for different services you may find that you don't have enough to give a proof of address for one specific place. Most will expect to see utilities bills, but as boaters don't use gas, electric or water supply companies these aren't an option. Most companies will not recognise correspondence from CRT as official proof, and the lack of a landline, broadband and TV service providers narrows the field even more.

Given the headaches that proof-of-address requests can cause, it's worth keeping a log of all the organisations you need to notify when you change your mooring. Keeping them up to date with your current whereabouts will ensure that you have as many options as possible when providing proof of address. Thankfully, most commercial organisations are keen enough to attract and keep customers that they're happy to go the extra mile to accommodate those with unusual circumstances, and explaining your liveaboard lifestyle to the operative taking your application will usually bring about a satisfactory result.

BENEFITS

It is possible to claim benefits as a liveaboard boater, but with the introduction of Universal Credit and the tightening of criteria for claimants, this can be a minefield. Housing benefit to cover mooring fees appears relatively simple to claim and some boaters have even managed to have their licence fee awarded too. When claiming these benefits it would make sense to claim council tax benefit too, if indeed you're one of the few boaters who actually pay it. And therein lies the problem. By claiming housing benefit and council tax your liveaboard status becomes obvious, official and undeniable. A mooring provider that does not have the relevant planning permission for residential moorings would understandably take exception to any official statement that they're harbouring a liveaboard, often resulting in them tightening the mooring rules.

The consequences for liveaboards down on their luck and reliant upon benefits might be severe, as the likelihood of losing a mooring should not be underestimated. While there are many cases of liveaboards finding a niche in the system where claiming benefits is possible, there's often an inherent stress and vulnerability that come with the situation, and caution should be employed. Tax credits are the responsibility of HMRC rather than the local council and there appears to be little communication between the two agencies.

In short, if you're in a situation where you're entitled to claim benefits then you certainly should. That's what the benefits system is there for. However, you should be prepared for the usual headaches surrounding the making of a claim to be amplified because you live aboard. It can be done, and many liveaboards do it, but it's a nightmare, to say the least.

TV LICENSING

There are no specific rules regarding TV licensing for liveaboard boaters, and even those who attempt to obtain one often run into problems. If you have a land address with a TV licence your viewing aboard is covered by this. If you have a residential mooring where you're permanently dwelling you will need (and can easily acquire) a TV licence specifically for that bona fide address. However, those boaters without a specific address seem to slip between the gaps of the licensing regulations.

Interestingly, TV licence inspectors have few powers to investigate licence evasion, even when investigating those watching TV in a land-based house. Mere ownership of a TV, aerial or set-top box does not necessitate a licence; a licence is only required to receive and view a TV programme, so unless it can be proved that someone was actually watching, enforcement of the licence regulations is difficult. Licensing officials have no right to enter a property without a warrant, and ownership of TV broadcast-receiving equipment is no proof of licence evasion. Moreover, it seems the TV licensing authorities have decided that the cost and inconvenience of enforcing the regulations within the boating community aren't worth the hassle considering the small numbers involved.

DATING

Boaters often live aboard alone, not only because of the constraints of space, but also as a consequence of a rambling 'free-spirited' nature. However, that's not to say boaters are inherently sad and lonely. Many boaters live aboard with a partner and occasionally whole families live aboard too. Neither are most boaters single. In fact, the novelty of living aboard is often an attractive positive in the dating stakes, and given that most boat folk are 'interesting' people, there's usually no shortage of dating opportunity. On the flip side, it can be difficult to reconcile a constant-cruising or itinerant boating lifestyle with a house-living, land-loving partner. Short-range relationships soon become long-range relationships and usually something has to give.

CLEAN CLOTHES

Previously considered a luxury too far, washing machines are now commonly found aboard many craft. The power consumption and space constraints were the most common reasons for their former lack of popularity, but as more people move aboard, more see a washing machine as a must-have if they're to enjoy life on the waterways.

Washers are easily accommodated by those who are regularly hooked up to onshore power, and some people are even happy to use washer-dryers as a result. The real issues begin when you're away from shore power while out and about cruising the network, but there are options.

Assuming you have room for a washer aboard, the challenge then becomes one of power availability. It's not the running of the machine that is the main use of power, but the heating of the water. While there are a few rudimentary options available on the market that can solve this issue, most are good for occasional use only and using them on a regular basis would become an onerous chore. They're more suited to camping, and aboard a boat are good for occasional or emergency use only.

Instead, many boaters sing the praises of twin-tub units. These not only are cheap to buy but also negate the need to heat water inside the unit by using hot water pumped from elsewhere. Some boaters plumb the water feed to their hot-water system – a gas boiler or diesel heater. Others fill the washer with a hose using

Compact automatic washing machine.

Whirlygig washing line fixed to the tiller.

hot water, and some even use buckets full of hot water to fill them. These twin tubs look as if they were made by Fisher-Price, but they're a wonderful and reliable low-cost way to get your laundry done, although a little more hands-on than an automatic washer.

If you don't want to dedicate hours of your life to twin-tub washday blues, then there's the option of fooling your automatic washing machine with a hot-water supply. This tactic essentially eliminates the machine's power-hungry need to heat the water, thereby minimising the energy used for a wash cycle.

For those without a washer, unless you know a friendly neighbourhood washing machine owner you will need to take your dirty washing to a launderette. Prices vary a little but probably outweigh the cost

and inconvenience of running a washing machine on board. 'I always leave my laundry as a service wash,' says Darren from Nb Dunster. 'I've much better things to do than spend two hours watching my underwear go round. I'd rather pay an extra couple of pounds and collect it later, washed, dried and folded.'

Some mooring providers, usually the more expensive and luxurious ones, have self-service laundry facilities on site, but these are rare. Usually these are coin-operated launderette-style machines, but sometimes they're simply standard household models and cost a couple of quid in cash paid to the marina owner. In a bid to solve the problem of not having access to a tumble dryer, some boats even have collapsible clotheslines installed near the tiller on their boat. Google 'brolly mate' and you'll see how it's done.

BEEN THERE, DONE THAT
WENDY'S WASHDAY

CHARLIE AND WENDY
Nb *Philip George*

Charlie plumbed the washing machine's water intake to my Webasto heated water supply. The installation of a thermostatic valve regulates the temperature to 40°C which almost completely stops the washer's water heater from kicking in. The heater does sometimes kick in to heat up the last few degrees, but this is for no more than 15 seconds or so and isn't much of a consideration in power terms.

💡 Launderette list

The Aylesbury Canal Society publishes a list of launderettes conveniently located near canals and rivers. Find out more at: aylesburycanal.org.uk.

TRANSPORT

Cruising the cut is great so long as you aren't reliant upon a car for the duration. Otherwise it can be quite a headache to ensure that both car and boat are in the same place. Once your day of boating fun is over you will need to factor in some way of collecting your car from where you left it, which can mean getting a lift, using a bicycle or public transport.

Either way, collecting a car will cost you time, money, favours or energy and possibly a combination of each. Once again, preparation is key. Finding out about local bus and rail services is probably the easiest solution, providing the services are reliable. Weekends and evenings can often make a mockery of the timetables, especially in rural areas. Cycling back to your car might be an option if you only moved your boat a short distance, and those fit enough to undertake longer journeys might not need to use a car in the first place. The recent advent of electric bikes is a potential solution, but don't forget that those bike batteries need to be charged somehow. And if all else fails you can always bite the financial bullet and call an Uber.

Tony's *towpath tales*

It's interesting to see people's reactions when they find out I live aboard a narrowboat. They range a full spectrum, from a fanciful appreciation to downright disgust and incomprehension. It's never a dull conversation. As a writer I work mostly online, so I'm able to travel wherever my mood takes me and work from there. To many, this seems an idyllic life, free from the everyday stresses of mortgages, soul-sucking jobs and school runs. They imagine I sit at my desk peering out of the window pondering, while the sun is shining, the cows are chewing the cud and I have a glass of beer permanently to hand.

Rest assured, only a handful of days each year are like this. But, nevertheless, many people express a wistful yearning for a life like mine, and it's difficult to explain the sacrifices I've made to arrive here after many years of hard work and hardship. Now that I am here I am enjoying living aboard to the full, but life isn't always a bed of roses.

Then there's the other perspective I experience. I don't know why some people think liveaboard boaters are the 'great unwashed', but I've seen residential boaters treated like they're the scum of the earth. Indeed, I've been told to 'get a job' and that I should move on elsewhere as my 'kind' are not welcome in the area. This was especially true when my boat was in need of a paint job. It's amazing how much more friendly people became when my boat had a shiny new finish. I'm still the same guy, but now I am somehow more acceptable. I don't understand it, but I can see how people might form these opinions. There are plenty of rough looking boats with unconventional people living aboard.

Although the CRT and the waterways have inadvertently taken on a housing role, CRT is not officially a social housing network. Many people have found cheap ways to live on the waterways, which often includes living on badly maintained boats. Those with low incomes avoid fixed expenses such as mooring fees, even when that means flouting the rules that govern overstaying on visitor moorings. Yes, it's wrong and yes, it's a pain for the rest of us, but I do have some sympathy for those who have been caught up in a downward spiral of poverty and social issues. People who have gone through a divorce and ended up with just enough money to buy a boat. Those who can't afford a mooring but need to stay in the area where their kids live or their low paid job is based.

Cont.

Those with mental health issues who don't function as well or as considerately as we would like. Or those who tried to live the dream on the inland waterways, but didn't quite make it.

Neither our canals nor CRT are equipped to care for those who find themselves in these desperate situations, but here they are nevertheless. I don't have a solution for the problem. I just know that I, for one, should not judge these people too harshly.

I remember the days when I couldn't pay mooring fees or fix my leaking window, let alone paint my rusting boat shell in pretty colours. Thankfully, I was free to move my boat as often and as far as I liked, so long as I could afford the diesel. If I'd had a proper job or children in the area, I would also have been left with little choice about where I went and how long I stayed.

The option of boating on the cheap gave me an escape route from the daily grind I found myself enduring at the time. I bought an old boat which was liveable but needed lots of work, and I spent the next five years developing my writing career and doing up the boat in small stages whenever I could afford to. And now, I'm sitting here, looking out of the window, watching the cows chewing the cud and drinking Pimms. And I'm thankful, because I've been lucky. I know how close I came to failing. I'm thankful because, nowadays, my life is idyllic. But, oh my! It very nearly wasn't. There, but for the grace of God, go I.

> 💡 **Vulnerable boaters**
> **CRT welfare team:**
> Tel: 0303 040 4040
> www.canalrivertrust.org.uk
>
> **Waterways Chaplaincy:**
> www.waterwayschaplaincy.org.uk

GROCERY SHOPPING

You'll find a rudimentary listing of grocery shops in waterways maps. But, as usual, Google is your friend here and it's reasonably easy to plan your mooring spots to be near a shop. Sure, you'll often need a trolley, or Popeye-sized arms to get your groceries back to your boat, but it's usually doable.

A much easier way to fill your cupboards is to sign up for online shopping with one of the big supermarket delivery services. Moor up near a roadside landmark and provide the address when you place your order. Canalside pub car parks are a good choice, but the delivery driver will usually call if they can't find you. It's an efficient and effective service – especially if you can load the groceries straight off the van into your cupboards.

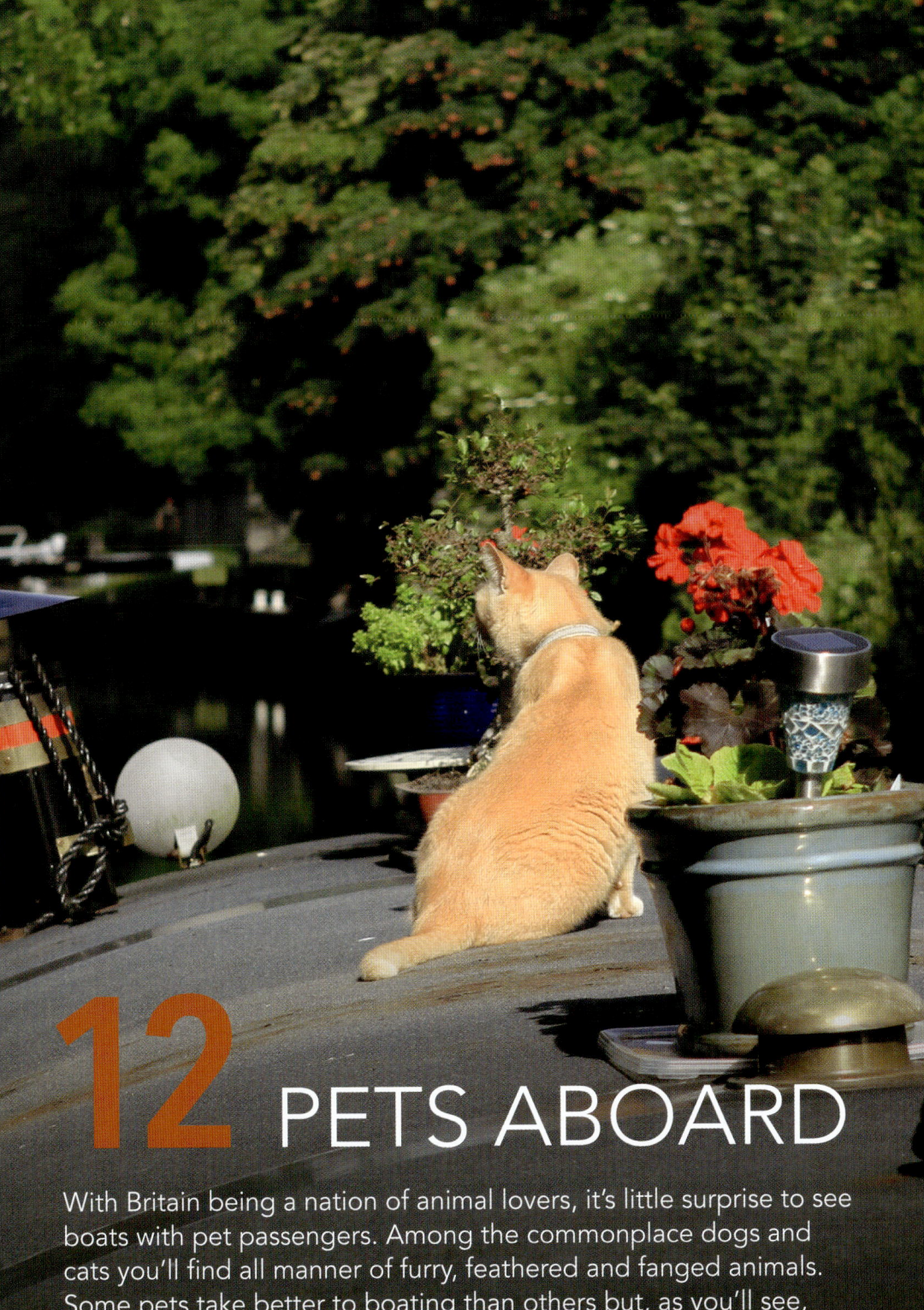

12 PETS ABOARD

With Britain being a nation of animal lovers, it's little surprise to see boats with pet passengers. Among the commonplace dogs and cats you'll find all manner of furry, feathered and fanged animals. Some pets take better to boating than others but, as you'll see, where there's a will there's a way!

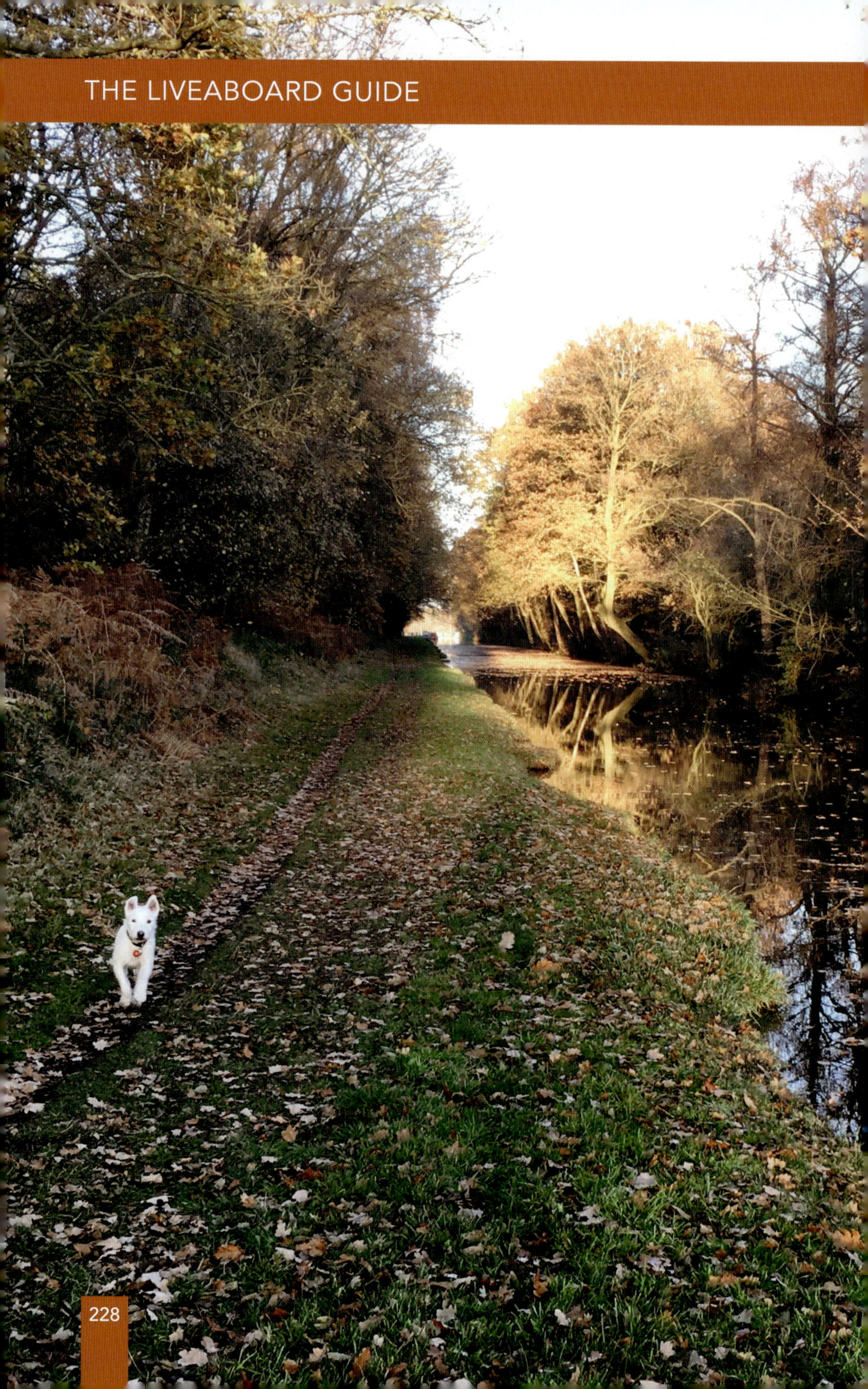

DOGS ON DECK

Dogs are by far the most popular pet to bring aboard, and most make good boaters. They tend to acclimatise easily and know how to stay safe and dry, usually after a couple of unplanned dips in the canal. Once they learn to stay on the dry bits there's not much else that can go wrong for a well-behaved and well-trained dog. It's usually the mischievous ones that will cause frustrations.

It's worth remembering that some breeds of dogs typically can't swim. The most common non-swimmers are breeds with flat muzzles, such as bulldogs, pugs and boxers. Others with disproportionate body dimensions, such as big-headed staffies and short-legged dachshunds, can have trouble too.

DO

- Do think about using a lead when walking the towpath. Read the law about controlling your dog in public here: https://www.gov.uk/control-dog-public/overview.

- Do have a generous supply of dog poo bags, for your own use and to offer to others who 'forgot'.

- Do use a gate or other means to stop your dog from escaping from your boat when moored.

- Do provide fresh water, especially after exercise and on hot days.

- Do provide a raised bed that is insulated from the cold floor, particularly during the colder months.

- Do make sure your boat is well ventilated on hot days.

DON'T

- Don't risk a 'dog overboard' situation. If you're underway, the last thing you need is a dog in the water. If they're likely to chase after wildlife, livestock or other people's pets, then keep them indoors.

- Don't tie your dog to the boat. If they fall overboard you risk strangulation, drowning or injury from the propeller.

- Don't put your dog onto a scorching hot steel roof.

- Don't let your dog near frozen canals. Ice is one of the biggest risks for dogs and their owners during winter. Frozen waterways can look a lot like solid ground to a dog, particularly when the ice is covered with snow. Every year several dogs die after falling through ice and some owners also die in their efforts to rescue them. Pet owners are advised to stay on dry land and call emergency services instead.

CATS ON THE CUT

Boating cats are usually in the care of liveaboard owners who rarely leave their home mooring. Fair-weather boaters and hire boaters are understandably reluctant to take their cats cruising for fear that their pet will not find their way back to the boat. However, some cats seem to adapt quickly, exploring new areas and returning each evening for their dinner. It's a case of trial and error.

DO

- Do keep your cat indoors for a few days before letting them out into a new area.

- Do provide a ramp so that they can escape from the water should they fall in.

- Do assess prospective mooring spots with your cat in mind before you tie up. Look for unknown dogs, busy roads and busy towpaths. If any of these are present, you might want to find another place to moor.

DON'T

- Don't take your cat cruising if you have to stick to a tight schedule. They may stay out longer than you're able to wait.

- Don't automatically assume that an older cat will not take to boating. If you slowly and carefully introduce them to the sound of the engine and the feeling of movement, most cats are happy boaters.

- Don't forget to have your cat spayed or neutered before they go wandering into another cat's territory.

SMALL FURRY FRIENDS

Rabbits, hamsters, guinea pigs, gerbils, mice and even rats are kept as pets aboard. They're certainly one of the less troublesome choices given that they'll usually be either supervised or in their enclosure. Cleaning and feeding are easy and they don't take up too much space, need walking or murder the local wildlife. Keeping them out of your bilges is probably your only worry. You might be surprised by the number of pet rabbits on the cut. Most are kept indoors as 'house rabbits', but some bunnies get to roam on deck or are even taken for walks on the towpath!

MINI BEASTS ABOARD

It's good to see that boaters are generally fond of most animals. We've heard of several unusual pets on boats, including fish, parrots, hedgehogs and even giant stick insects.

It goes without saying, that living on a boat brings an additional set of considerations for pet owners, so do plenty of research before bringing a new pet aboard.

BEEN THERE, DONE THAT
PETS ABOARD

POLLY – VETERINARY NURSE
Nb *Springy*

Cats roam away from a new point concentrically, and unless they get scared, they're unlikely to fail to return or find their way home. I have wind chimes on the boat to orient them, though I am not convinced that this does anything that they can't do themselves.

Some people think that a litter tray will act as a homing scent for cats exploring new places. Of course, each cat will be different, but most don't tend to approve of the smell of their own funk! I'll generally put a litter tray on the stern deck until the cat gets comfortable in a new area, but apart from that I don't use them otherwise.

KERRY
Nb *Linnet*

Kerry lives aboard a historic wooden boat called *Linnet* and sells coal and diesel from another historic boat called *Ariel*.

My pet rabbit Paddy wears his harness when he's on the roof and I hook the lead to the speedwheel just in case. But he's a good lad and he remembers his training. It took months of solid training and dozens of Weetabix to get Paddy trained, and there are still days when all the Weetabix in the world won't budge him!

SARAH
Nb *The Book Barge*

(Bookshop by day and liveaboard vessel by night, Sarah's boat is also home to a lop-eared rabbit named Napoleon Bunnyparte. Sarah is also the author of a splendid book called *The Bookshop That Floated Away*.)

When my boat was a full-time bookshop I brought Napoleon with me to work each day. When we moved onto *The Book Barge* I initially worried he'd miss the space (and courtyard) he'd enjoyed when he lived in a house. But I didn't count on the compensatory closeness narrowboat living affords. Rabbits are sociable animals and they rather like having a human around. Napoleon definitely enjoys this proximity. The boat is open plan and he seems to revel in the lack of privacy and close quarters where my boyfriend and I sometimes struggle.

Problems arise because the boat still doubles as a bookshop. Having a rabbit here puts stock and potential sales in constant jeopardy. Napoleon has a taste for expensive antiquarian book spines and an unpredictable bladder. On the flip side, he's rather brilliant customer-luring collateral. His ear-washing routine has earned him a dedicated fan base of under-fives, who regularly visit to 'awww' over him, parents (and their purses) in tow.

*Napoleon Bunnyparte aboard
Sarah's floating bookshop.*

BEEN THERE, DONE THAT
PETS ABOARD

LAURA
Nb *Saving Grace*
I live aboard with my boyfriend Owen, a cocker spaniel called Jonty and two guinea pigs – Bean and Pea. We had the guinea pigs before we moved aboard and were planning on rehoming them but thought we would see how it worked out. We're glad we did because they seem to love life aboard! We open the cage in the daytime to let them run around in the bow and they get plenty of grass cuttings when the grass nearby has been mowed. We have been on a few cruises with them. Passers-by stop and smile when they notice that we have guinea pigs in the bow. Jonty the dog tends to ignore them.

HOLLY
Nb *Gertruda*
I have a rabbit called Ziggy and a hamster called Trabby on board. Trabby is fine on the boat and it's not much different from looking after a hamster in a house, although he bumps into things in his ball more often. The rabbit does fine too. I've even heard of people letting their rabbits swim in the canal but I'm too scared to see if Ziggy would.

SUE
Nb *Billy G*
We have a boating tarantula! Sidney is a female Chilean Red Tarantula and she's quite gentle. She lives in a large fish tank and eats crickets, which can get on your nerves as they chirp constantly. When people come to visit they expect to see fish when they look in the tank. Some visitors stay and some make an excuse and leave. She did go missing once when she dug the cork out in the corner of the top of the tank and decided to climb the curtains. She wasn't impressed at being put back in the tank! We also have two dogs and a budgie called Naughty Boy.

IVAN *(via Facebook)*
Our dog didn't understand the difference between green grass and the green pondweed covered canal!

FIND OUT MORE

BOOKS

Adlard Coles Book of Diesel Engines
by Mel Bartlett
Adlard Coles Nautical
Explains in clear, jargon-free English how a diesel engine works, and how to look after it, and takes into account developments in engine technology.

Narrow Boats: Care and Maintenance
by Nick Billingham
A useful breakdown of boat maintenance, and although written in 1995, not much changes on the cut.

Essentialism: the Disciplined Pursuit of Less
by Greg McKeown
Not specifically aimed at boaters, but the philosophy is well suited to liveaboard life.

The Inland Waterways Manual
by Emrhys Barrell
Adlard Coles Nautical
This book will tell the reader all they need to know about how to get afloat – which boat to choose, whether to hire or buy, how much it will cost, and where they can go.

Going It Alone by Colin Edmondson
A boater's guide to working a narrowboat single-handed. 'I've been asked the question "how on earth do you manage on your own?" so often that I decided to write this booklet to share ideas with others who boat alone, and with those who maybe would like to do so but need a bit of encouragement.'

Canals of Britain by Stuart Fisher
Adlard Coles Nautical
An inspiring, practical guide, which is popular with all canal enthusiasts and boaters wanting to get the most out of Britain's canals.

Voyaging on a Small Income
by Annie Hill
About yachting, but contains some fabulous advice and was the inspiration for this book.

London's Waterways by Derek Pratt
Adlard Coles Nautical
With its stylish design, beautiful photography and quirky captions, this gorgeous coffee table book is the perfect gift for inland waterways enthusiasts, as well as tourists and Londoners.

Sell Up and Cruise the Inland Waterways by Bill and Laurel Cooper
Adlard Coles Nautical
With anecdotes from their own experiences to illustrate their points, as well as maps, sketches and photographs, the Coopers can help anyone dreaming of selling up and cruising the inland waterways to make that dream become a reality.

The Boaters' Handbook
A brilliant concise guide to boat handling and safety. Available as a free download at: https://canalrivertrust.org.uk/boating/go-boating/a-guide-to-boating/boaters-handbook

MAGAZINES

Waterways World
The biggest-selling and longest-established inland waterways magazine.

Canal Boat
Another monthly magazine championing our wonderful waterways and boating.

Towpath Talk
A popular free monthly newspaper about the UK waterways featuring the latest news, trader ads, waterways stoppages and events.

ORGANISATIONS

Inland Waterways Association
www.waterways.org.uk
The IWA is a registered charity, founded in 1946, which advocates the conservation, use, maintenance, restoration and development of the inland waterways for public benefit.

Residential Boat Owners' Association
www.rboa.org.uk
Established in 1963, the Residential Boat Owners' Association is the only national organisation which exclusively represents and promotes the interests of people living on boats in the British Isles. Representing all those who have chosen to make a boat their home – whether that boat is static or cruises; is based inland or on the coast; has a permanent or temporary mooring (whether residential or not) or continuously cruises – all are residential boaters.

National Bargee Travellers Association
www.bargee-traveller.org.uk
The NBTA represents the interests of all itinerant liveaboard boat dwellers.

National Association of Boat Owners
www.nabo.org.uk
NABO is dedicated to promoting the interests of private boaters on Britain's canals, rivers and lakes, so that their voice can be heard when decisions are being made which might affect their boating.

Association of Waterways Cruising Clubs (AWCC)
www.awcc.org.uk
A grouping of individual and independent boat clubs which offer their members facilities related to boating on the inland waterways of the United Kingdom.

Canal & River Trust
www.canalrivertrust.org.uk
The Canal & River Trust cares for a 2,000-mile (3,220km) long, 200-year-old network of canals, rivers, reservoirs and docks because it believes that life is better by water. Its work involves not only looking after our waterways but promoting them to the people who have waterways on their doorstep so that they can benefit from this free, accessible and local source of wellbeing.

Environment Agency
www.gov.uk/government/organisations/environment-agency
After the Canal & River Trust, the Environment Agency is the second largest navigation authority in the UK, managing navigation for 634 miles (1,020km) of England's rivers.

Boat Safety Scheme

www.boatsafetyscheme.org

The Boat Safety Scheme, or BSS, is a public safety initiative owned equally by the Canal & River Trust and the Environment Agency. Its purpose is to help minimise the risk of boat fires, explosions or pollution harming visitors to the inland waterways, the waterways' workforce and any other users.

British Marine Federation

www.britishmarine.co.uk

British Marine is the trade association for the UK leisure, superyacht and small commercial marine industry. Its 1,500+ members come from a broad range of businesses including boat builders, chandlers, brokers, marinas, passenger boats and engines.

Waterways Chaplaincy

www.waterwayschaplaincy.org.uk

The Waterways Chaplaincy was formed to provide help and support for those who find themselves struggling. The chaplains are all volunteers from local churches who regularly visit the waterways, offering help, companionship and a listening ear to anyone they may meet at the waterside. This might be boaters, cyclists, walkers and runners, or anglers, magnet fishers and canal workers.

River Canal Rescue

www.rivercanalrescue.co.uk

River Canal Rescue is a membership-based organisation that offers 24/7 support in breakdown assistance and recovery across the UK's inland waterways.

BOAT BROKERAGES

Braunston Marina

www.braunstonmarina.co.uk

Braunston Marina offers an extensive range of second-hand and new narrowboats for sale. Their central location and easy accessibility makes them an excellent choice for anyone wishing to buy or sell a boat.

Whilton Marina

www.whiltonmarina.co.uk

Whilton Marina is located at Whilton Locks near Daventry on the Grand Union Canal. The company has been buying, selling and caring for narrowboats since 1971 and have a large selection of narrowboats for sale at the marina for viewing.

Apollo Duck

www.apolloduck.co.uk

Online – large site with thousands of boats and related items for sale.

Boats and Outboards

www.boatsandoutboards.co.uk

Online – find thousands of boats for sale and other boating related ads.

BOAT TRAINING

Narrowboat Escapes

www.narrowboatescapes.co.uk

One and two day courses, covering safety, rights of way, setting off, stopping, steering, turning, mooring, locks, bridges, tunnels, going aground and more.

ONLINE RESOURCES

CanalPlanAC
www.canalplan.org.uk
An interactive guide to the inland waterways of Europe. Plan journeys or holidays and calculate the length of a trip including information on the number of locks and bridges you'll encounter.

Canal Junction
www.canaljunction.com
Information and advice on all aspects of narrowboating, canal heritage and arts and crafts. Holiday boat hire information with links to hire companies across the network.

The Considerate Boater
www.considerateboater.com
Promotes considerate boating and good boating etiquette on the inland waterways.

Canal & River Trust Licence applications
https://licensing.canalrivertrust.org.uk
All the information needed to decide which licence is right for you, with facilities for applying online.

Waterside Mooring
www.watersidemooring.com
Canal & River Trust's official website of CRT-owned waterside moorings. Set up an account and register interest in a mooring to be notified when one becomes available.

FACEBOOK GROUPS

Narrowboat Users Group
Useful advice and support from fellow boaters.

The Friendly Narrowboat Forum
Extra friendly useful advice and support from fellow boaters.

Narrowboat Network Issues stoppages and incident group
Information and advice on network issues from boaters down on the 'ground'.

Compost Toilets for Boats and Off-grid Living
A valuable resource for anyone wishing to take their ablutions off-grid.

Narrowboats for Sale UK
The Autotrader equivalent for the narrowboat community.

Canal Market Place
A place to find businesses and tradespeople who are linked to/trade from the canals. Mixed in with lighthearted chat and photography.

12 volt boating group
An excellent resource for any 12V electrical problems and projects you might have. With over 5,000 members you're bound to find the answer on here.

YOUTUBE CHANNELS

Robbie Cumming

www.youtube.com/@RobbieCumming
My mate Robbie lives aboard his 42ft
(12.8m) narrowboat, *Naughty Lass*, and
spends his time touring as many of the
canals and rivers of the UK as he can. It's
real boat life, exploring local towns and
cities, and he's always on the lookout for
'Pub of the Week'. He even has a BBC
TV series called *Canal Boat Diaries*.

Art in The Corridor

www.youtube.com/@Artinthecorridor
Artists Ant and Hannah live and work
aboard their narrowboat *The Corridor*.
Boat-life chit chat, with a generous
helping of art tutorials.

Myles McDowell #Flow with Mylo

www.youtube.com/@MylesMcDowell
Boating advice and anecdotes told in an
engaging and gentle style.

The Mindful Narrowboat

www.youtube.com/@themindfulnarrowboat
Vanessa and her dog, Zephyr, navigate
life on *Alice Grace*. She focuses on slow
living and mindfulness, often including
nature journalling and poetry.

Cruising The Cut

www.youtube.com/@CruisingTheCut
Cruising The Cut is about the historic
canals of the UK. The videos are made
by David Johns, a man who in 2015 quit
his job, sold his house and went to live
on a narrowboat.

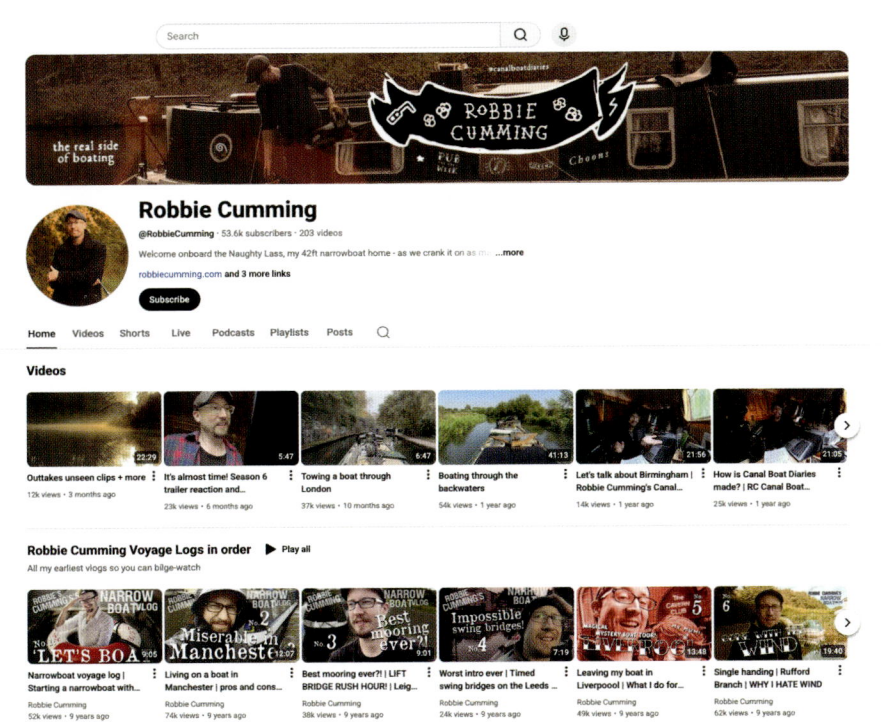

Air draft
The height of the boat above the waterline – worth knowing when approaching low bridges.

Anode
Also known as sacrificial anodes. In fresh water, these are a large piece of magnesium welded to the narrowboat's steel hull beneath the waterline. They protect the hull from corrosion caused by electrolysis.

Beam
The width of a boat at its widest point.

Berth
A bed on a boat.

Bilge
The section at the bottom of the boat, usually under the floor, where water can collect.

Bilge pump
A pump for removing water that has collected in the bilges.

Blacking
A protective coat of specialist bitumen-based paint which is applied to steel hulls to prevent rusting. Other protective coatings are sometimes used.

Boat Safety certificate
The equivalent of an MOT for canal boats. They are valid for four years.

Bow
The front of the boat.

Bow thruster
A small propeller located in the bow which is used to help steer the boat.

Bulkhead
An upright wall inside the boat.

Butty
An unpowered narrowboat, often towed behind a motorised narrowboat.

Calorifier
A water tank, usually heated by the running engine.

Cassette toilet
A toilet with a removable sewage-storage cassette.

Cratch cover
A canvas cover fitted over the forward well deck.

Cruiser stern
A boat with a back deck of between 4ft and 8ft (1.2m and 2.4m) in length, providing lots of space for several people.

Dinette
An arrangement of a dining table and seating that can be converted to become a bed.

Draft
The amount of the hull that is below the waterline – another useful measurement to know.

Elsan point
A sewage disposal facility where boaters can empty the contents of a cassette toilet.

Fiddle
A raised lip or rail around the edge of a shelf to prevent items from sliding off.

Galley
The kitchen area of a boat.

Galvanic isolator
An electrical device that prevents hull corrosion.

Gunwale
The top edge of the hull where it joins the cabin side – pronounced 'gunnel' similar to tunnel.

Hull
The main part of the boat that sits in the water and gives a boat its buoyancy.

Inverter
Electronic device that converts 12V DC battery power into 230V AC for appliances with three-pin plugs.

Mushroom vent
A mushroom-shaped vent in the roof which provides airflow.

Overplate
To weld new steel onto the corroded hull.

Pump-out toilet
A type of toilet where sewage is stored in a large holding tank, which can be later pumped out at a pump-out facility.

Saloon
The living area on a boat.

Semi-traditional
A style of narrowboat or wide beam with a large back deck surrounded by cabin sides, but no roof. These are a compromise, boasting the looks of a trad but with the space of a cruiser.

Shoreline
An electrical cable that connects the boat to a 230V electricity supply on the shore.

Skin tank
A steel tank welded to the interior of the hull which provides engine cooling.

Stern
The back of the boat.

Stern gland
The threshold that separates the inside of the boat from the water outside, and where the propeller shaft passes through the hull. It is usually a tightly packed combination of dense rope and grease.

Stretching
When a boat is cut in two and a new section is welded in place to make the boat longer.

Superstructure
The structures on a boat that sit above the deck.

Traditional style
A style of narrowboat or wide beam with a short back deck of usually 2–3ft (0.6–0.9m).

Tumblehome
The angle of the inward slope on cabin sides.

Weed hatch
A hatch with a watertight lid through which boaters can access the propeller.

Windlass
A handle used for opening and closing lock paddles.

INDEX

ACKNOWLEDGEMENTS

Huge thanks are due to everyone who contributed information and expertise to this book. Thank you all, particularly the boaters who provided information, advice and data for the case studies – I couldn't have done it without you.

Bobby Cowling and Andrew Denny – *Waterways World* magazine

Chris and Fran Salisbury – Canvasman boat covers

Matthew Symonds and David Helliwell – Canal & River Trust

Pete and Karen Flockhart – Tradline Ropes and Fenders

David Hull

Gary Smales – boatsafeteyexaminer.com

Tim, Adrian, Mandy and the team – Braunston Marina

Paul – Haven Knox-Johnston

Colin Ives – composting expert

Karen, Pete, Kim, Dom, Brett and Charlie – Canal Cruising Company

Michael Punter – Lee Sanitation

Tim Davis – Onboard Solar

Tony Preston – Mercia Marina

Jo and Troy Dortona – Snaygill Boats

Andy Russell – boat painter

Peter Dawson – Dawson's Fuels

Kevin Wilmott – Angling Times

Kathy Tedcastle – GP

Ceri Hughes – Benefits advisor

And special thanks to my boating buddies:

Martin and Jules Grimwood

Richard and Lucia Holdsworth

Robbie Cumming

Kate Hughes

Paresh Ahir

PHOTOGRAPHY CREDITS

Alan Barber

Apsley Marina

Bobby Cowling

Bosworth Marina

Chris Beesley

Chris Salisbury

Dave Fletcher

HOTBIN Composting

Jabsco

Jo Bowling

John Stroud

Kate Hughes

Kevin Still

Lee Sanitation

Marineware

Mark Wilson

Margaret Holmes

Mercia Marina

Pilling's Lock Marina

Sarah Henshaw

Separett waterless toilets

Simploo waterless toilets

Steve Rayner

Tankbusters

Tim Coghlan

Tradline Ropes and Fenders

Vickie Wigley